IMAGES
of America

GRAHAM COUNTY

On the Cover: The Graham County Fair started in 1900. It has been the center for social, cultural, educational, industrial, and agricultural interests without interruption for over a century. With a sense of pride and competition, the fair has attracted residents and visitors with bright colors, music, and family-oriented attractions. Here five young ladies demonstrate the advantages and proper usage of pressure cooking in 1916. Pictured from left to right are Nora Allen, Cleofa Duke, Effie Killian, Dessie Morris, and Thressa Layton. (Courtesy Graham County Historical Society and Museum.)

IMAGES
of America

GRAHAM COUNTY

Harold E. Herbert and the Graham County
Historical Society and Museum

Arizona Historical Foundation

ARCADIA
PUBLISHING

ISBN 978-0-7385-4848-7

Published by Arcadia Publishing
Charleston SC, Chicago IL, Portsmouth NH, San Francisco CA

Printed in the United States of America

Library of Congress Catalog Card Number: 2007937551

For all general information contact Arcadia Publishing at:
Telephone 843-853-2070
Fax 843-853-0044
E-mail sales@arcadiapublishing.com
For customer service and orders:
Toll-Free 1-888-313-2665

Visit us on the Internet at www.arcadiapublishing.com

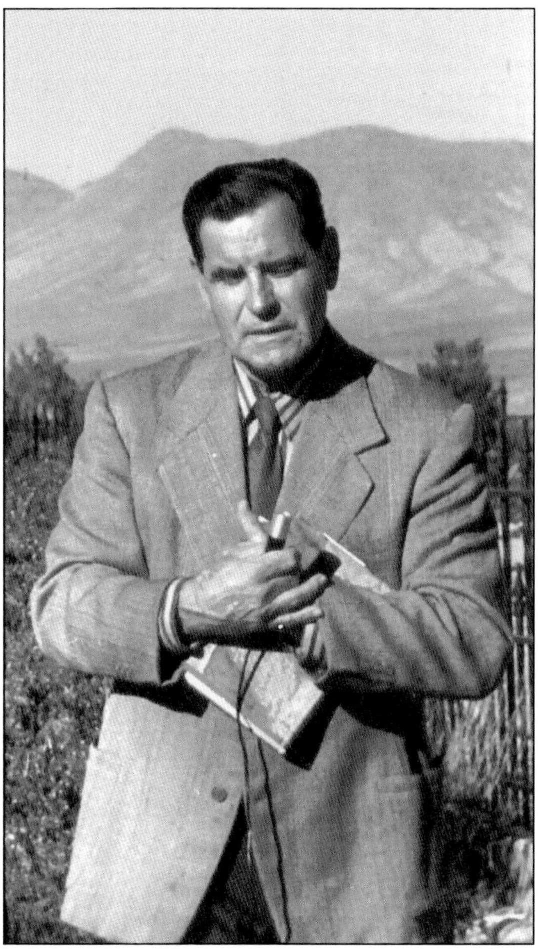

This book is dedicated to the memory of Ryder Ridgway (1909–1985), whose name has become synonymous with the history of Graham County. Ryder started publishing history articles in the Eastern Arizona Courier *in 1974. With a column titled "Arizona Days and Ways: Highlights of the Past," he memorialized people, places, and events both mundane and historic. His contributions to* Arizona Highways *and his ability to speak for and about Graham County have been widely acclaimed. No one can start researching any topic connected with Graham County without first asking, "What did Ryder write about this?"*

Contents

ACKNOWLEDGMENTS

This book is the result of the combined efforts of the board and members of the Graham County Historical Society and Museum. The author particularly wants to thank five people who helped make the final selection of photographs from more than 2,000 owned by the society: Ralph Smith, president of the board; Toni Williams, assistant director of the museum; board members Ben Bryce and Keith Crocket; and member Frank Sainz. If not noted otherwise, all photographs featured in this book appear courtesy of the Graham County Historical Society and Museum collections. Mel Jones, director of the museum, provided space, open access, and enthusiasm for the project. Additional photographs were obtained from Amelia Sainz, Sharon Hinton, and Ray Ferguson. Editing the text fell to Toni William, who spent 15 years as an editor for the *Eastern Arizona County Courier.* The author also expresses a heartfelt thank-you to his father, Heber Ray Herbert, a World War II veteran, who patiently sat in his wheelchair next to the scanner while hundreds of images passed before him.

INTRODUCTION

The land now known as Graham County and Greenlee County has a unique history among Arizona counties. The Mexican-American War in 1848 resulted in the addition of the areas of California, Arizona, and New Mexico to the United States. Not until the Gadsden Purchase in 1853 was the area containing Graham County added to the territory. It was originally part of Doña Ana County of New Mexico Territory until that huge region, which reached all the way to the Colorado River, was split into four counties.

Reorganization toward the end of the Civil War resulted in the designation of judicial districts, with the southern portion of the state designated as Judicial District 1, known as Pima County. In 1881, Pima County was reduced in size with the creation of Graham and Cochise Counties. At that time, Graham County included Greenlee County, which was not separated until 1909 (with Clifton as its one and only county seat, recognized as such in 1911).

A unique historical fact about Graham County is that it was the first to be named for something other than a native tribe. In 1848, Graham County was named by William H. Emery, a member of the Topological Corps of Engineers, for his friend James Duncan Graham. Greenlee County was the first to be named after an Arizona pioneer, Mason Greenlee, an early prospector in the area. The original Graham County seat was Safford, named after territorial governor A. P. K. Safford, primarily because of the financial prowess of Safford's founder, Josh Bailey.

Two years later, in 1883, I. E. Solomon's financial fortunes and the businesses built around his charcoal, farming, and real estate interests far outweighed those of Josh Bailey. Consequently the county seat was moved five miles to the east and was invested in the community of Solomonville (locals often called it Solomonsville). Much of the growth and exciting boom days of the Gila Valley occurred while Solomonville was serving as the seat. A wooden courthouse was built after Solomon's Hotel became too small and busy to hold trials and conduct county business.

I. E. Solomon was a founder of the Gila Valley Bank, which eventually evolved into Valley National Bank. Solomon became active in local and territorial politics. He was instrumental in getting the Gila Valley Globe & Northern Railway built from Bowie to Globe, but failed to get the railroad to pass through downtown Solomonville. As a result, Solomonville began to lose population while that of Safford increased. As the prospects for statehood mounted, merchants and citizens in Safford and Pima worked earnestly to get the territorial and state governments to recognize a change in location of the county seat. In 1912, a petition issued for that purpose was circulated amongst the property owners of the county. In the end, Safford won out over Solomonville and Pima, and the move was made.

The growth and development of Graham County and Greenlee County has been entwined. Graham County has, over the years, supplied labor, goods, and services to the mines in Greenlee County and continues to do so today. The increasing property value of the mines around Clifton and Morenci resulted in a disparity of tax revenues. Clifton and Morenci realized that their tax revenues were unfairly benefiting the Solomonville-Safford area more than the mining area. That realization resulted in a demand to split the county. From the time of the creation of

Greenlee County in 1909 through World War II, both counties grew at a similar rate. Some of the photographs about the mining industry were taken in what is now Greenlee County. This book will concentrate on the time from the start of the 20th century to the post–World War II era, when the interests and growth of the two counties began to diverge.

A parallel military-political entity was established within Graham County in the early 1870s. The construction of numerous military forts—stretching from Fort Bowie in the south to Fort Apache in the north—resulted in members of Native American tribes being forced onto reservations. The area between Fort Apache and the Gila River was designated the San Carlos Apache Reservation. It consisted of thousands of acres that were eventually divided into two distinct reservations. The smaller, northern portion became the Fort Apache Reservation. The larger, southern San Carlos Apache Reservation was contained primarily within Graham County. The post–Civil War years constituted a period of armed aggression between citizens and the military against the Apaches, whose way of life was being forcibly changed by political and military action. Not as many lives were forfeited as has been portrayed in film and fiction, but the fear of the Apaches was palpable until Geronimo surrendered in 1886.

The 20th-century changes that occurred within Graham County were more acutely felt by the Apaches than by Anglos and Mexicans. The Apaches were forced to give up everything that was dear to them. They were expected to cease the nomadic existence that had allowed them to hunt and gather in a vast terrain stretching from the White Mountains in Arizona to the Sierra Madre Mountains in Mexico. They were forced to give up their native religion and language. But a strong sense of identity and pride allowed them to resist changes. Unlike other Native American tribes, most Apaches retained their native language and the women continued to dress in native attire. Throughout the period covered by this book, Apaches were commonplace on the streets of all the towns and villages between Globe and Clifton. Their distinctive dress, language, and manners were most often welcomed in businesses and on the road. Some antagonism popped up from time to time; for the most part, however, peaceful coexistence dominated.

One

The Apaches

After decades of Spanish incursions into the homeland of the Western Apaches, the area within the Gila River Valley and northward to the White River was referred to as Apacheria. The Spanish declared this vast territory out of bounds for exploration and settlers for almost a century. Several bands of Apaches used the foothills of the valley as access ways to southern hunting and gathering grounds. Their traditional routes of passage crossed over an imaginary line that separated Mexico and the United States. Of course, the Apaches could see no such line and refused to recognize changes to their traditional sojourns.

Fear of Apache depredations did not greatly interfere with settlers, trappers, and adventurers until the time of the Civil War, when most of the U.S. military was withdrawn from the area. Some trappers and adventurers who traveled into the territory became accepted by the Apaches. One, James Hinton, married an Apache woman. His children were raised as Apaches, and several rose within the tribe as respected spiritual singers. Other Apache Hintons have become businessmen, farmers, and members of the tribal government.

During the 1870s and 1880s, a series of military camps and forts was established throughout the area. The U.S. military established Fort Bowie, Fort Grant, Camp Goodwin, Fort Thomas, the San Carlos Sub-agency, and Fort Apache to contain and control the Apaches. During this era, the Apaches caused few deaths within Graham County, but those that did occur were widely publicized and resulted in the spread of fear and loathing amongst Anglo and Mexican residents. Locals both welcomed and resented the U.S. military for its failure to prevent Apaches from leaving the reservations and threatening early settlers. Those fears and concerns slowly faded away after the surrender of Geronimo in 1886. By the start of the 20th century, Apaches, Anglos, and Mexican Americans had developed a high degree of accommodation that has since waxed and waned over the years.

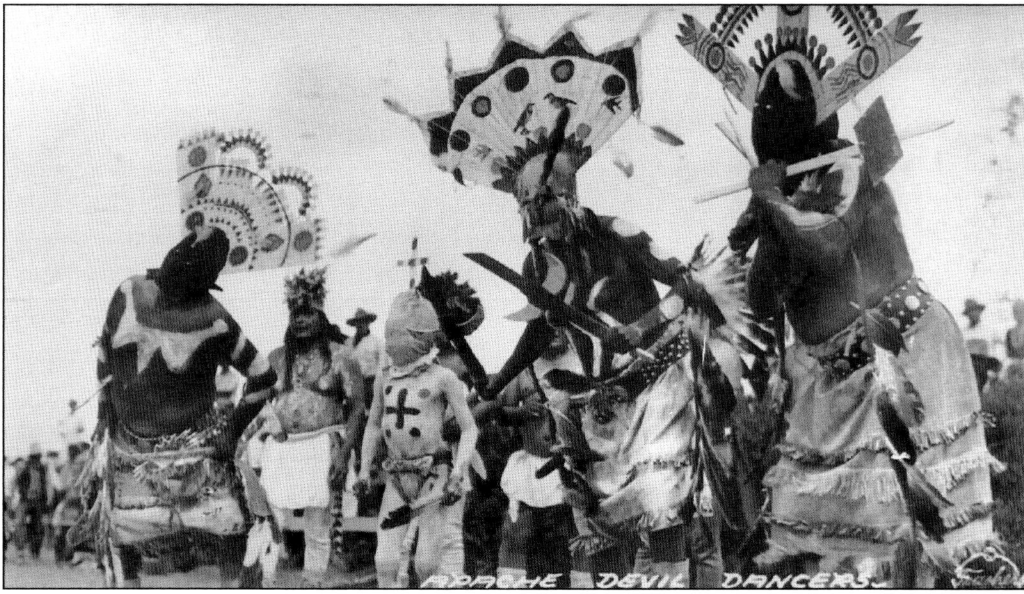

The Apaches and their cousins the Navajos constituted hundreds of tribes and thousands of bands spread all across the Southwest, from Texas to Arizona. Pushed westward, they persevered by mastering survival in the foothills of the western mountain ranges.

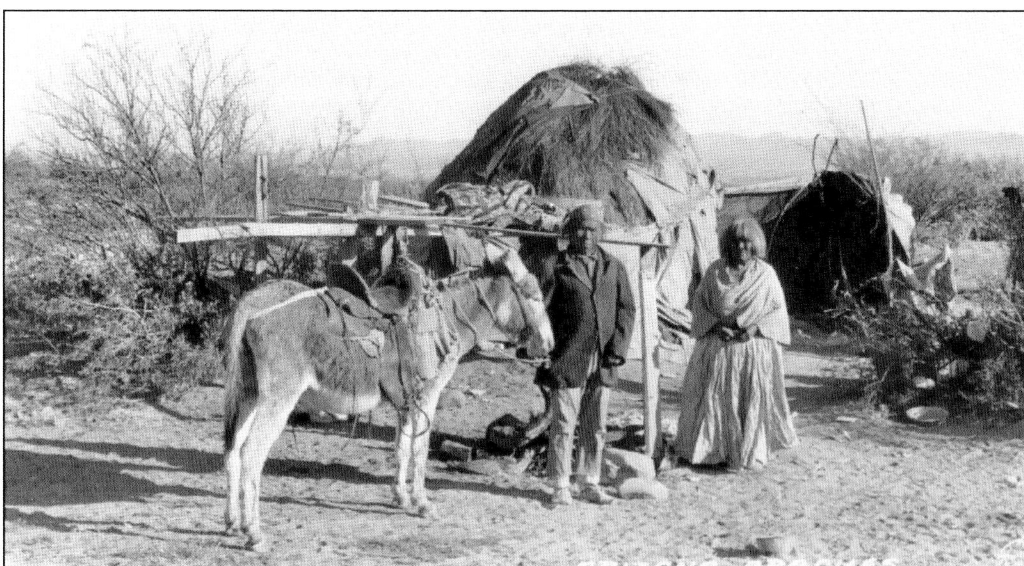

This postcard depicts the lifestyle of an Apache family around 1900. For decades, the Apaches were kept on the brink of starvation because food supplies at the San Carlos Sub-agency were susceptible to corrupt Indian agents. Military contractors often delivered rotten or spoiled meats, beans, and rice with shortages they were seldom challenged to explain. (Courtesy Harold Herbert.)

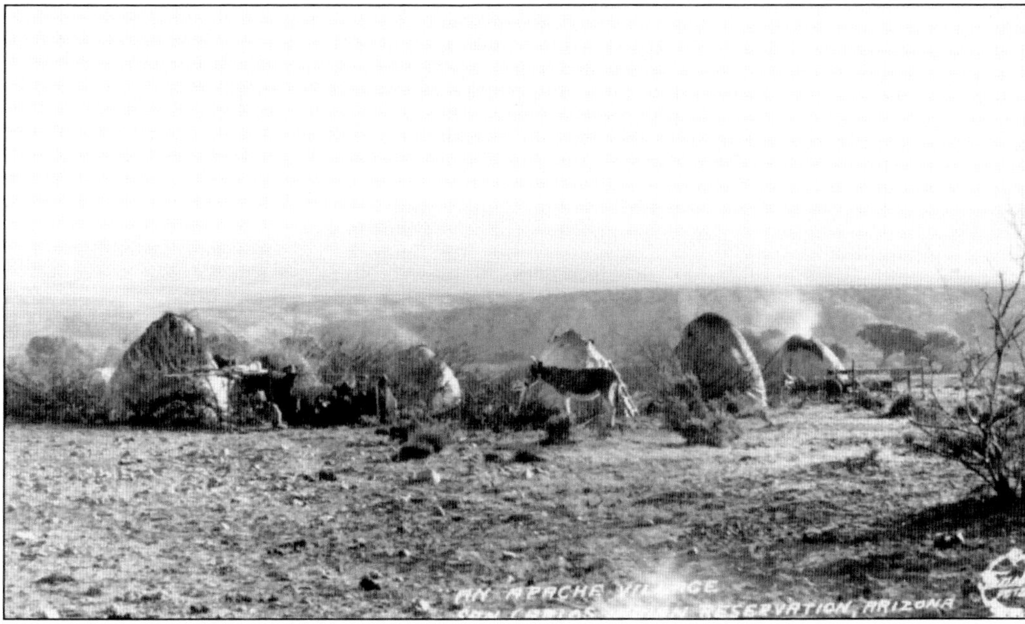

Shown in this postcard is an Apache village. Apache culture is matrilineal, meaning kinship is passed down through mothers. Apaches also endow women with possession of property, including homes and farming plots. The federal government never recognized that tradition and instead insisted on giving authority to male heads of household and recognized tribal chiefs. (Courtesy Harold Herbert.)

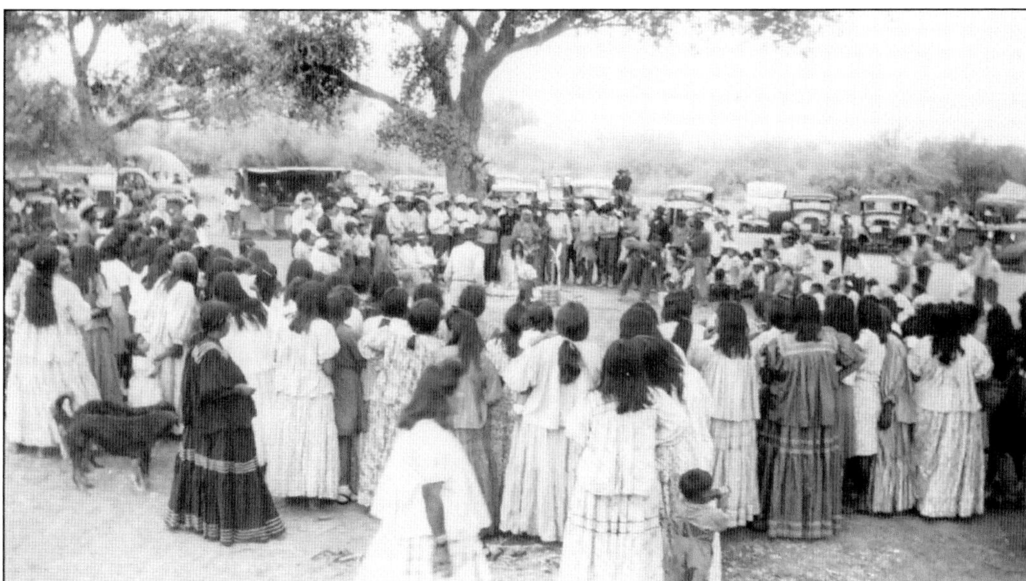

The Changing Woman ceremony has long been one of the Apaches' most important traditions. Not only a puberty rite, it is also a spiritual event involving a young lady's family and large portions of the community. The ceremony is conducted by a spiritual singer (often misidentified as a medicine man or shaman) whose long and varied songs give the honoree temporary powers of healing and authority. (Courtesy Sharon Hinton.)

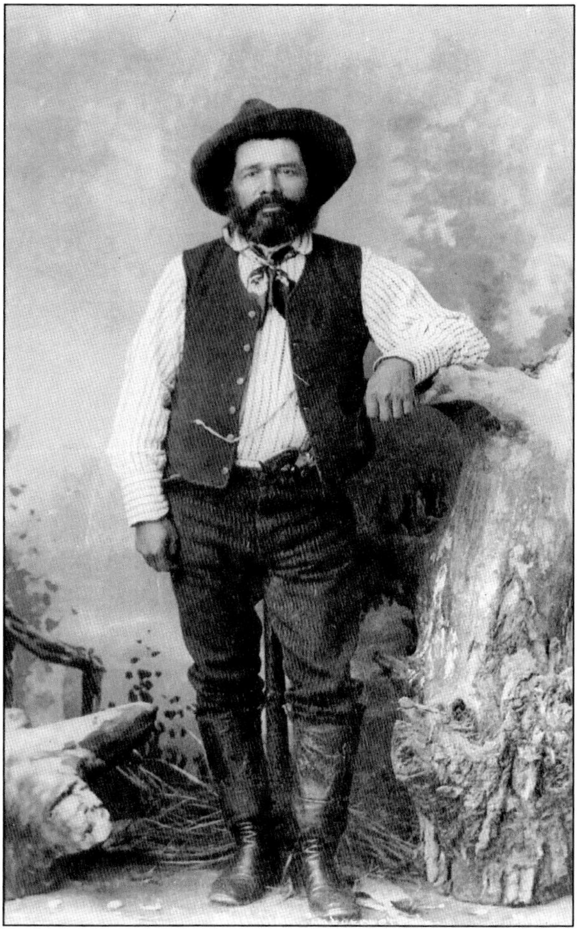

Merejildo Grijalva was a representative of the Apache conflicts in Graham County for three decades. As a child, Apaches had kidnapped him from his village in northern Mexico. He survived to adulthood, at which point he was able to escape. His mastery of Spanish, English, and Apache and his willingness to help the U.S. cavalry led Grijalva to become a renowned scout and translator.

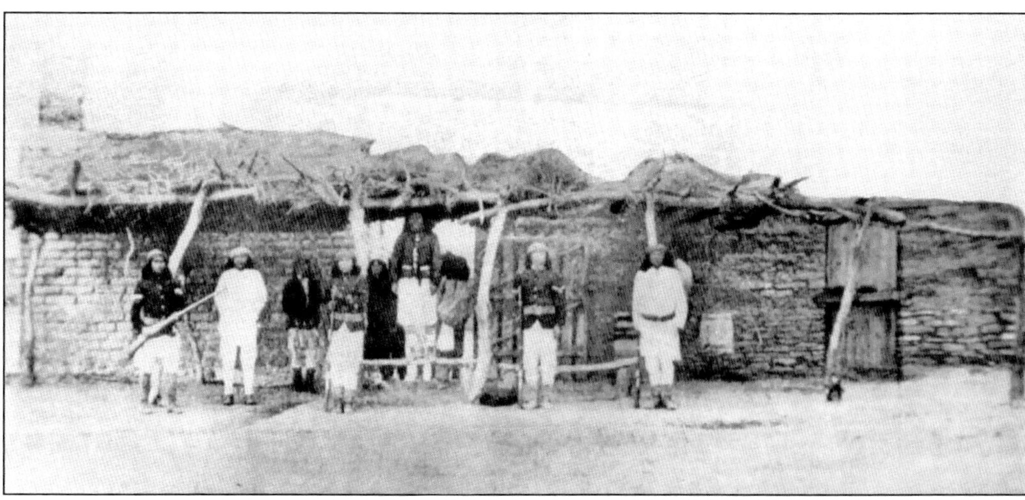

Apache scouts guarded the San Carlos Reservation jail. At one time or another, all Apaches felt they were locked in jail, as the U.S. military worked hard to prevent them from leaving the reservation. The cultural traditions of gathering acorns and piñons, hunting in the foothills, and planting corn on creeks flowing from the surrounding mountains were denied by their confinement.

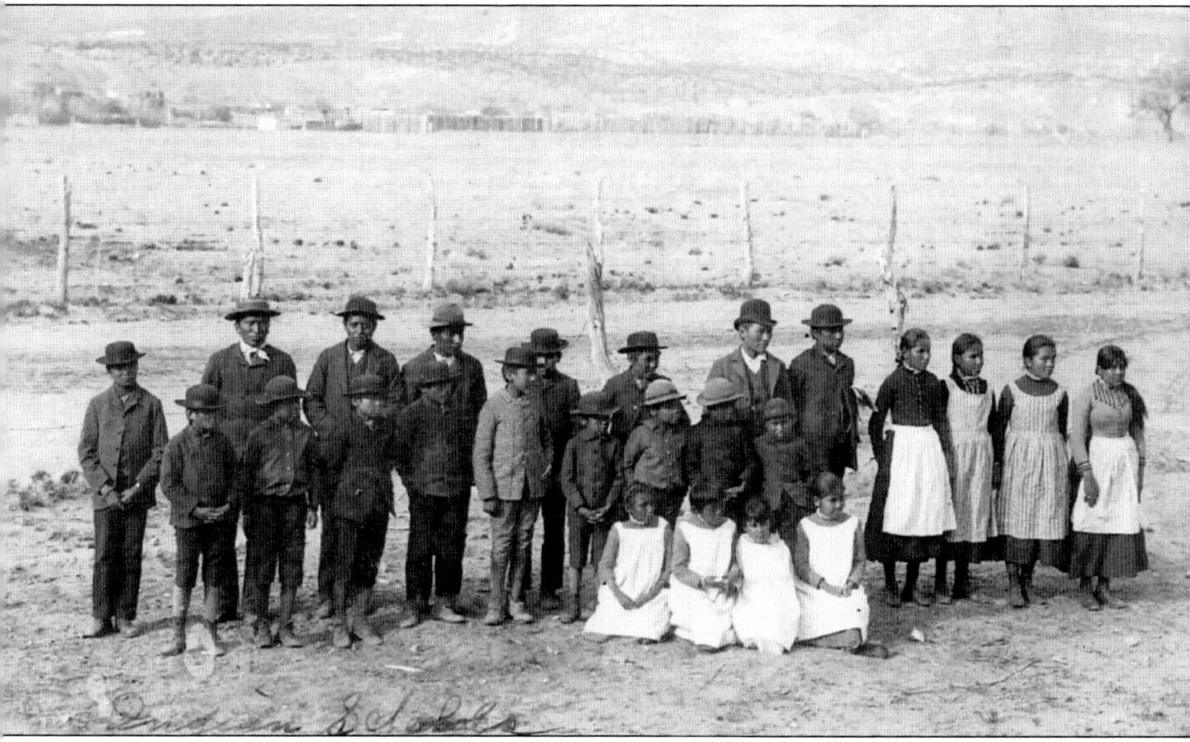

The period of time most resented by Apaches was when the federal government attempted to destroy Native American culture by forcing the abandonment of their tribal identity, traditional dress, and language. Education was used to implement these changes. The Apache schoolchildren pictured here in the 1930s had been taken away from their parents and required to live in school dorms. The Lutheran and Catholic Churches sponsored such schools.

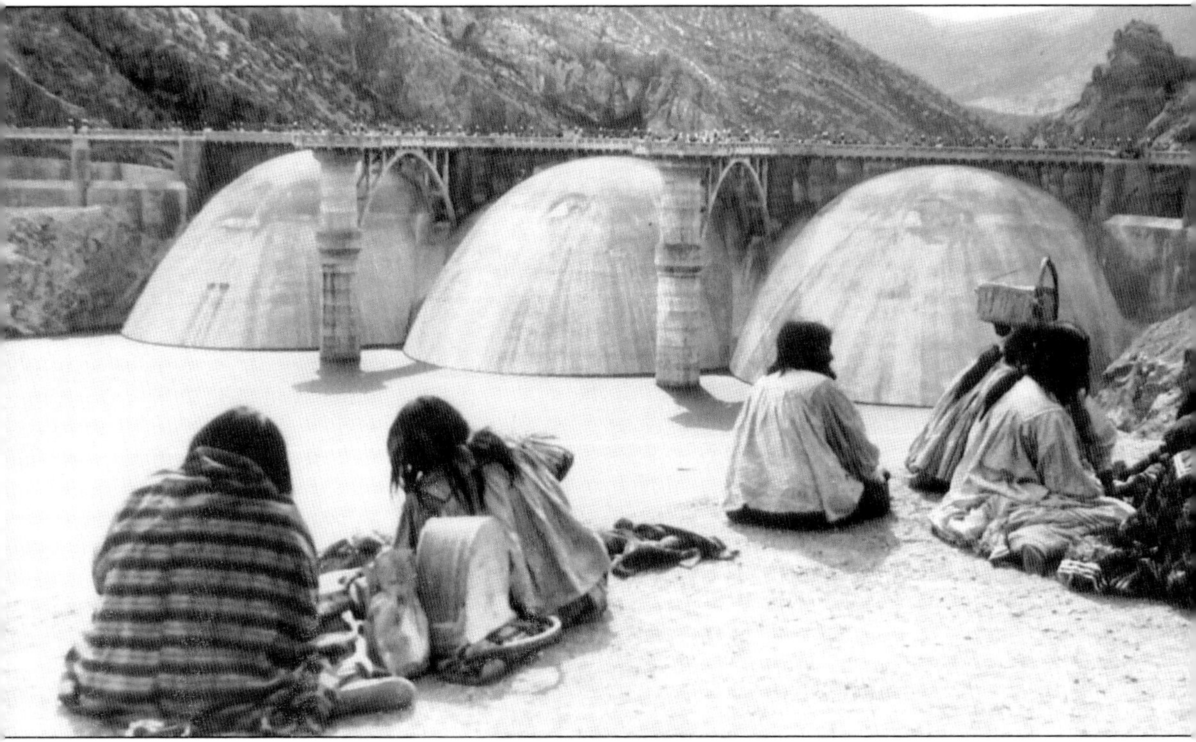

Apache women sit on a bluff overlooking the developing San Carlos Lake after the Coolidge Dam was completed in 1928. Unfortunately the pay schedule allowed contractors to give Mexican and Apache workers lower wages than Anglos. When construction ended, so did the jobs, and since there were no Apache communities capable of using electric power, it took years for them to benefit from a promise for a better life.

Two

SOLOMONVILLE EARLY GOVERNMENT AND LAW ENFORCEMENT

Apache conflicts with Mexicans and Anglos occurred sporadically, but that did not deter Mexican families from Texas, New Mexico, and the Mexican states of Chihuahua and Sonora from settling in the Gila River Valley. Two waves of migration, each associated with civil unrest in Mexico, caused the Mexican population to increase. The first migration occurred in 1848 after the Mexican-American War. A few Mexican peasants fled Texas and New Mexico and found refuge on the Gila River; forming a community they called Buena Vista, later to become San Jose. The second wave came in the 1870s during the Mexican war against France. Copper was discovered near Clifton, attracting even more Mexicans to the area.

Jewish businessman Isador E. Solomon moved to Clifton in 1876. Gambling on the demand for charcoal for the mines in the area, Solomon settled 20 miles down the Gila River. He hired locals to build kilns and harvest the thick forests of nearby mesquite. He bought a store from Bill Munson and started a community that came to bear his name. Solomonville attracted other businesses and farming in the area. Its growth so outstripped Safford that the county seat was transferred there in 1883. Itinerate lawyers and judges, sheriffs, jurymen, and all the staff required to conduct trials, inquests, and hearings helped cause the community to expand. After the county courthouse was built in Solomonville, things appeared to be settled until the construction of the Gila Valley Globe & Northern Railway.

Solomon was intimately involved in getting the railroad built but, in doing so, failed to convince the owner to pass the line through Solomonville. A Solomonville railroad depot was constructed south of Solomonville, but as new businesses began expanding in Safford and communities westward, Solomonville waned in importance and population. After statehood, in 1912, there was a concerted effort to get the county seat returned to Safford. In competition with Pima, Safford won. Solomonville rapidly declined but continued to exist with schools, businesses, churches, and closely knit families.

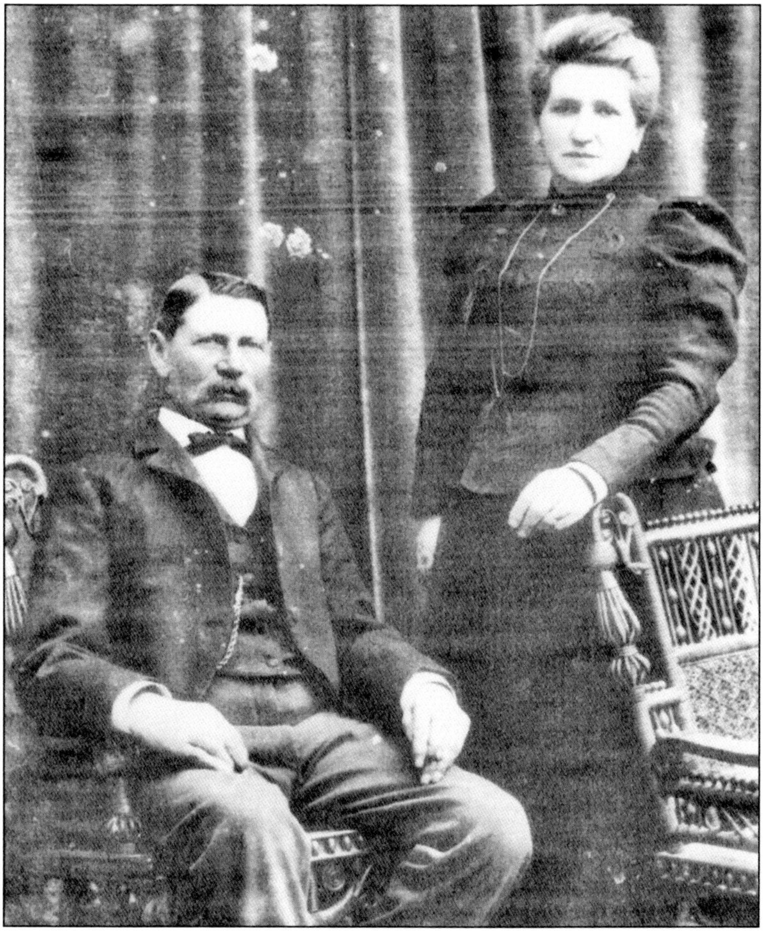

Isador E. Solomon foresaw a need for charcoal in the mines and thus started looking for a source of mesquite wood and a place to build kilns. He came upon the old Mexican village of Buena Vista, where he found willing laborers. The area's mesquite groves and adobe clay were ideal for his purposes. He hired locals, built kilns, and started freighting along the Gila River to deliver charcoal to the mines. His wife, Anna, ran the Solomonville Hotel and was active in local society. The community that developed around his store became known as Solomonville.

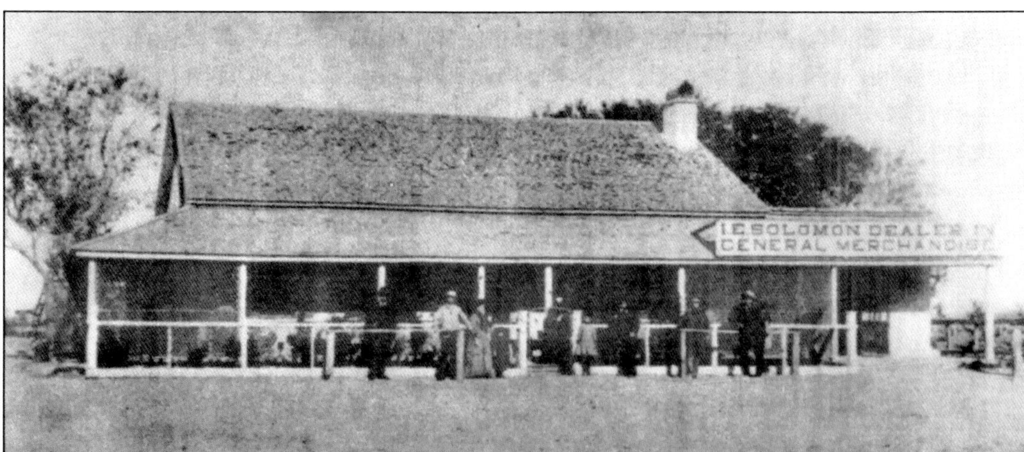

I. E. Solomon's General Merchandise store was a long-standing establishment in the community. Solomon expanded his home to include a hotel that provided space for lawyers and judges. The presence of legal personnel did not lessen the dangers in the area. In one instance, Solomon delayed a trip to Clifton because his daughter was ill. The stage that departed on that day was waylaid by Apaches and all the occupants killed.

The Solomon Hotel was recognized as the center of government until the construction of the county's first courthouse in 1883. Anna Solomon oversaw the hotel and organized social events for military officers and their wives. By the start of the 20th century, Solomonville included three stagecoach companies, three blacksmith shops, several saloons, hardware stores, restaurants, laundries, and stables—all of which provided goods and services to a permanent population of almost 1,000 people.

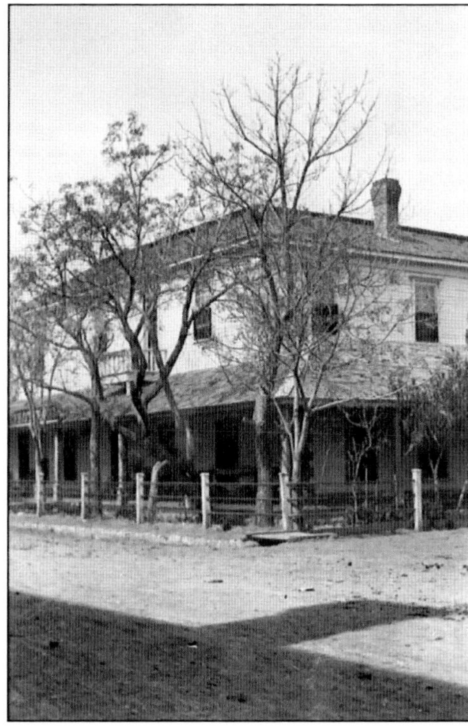

Fancy balls and fêtes were popular in Solomonville. This invitation to celebrate both Valentine's Day and Arizona statehood was issued by the Kickers' Klub in 1895. This ball took place at the courthouse, with the Grand March starting promptly at 8:00 p.m. Notice the name of the vice president of the club, one Arturo Elias, and then closely examine the invitation on the next page.

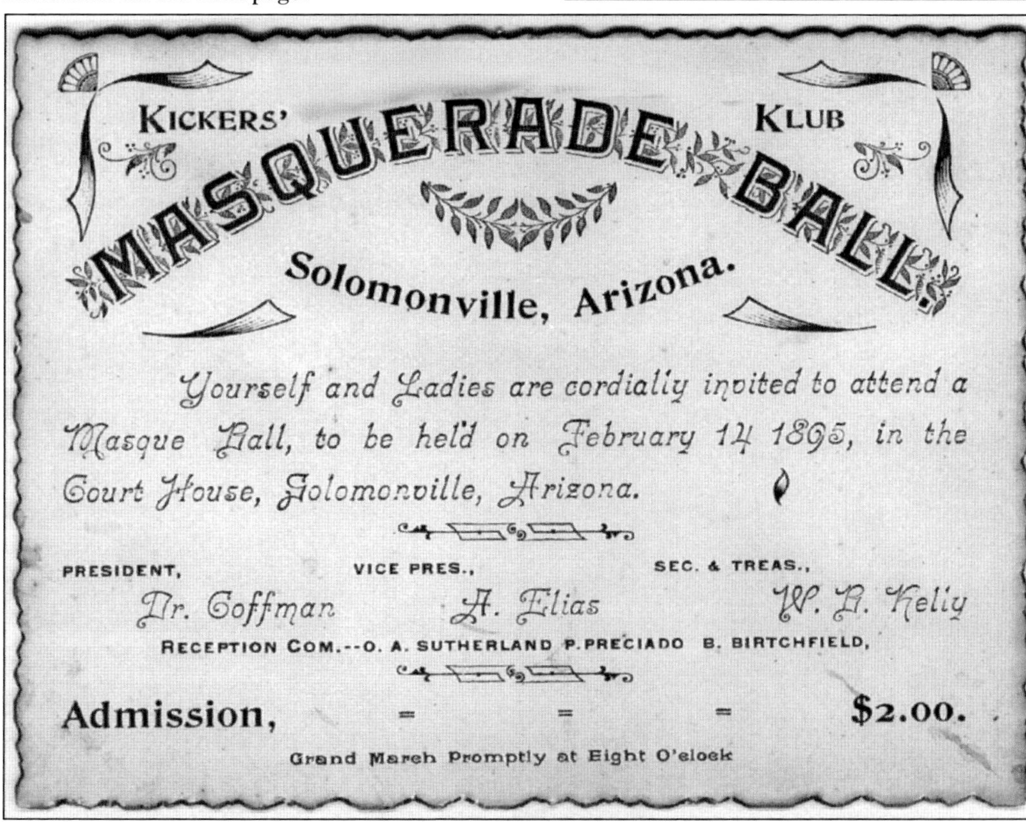

KICKERS' KLUB

MASQUERADE BALL.

Solomonville, Arizona.

Yourself and Ladies are cordially invited to attend a Masque Ball, to be held on February 14 1895, in the Court House, Solomonville, Arizona.

PRESIDENT, Dr. Coffman VICE PRES., A. Elias SEC. & TREAS., W. B. Kelly

RECEPTION COM.--O. A. SUTHERLAND P. PRECIADO B. BIRTCHFIELD,

Admission, = = = $2.00.

Grand March Promptly at Eight O'clock

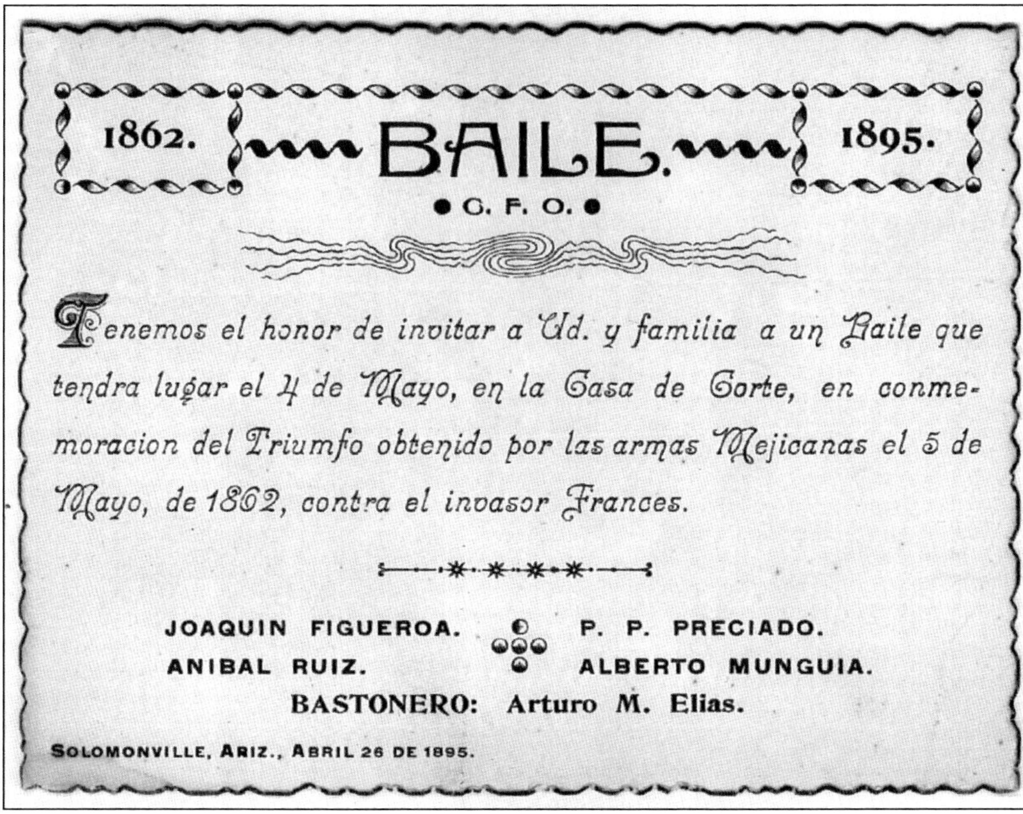

1862. BAILE. 1895.

O. F. O.

Tenemos el honor de invitar a Ud. y familia a un Baile que tendra lugar el 4 de Mayo, en la Casa de Corte, en conmemoracion del Triumfo obtenido por las armas Mejicanas el 5 de Mayo, de 1862, contra el invasor Frances.

JOAQUIN FIGUEROA. P. P. PRECIADO.
ANIBAL RUIZ. ALBERTO MUNGUIA.
BASTONERO: Arturo M. Elias.

SOLOMONVILLE, ARIZ., ABRIL 26 DE 1895.

Written in Spanish, this 1895 invitation celebrated Cinco de Mayo at the Casa de Corte. Spanish and English was universally spoken in early Solomonville. Even though some events were segregated, there were few strict rules of separation, and leading Mexican families were welcomed in all businesses in town. The *bastonero* (band director) for the event is the same Arturo Elias, vice president of the Kickers' Klub.

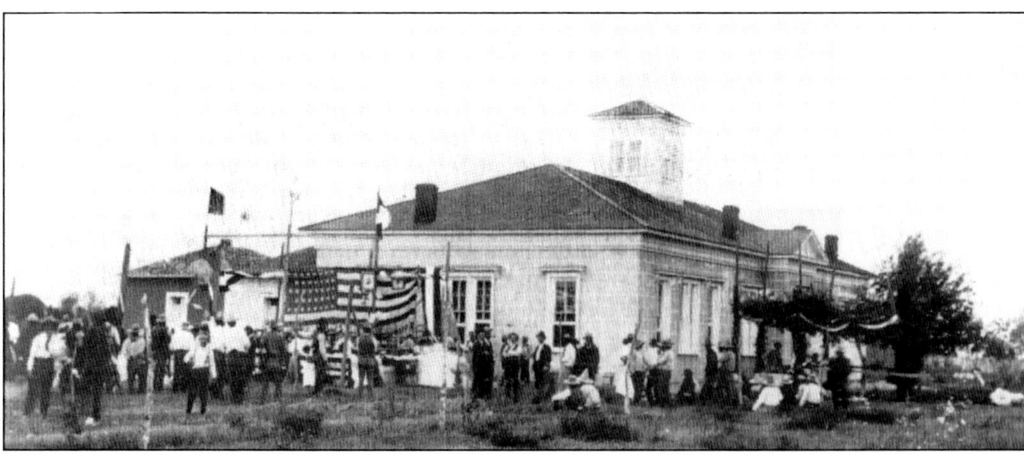

The courthouse's broad expanse of grass became the location of outdoor events. This Fourth of July celebration in 1900 graphically portrays the importance of the event to the citizens of Solomonville.

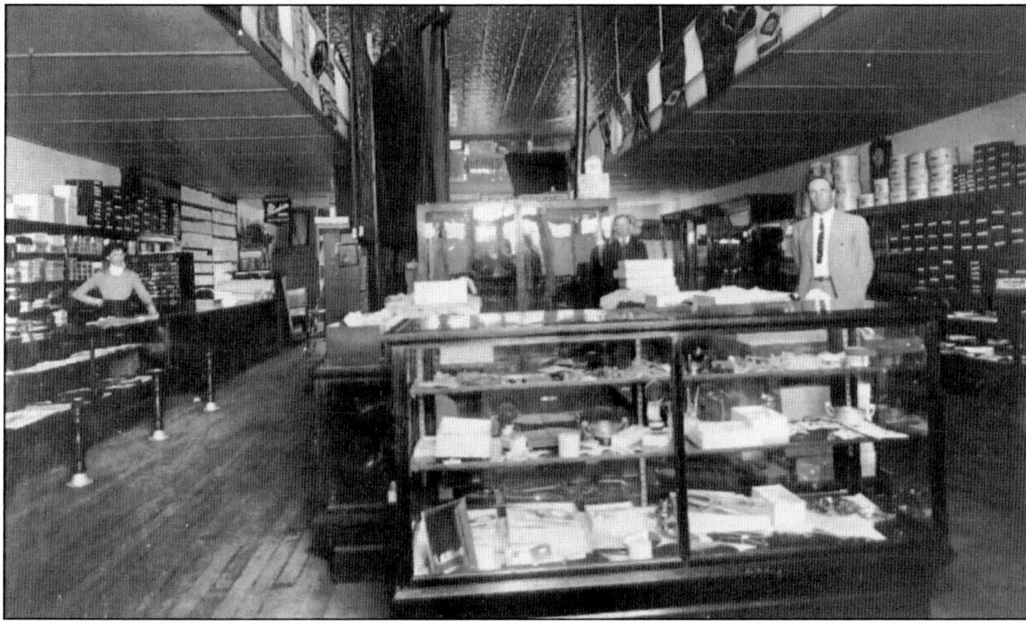

The interior of Solomon's Dry Goods and Hardware was spacious and clean. The two-story brick building also included balconies for the storage of inventory. Common to early-20th-century stores, there were no open shelves; instead, clerks were asked to select the merchandise, which was then laid upon the counter for customers to examine. Household delivery was common, and the manager and clerks were expected to make formal relationships with customers.

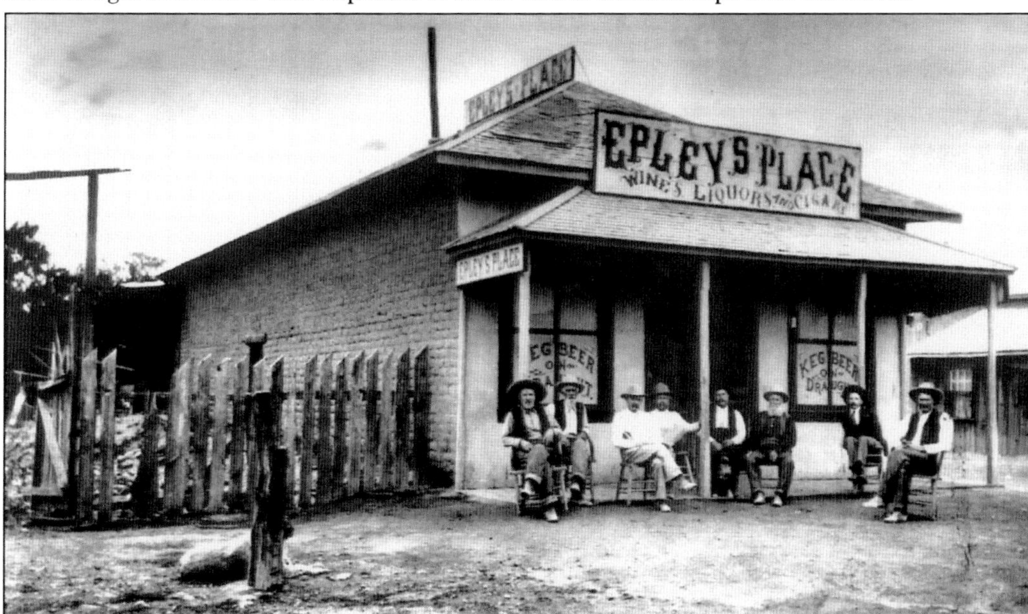

While the west end of the valley was home to Latter Day Saints communities, the eastern part was well supplied with bars. Epley's Place was owned by John Epley, who served as a deputy sheriff for a time. When renowned criminal Augustine Chacon was convicted and sentenced to be hanged, Sheriff Jim Parks offered Epley the privilege of springing the trapdoor to drop Chacon to his death. Epley replied, "I would damn sure shoot him, but I don't want to spring no trap."

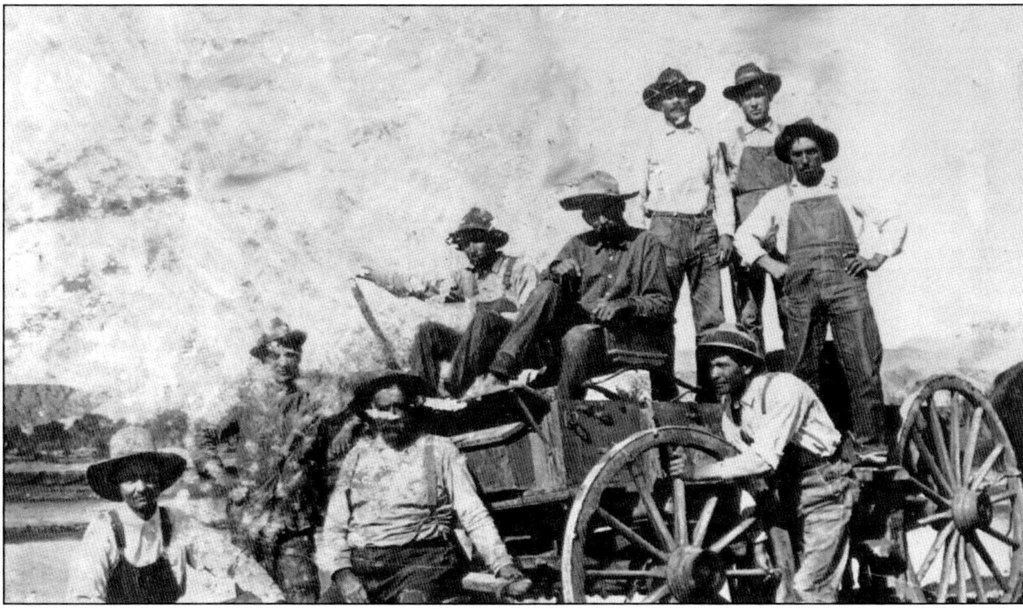

Hardy Mexican farmers pose for a photograph in the middle of the sugarcane harvest. Visible in the left background are the Gila River and the trees along the far bank. Sugarcane was a popular crop at the beginning of the 20th century, and a molasses plant in the area turned out both sugar and syrup. (Courtesy Amelia Sainz.)

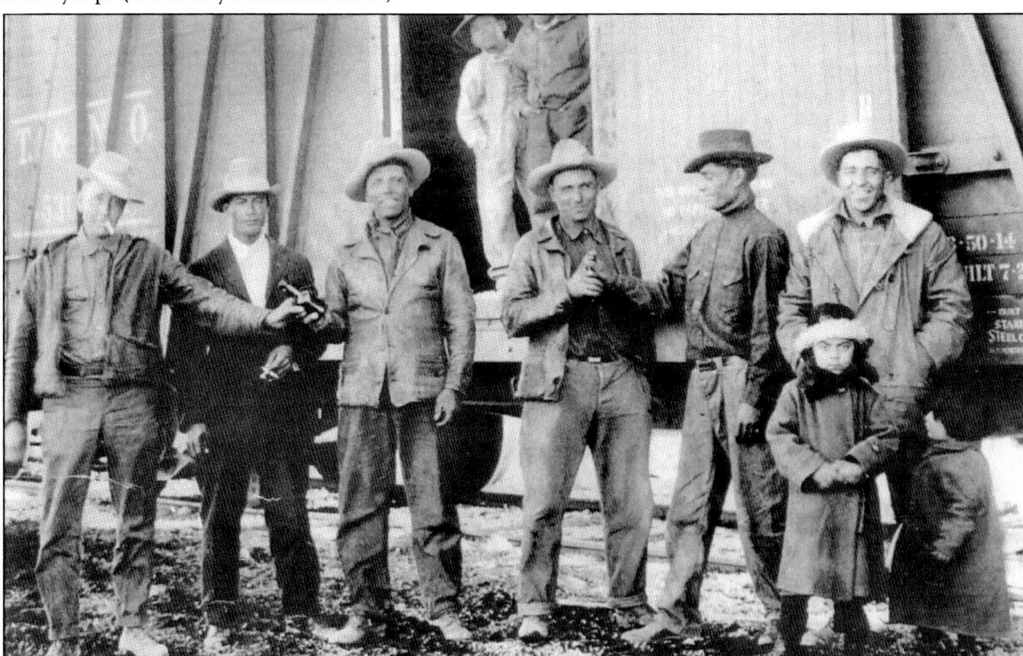

Men take a break in the loading and unloading of boxcars at the Solomonville railway station. Everyone except for the man in the dark suit (second from the left) was a native of Solomonville or San Jose when this photograph was taken in 1925. The gentleman at left is Chico Ariniz, who is handing a drink to Aurelio Hernandez. Fourth from the left is Epitacio Granillo. The two men to the right are Pablo Juarez and Julio Escabedo, with his two children. (Courtesy Amelia Sainz.)

Three

Mormon Pioneers and the Communities They Developed

In the late 1870s, Church of Jesus Christ of Latter-day Saints (LDS) pilgrims from Utah arrived in the Gila Valley. After a long march from northern Arizona, they arrived in a familiar place, as this land was known to the Mormon Battalion 30 years earlier. The pioneers immediately broke land and planted the precious seeds they had brought with them. They were more concerned about getting crops planted than building comfortable homes. Several families lived in their wagons and tents for a year or so before constructing permanent residences.

The LDS settlers had successfully traversed territory inhabited by warring tribes, bandits, and isolated military forts. They believed that miraculous intervention had protected them in their journeys. When they arrived in the Gila Valley, they eagerly began to conquer the land and plant deep roots. In San Jose and Solomonville, early Mexican farmers had discovered an ancient canal system that had delivered water from the Gila River to tillable land. Early on, they dug out the ditches and canals to irrigate their lands. The LDS pioneers found similar relics and continued the process, bringing precious water from upstream and east of Safford all the way to Pima and beyond.

The newcomers found much unoccupied land between Fort Thomas and Safford. Appropriately they named one of their first communities Eden. They subsequently spread out on both sides of the Gila River, creating communities called Bryce, Matthewsville, Smithville (later Pima), Central, Thatcher, Graham, Hubbard, and Layton. Communities like Pima and Central were laid out with orderliness and street names identical to Salt Lake City. The communal lifestyle of the LDS pioneers contributed to their collective success as settlers, farmers, merchants, and community builders. Leaders were easily identified, often serving as bishops and later as stake presidents of the Church of Jesus Christ of Latter Day Saints. Such leaders included Ebenezer Bryce, who farmed a scenic area of southern Utah that still bears his name (Bryce National Monument), and Christopher Layton, whose home and business enterprises became the cornerstone for the community of Thatcher.

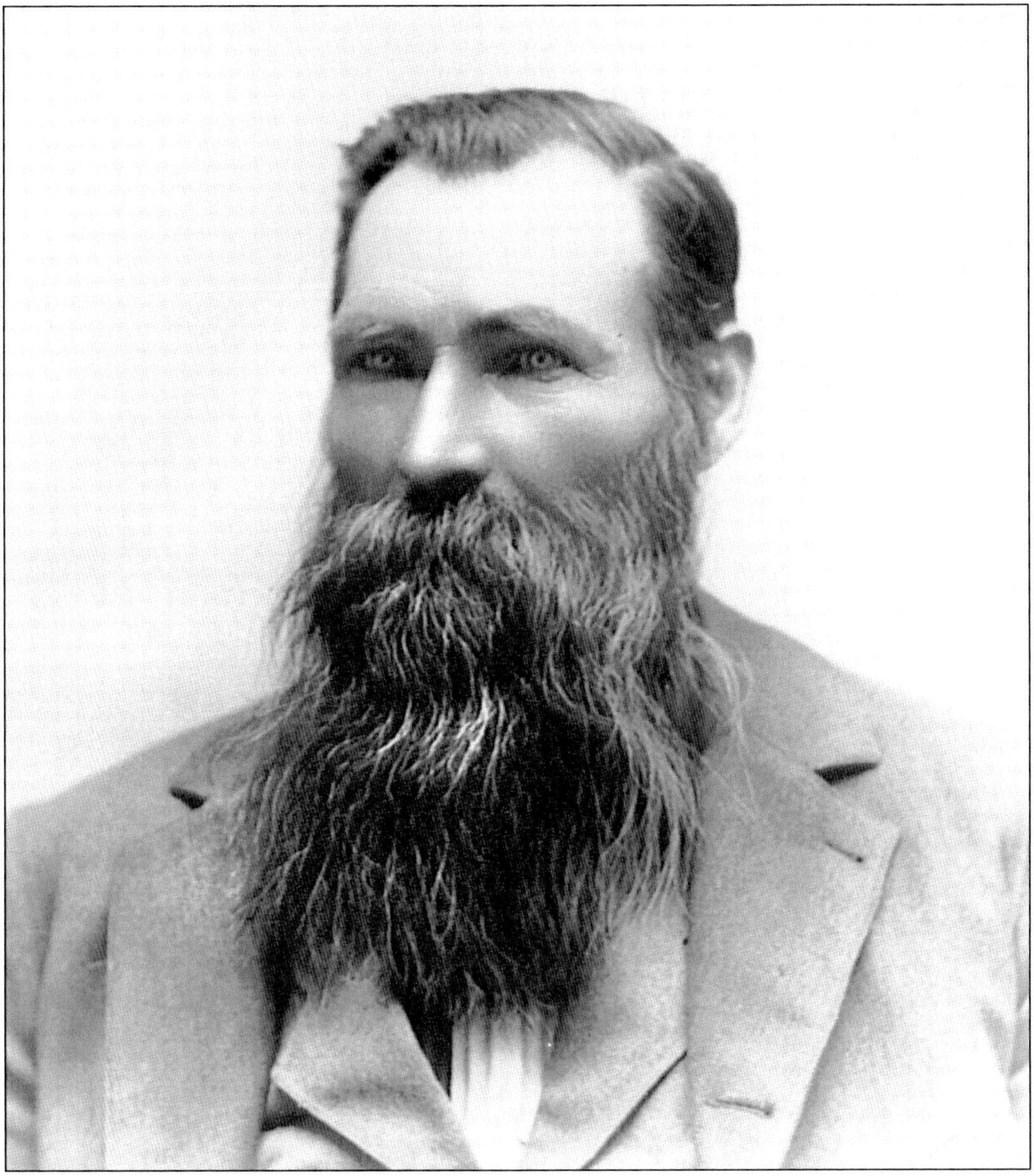

Official church directives to settle the Gila Valley came after early explorers reported "that the country looked good for stock raising and farming." On March 16, 1879, at the camp of Moses Cluff (pictured above), the proposed migration was approved by stake president Jesse N. Smith, who appointed Joseph K. Rogers to lead it. In the first company were Rogers, W. R. Teeples, Hyrum Weech, Henry D. Dall, William Thompson, and the families of all except Weech and Dall. To these were added John and Thomas Sessions and Earlton Haws, making 28 in all. Arrival occurred on April 8, 1879. The Cluffs (three families) came after the first party. Samuel Curtis, Heber Reed, Edgar Sessions, and William Asay formed a later migration.

Few Graham County pioneers have blazed a trail as brightly as that of Ebenezer Bryce. In 1875, he and his wife settled in Pine Valley, Utah, where Bryce built what is now the oldest Mormon chapel still in continuous use. The family moved to the Paria Valley below a spectacular canyon that was later named for him and is now known as Bryce National Park. In 1880, the family moved to Arizona. There Bryce established the community of Bryce, just across the Gila River from Smithville (Pima).

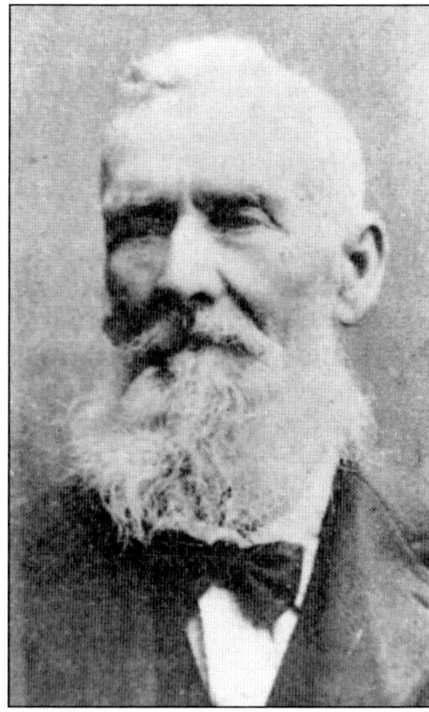

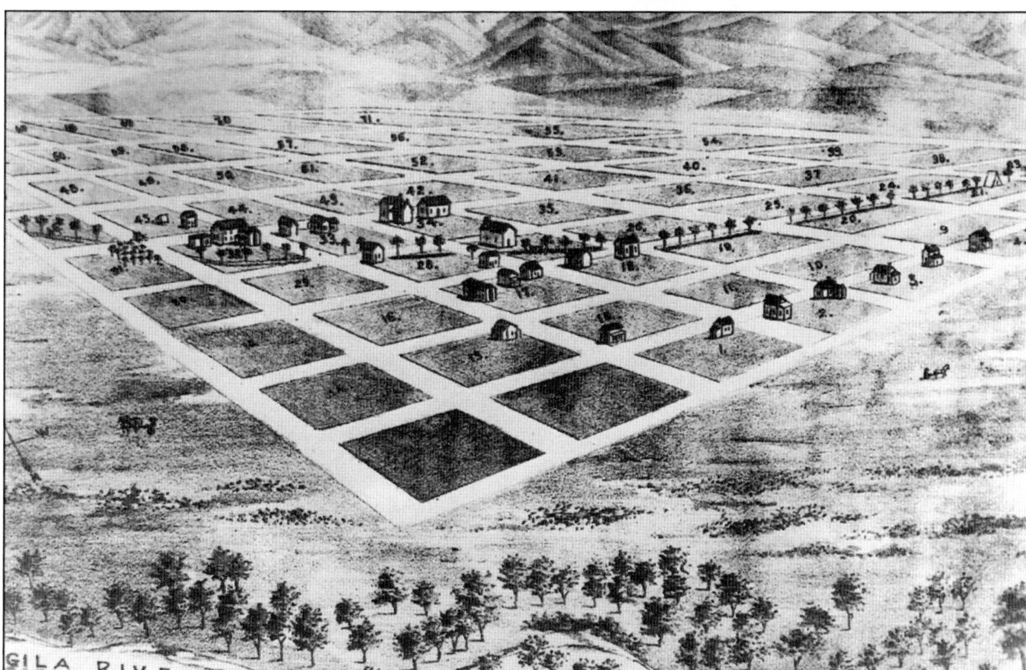

LDS pioneers came with animals, farm implements, seeds, dedication, and a vision of the future. They had in mind not just farms scattered across the landscape, but also rather orderly communities that they felt were necessary for growth and development. This view depicts the community of Central, just east of Pima. The pioneers chose to number the streets exactly as they were numbered in Salt Lake City.

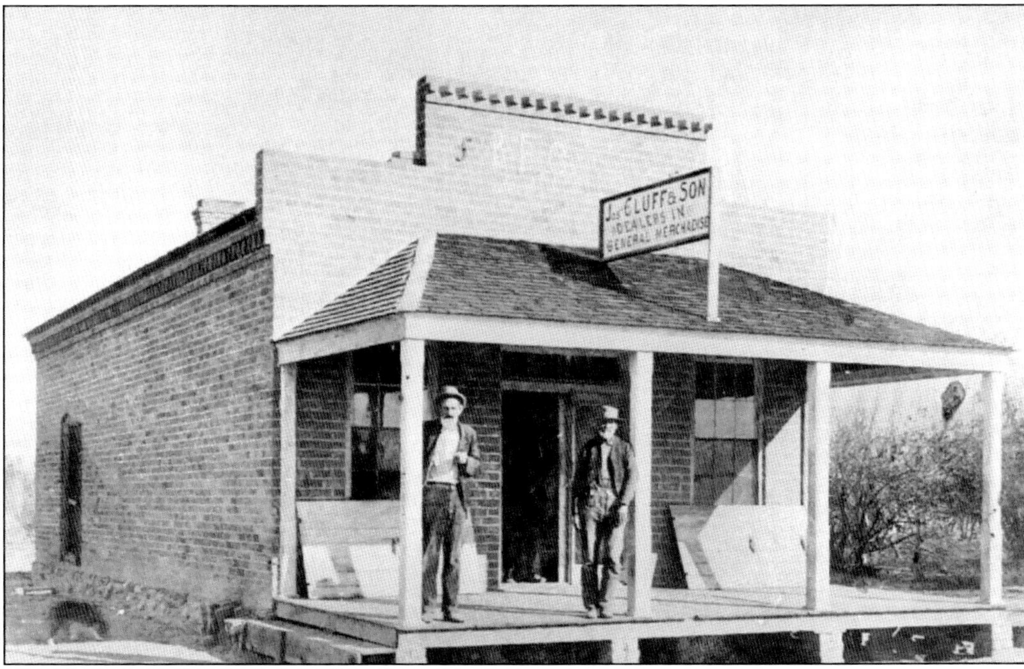

Central Market, located on what is now Highway 70, survived decades. Its earliest manifestation was this brick building owned and operated by Joseph Cluff and his son. Because most community stores also served as post offices, they were popular gathering places.

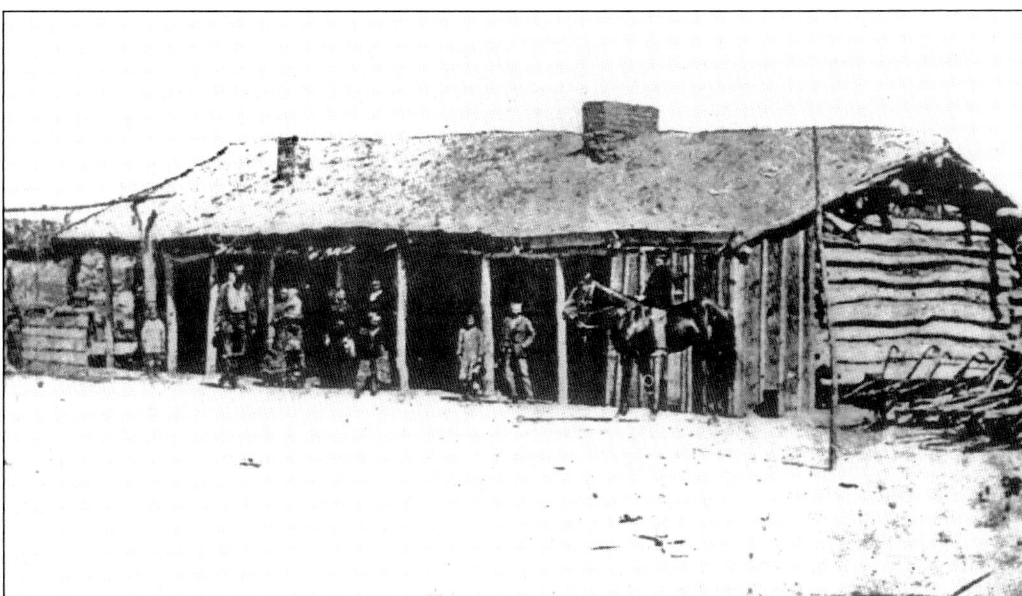

After living in tents and wagons for the first planting season, early pioneers constructed rough-hewn homes like the Teeples' first home in Pima. These sturdy but aesthetically unattractive structures were seen as temporary and often became bunkhouses, barns, or storage sheds when functional homes were built. Later arrivals often spoke of living in uncomfortable, older houses. The town of Pima assigned lots to the families due to arrive.

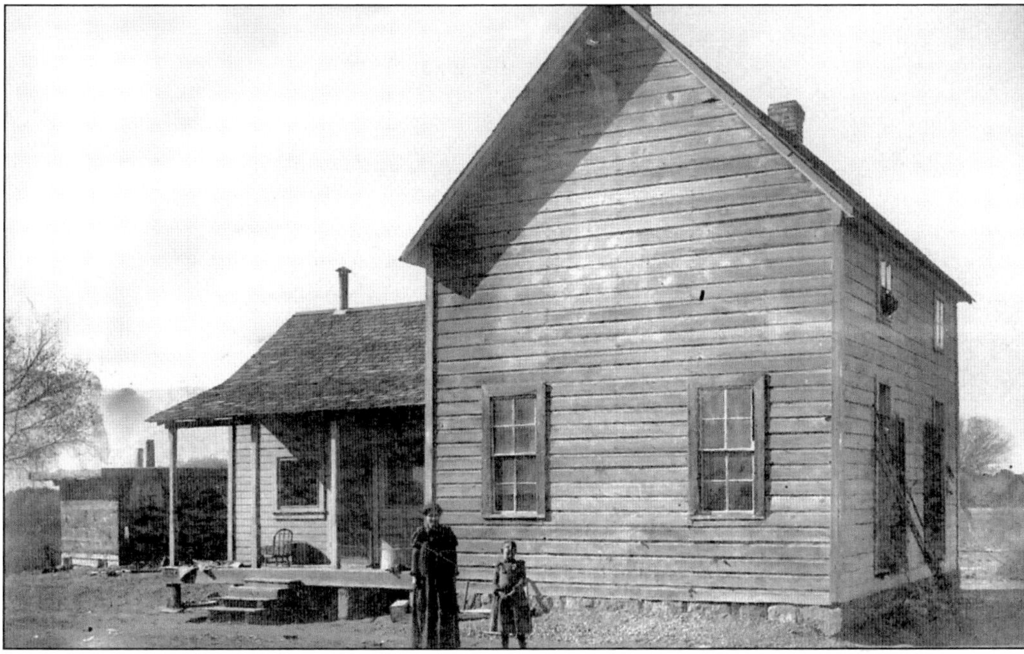

The permanent homes were stylish and inevitably included open porches that became summertime bedrooms. The demand for lumber and roof shakes resulted in the early development of lumber mills high up on Mount Graham. The Moroni Skinner home in the community of Graham was located north of the Gila River, across from Safford.

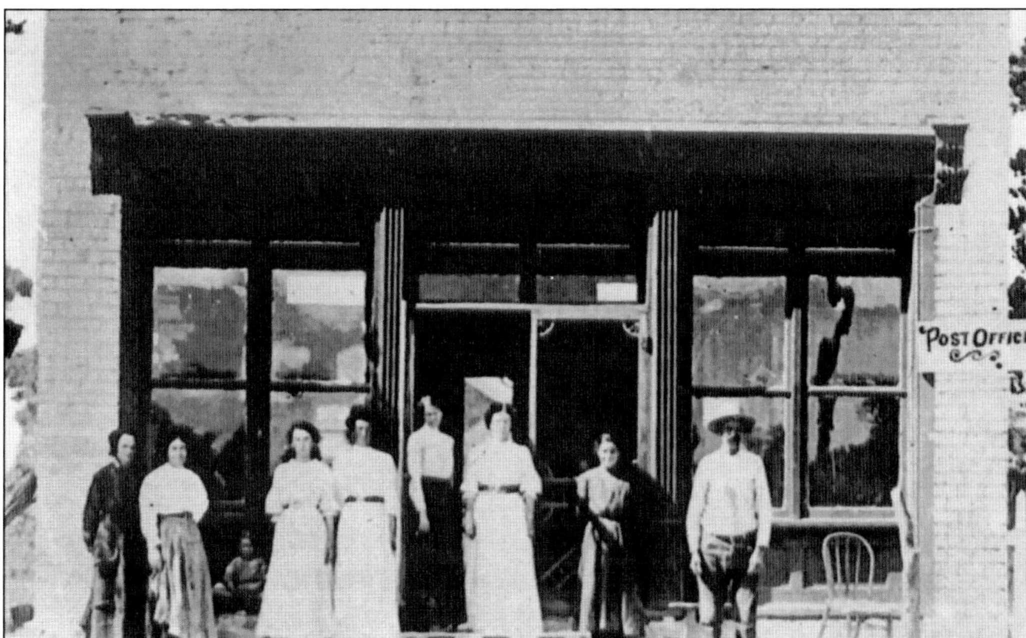

Communities were solidified around a local post office such as the Eden Post Office, pictured here. Quite often the postmaster or postmistress became one of the most popular and readily recognized people in the community. Mail delivery never developed, and the tradition of making daily trips to the post office has survived in most communities.

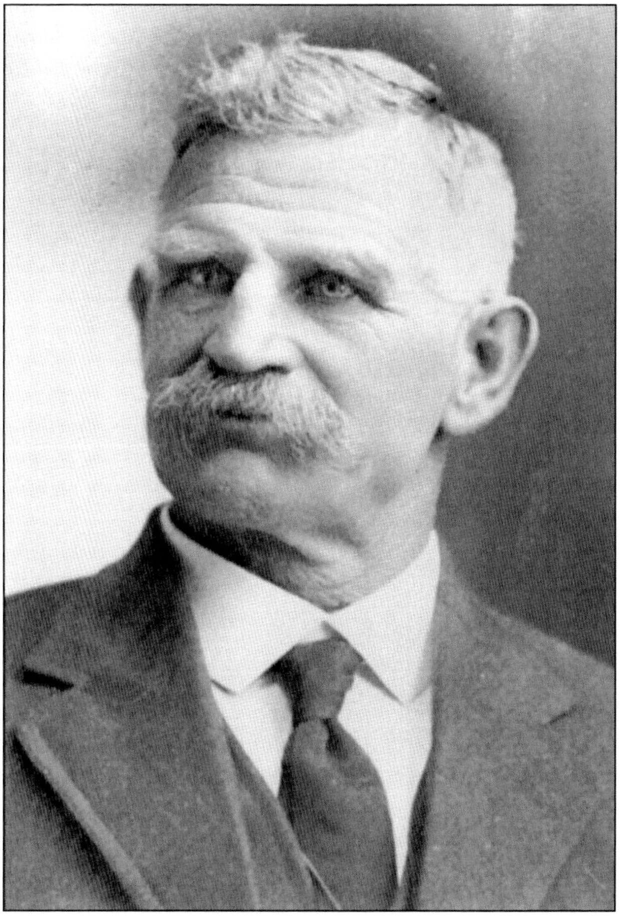

Known as "Mr. Bonita," Miles L. Woods was a longtime resident and shepherd of the community of Bonita near Fort Grant. Even though the Spanish word for pretty was applied to this community, it has a less than savory history, housing several bars and brothels for years. With the leadership of Miles Woods, though, the town was tamed. The first justice of the peace, he also proudly bore the title of judge. Within the community, Woods fulfilled military contracts for wood, hay, and beef.

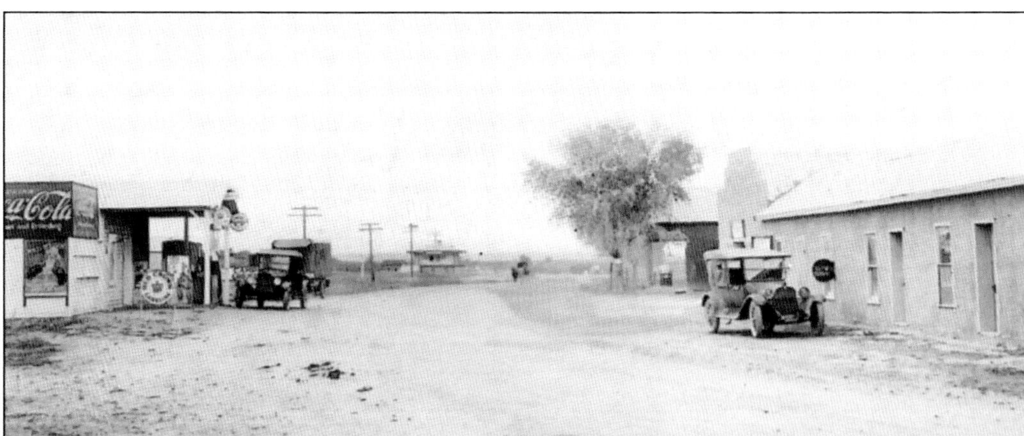

Like Bonita, a community developed near Fort Thomas in the 1880s. Called Maxey, it was a bawdy array of bars and brothels that serviced soldiers. After the fort closed, however, the town of Maxey disappeared and a new one developed into a prosperous farming and ranching area. Two markets straddled Highway 70 by the early 1900s. The left was owned and operated by Elkins and the other by W. O. Tuttle. In the 1920s, the little town of Fort Thomas was the home of three champion rodeo competitors: Breezy Cox, Everett Bowman, and Hugh Bennet.

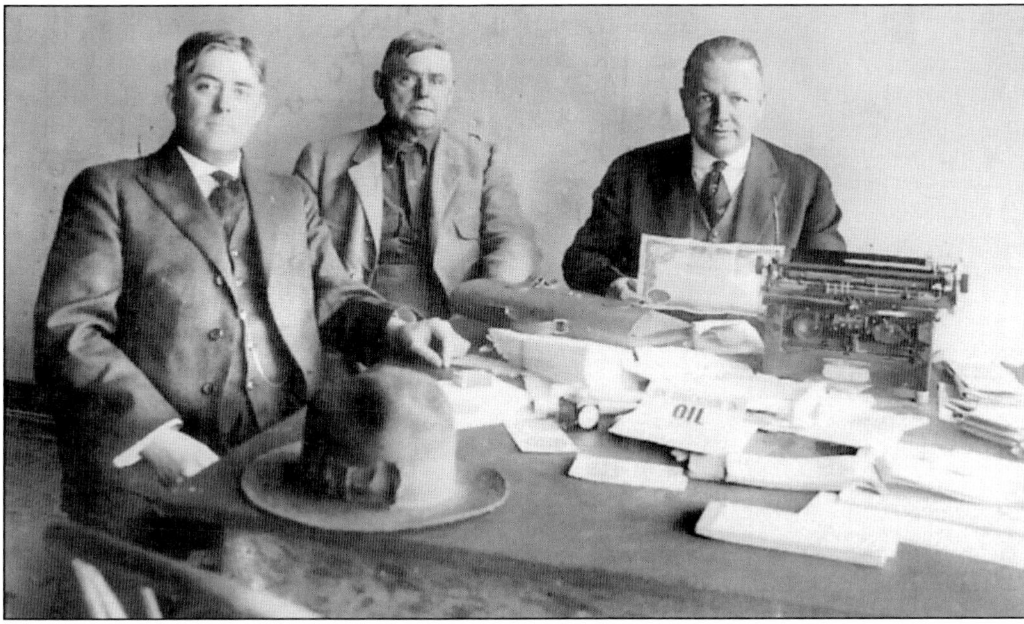

The wheeler-dealers of Fort Thomas, W. O. Tuttle (left) and two unidentified gentlemen, examine oil leases and stock certificates, possibly planning investments or loans. Tuttle, well known throughout the Gila Valley, was selected by the county board of supervisors to sit on the committee planning the celebration for the grand opening of the Graham County Courthouse, on Labor Day, September 6, 1916.

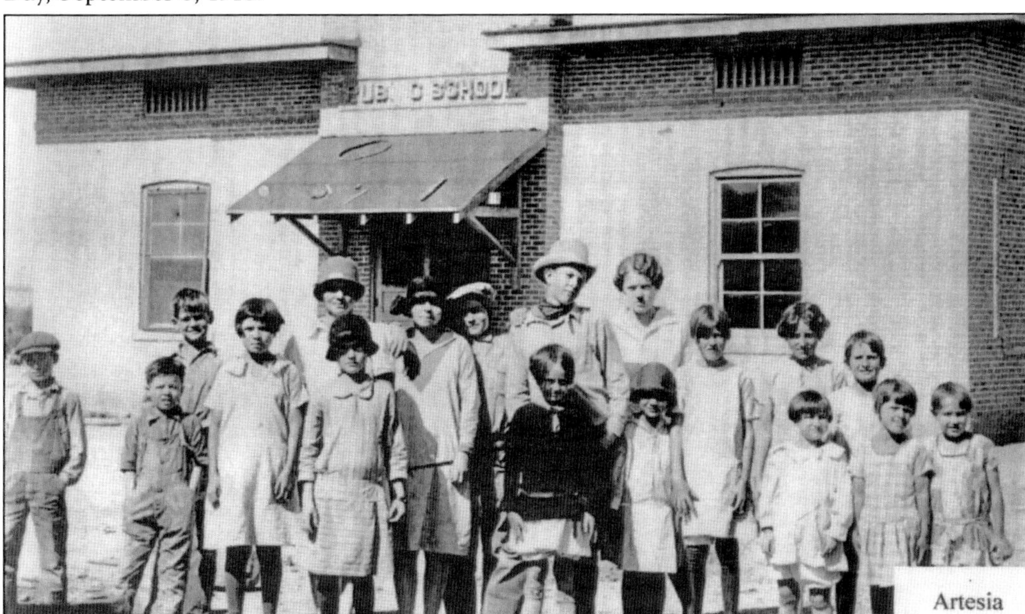

The Artesia School represents another of the communities south of Safford. In the 1930s, this school attracted students from the Lone Star area and the farmlands south of the road to Solomonville. Early farmers in the region recognized the importance of artesian waters. Those water sources allowed the irrigation of fields higher up on the valley floor that could not have been supplied with canals and ditches connected to the river.

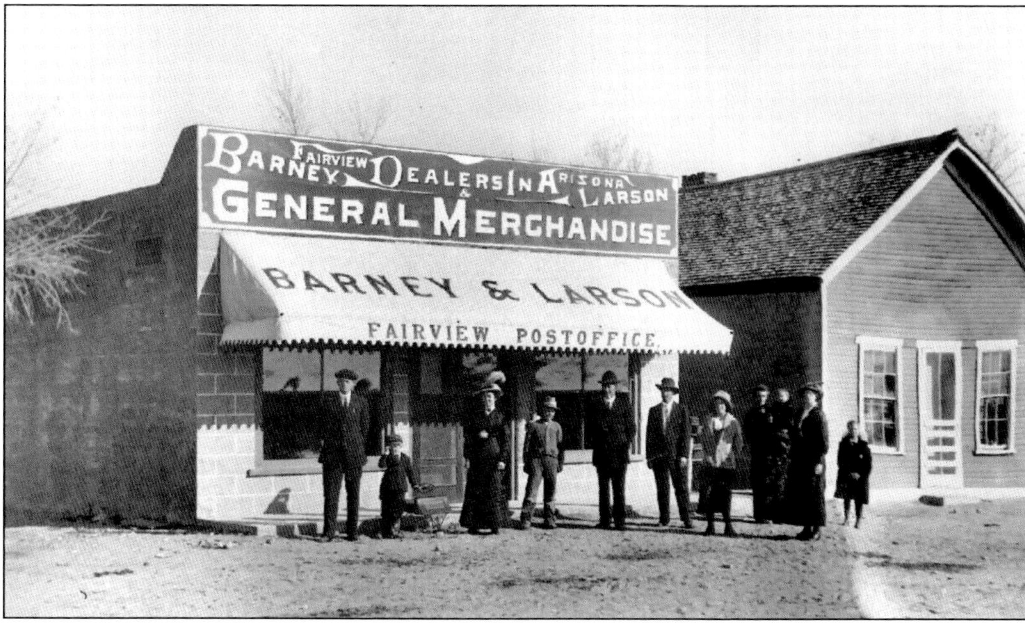

Fairview Market and Post Office, owned by Walter T. Barney, planned for a community of that name. But no town of Fairview ever developed. Instead, the community took the name of an early pioneer in that part of the valley: Joseph Matthews. Matthewsville never became a real town, only a market surrounded by farms. After the construction of the Gila Valley Globe & Northern Railway, the name again changed to Glenbar.

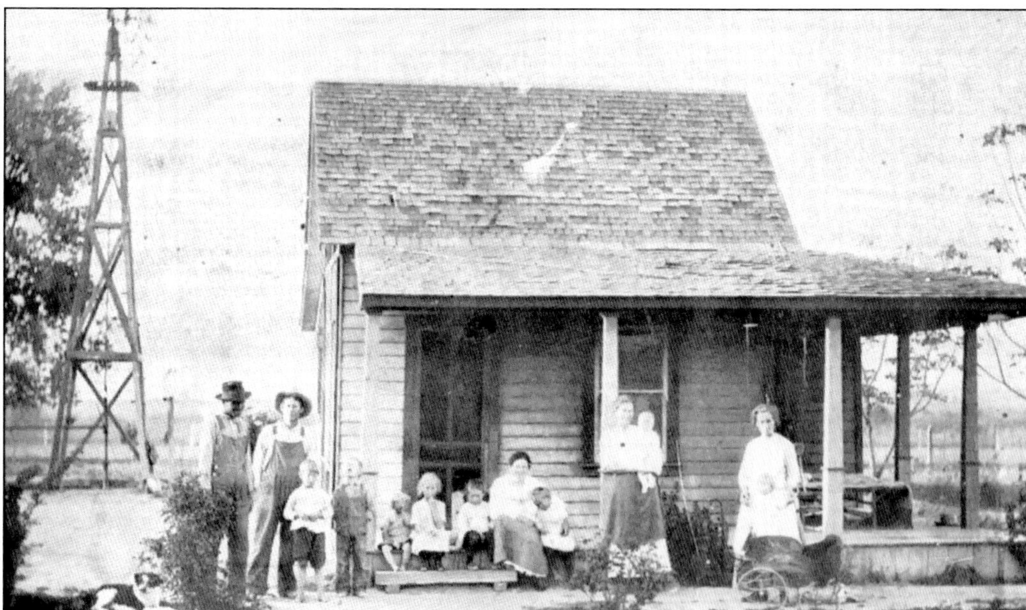

The farms around Glenbar provided sustenance gardens and cash crops like alfalfa, wheat, barley, and onions. Taking time out to visit neighbors was an important and necessary social event. Here neighbors gather at the Hyrum and Laura Smith home in 1916. Seen from left to right are Edward Moody, Hyrum Smith, Waldo Smith, Vernel Smith, Zella Moody, Hazel Moody, Gwen Moody, Grace Larson, Venice Larson, and Nello Smith.

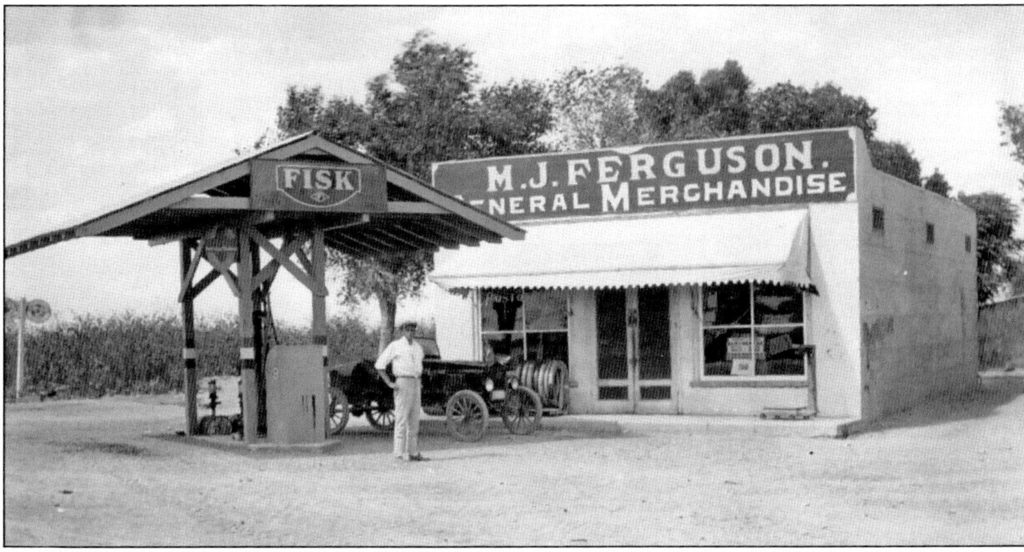

One of the most popular shops in the Glenbar area was the store, service station, and post office owned and operated by M. Jay Ferguson and his wife, Rose Emily. This is the same building originally known as the Barney & Larson Merchandise store. The couple built a home close to the store and successfully provided just about every type of merchandise and service customers could hope for. (Courtesy Ray Ferguson.)

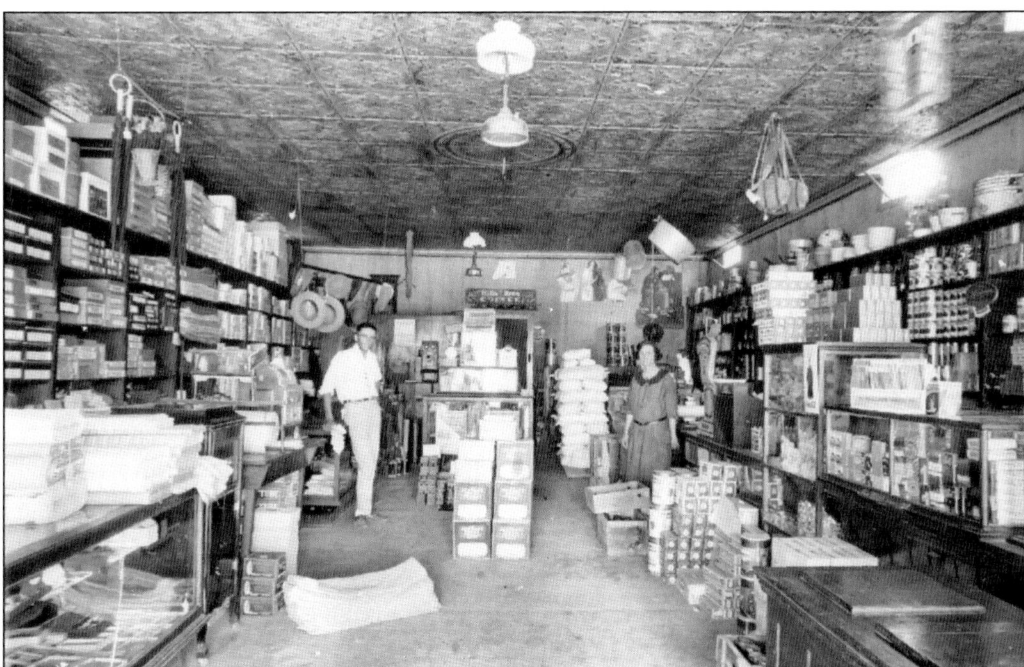

The Ferguson Store stacked merchandise from floor to ceiling. From canned goods to shoes, overalls to pocket knives, Jay could get it. The author's mother often remarked that when her family arrived in the valley in the 1930s, her father took her to Glenbar to buy a pair of school shoes. (Courtesy Ray Ferguson.)

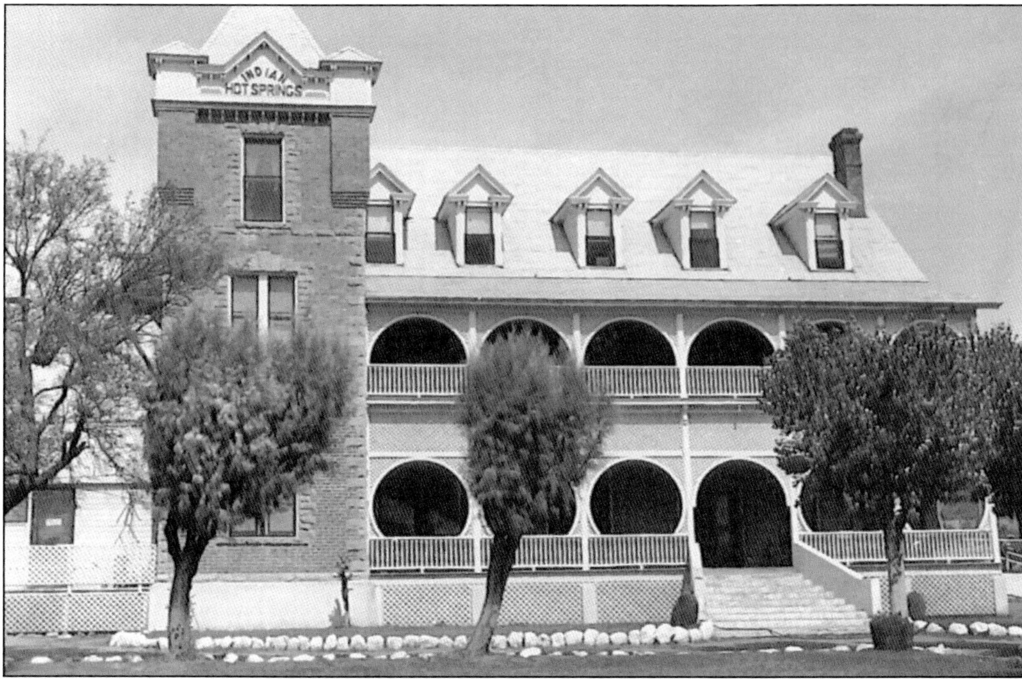

The most popular attraction in the Gila Valley was Indian Hot Springs. Fort Thomas merchants John and Andy Alexander built the hotel near some natural hot springs in 1903. Pictured here in its remodeled splendor, it attracted entertainment-starved miners from Globe. By 1916, each weekend would see 300 to 400 Globe residents board the Gila Valley Globe & Northern Railway. They would disembark at Cork Crossing, where they would board wagons to cross the Gila River to get to the hotel.

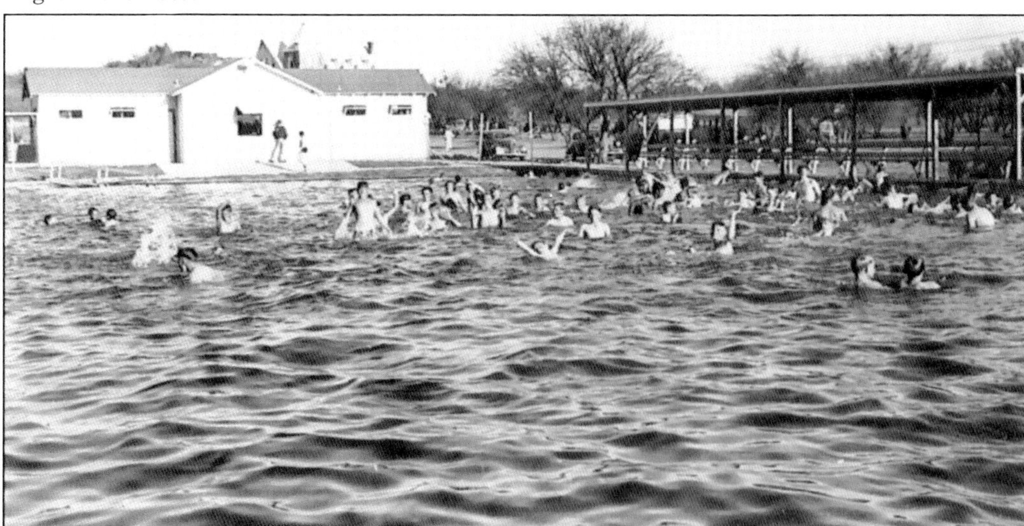

Fed by natural artesian springs, the Indian Hot Springs plunge offered bathing suit rentals, changing rooms, and a huge, slippery bottomed pool. At various locations were shallow ditches that emptied into small bathing tubs where visitors could lounge away the hours covered with slow-running hot water. The grounds were popular for weddings, family reunions, and weekend romps. Valley gals found beaus on these familiar grounds.

Four

Irrigation and Farming

From Grains to Cotton

Flat, rich land attracted all types of people to the Gila Valley. Early Mexican settlers in San Jose and LDS pioneers shared the quest with a group of farmers from Gila Bend whose dreams of building canals for irrigation in that region were destroyed by flooding. However, their renewed efforts in the Safford area resulted in the creation of the Montezuma Canal Company.

Early on, grains, grasses, and alfalfa were in great demand by the U.S. cavalry. Ready cash came from contracts to supply the military with fodder for their horses and beef for both the soldiers and Apaches on the reservation. The successful planting of sustenance vegetable gardens and orchards slowly grew into another source for cash. Great demand developed for soft-shelled pecans and wheat. The first industries were initiated with the freight delivery of farm produce and the establishment of flour mills. These enterprises were developed by farmers themselves and often became successful, thriving businesses.

Even though there is evidence that prehistoric tribes in the area harvested and used cotton fibers for weaving into cloth, large-scale cotton growing did not develop in the Gila Valley until after World War I. The long, hot growing season proved to be great for cotton production, but the increased demand for water required expansion of the canal system. The need for seasonal employees also became apparent.

Real expansion of cotton production began during the period of the Dust Bowl and the Great Depression. Migrant farmers and their families flowed westward looking for new opportunities and employment. Cotton hoeing, picking, and transport offered ready cash for locals and migrants.

During World War II, the demand for seasonal workers caused local cotton farmers to travel all the way to the Navajo Reservation in northern Arizona. In that era, the face of farming within the valley dramatically changed. Instead of hundreds of acres of wheat, alfalfa, and vegetable gardens, farmers expanded their cultivated fields into thousands of acres of cotton. Cotton gins were built and co-ops became commonplace.

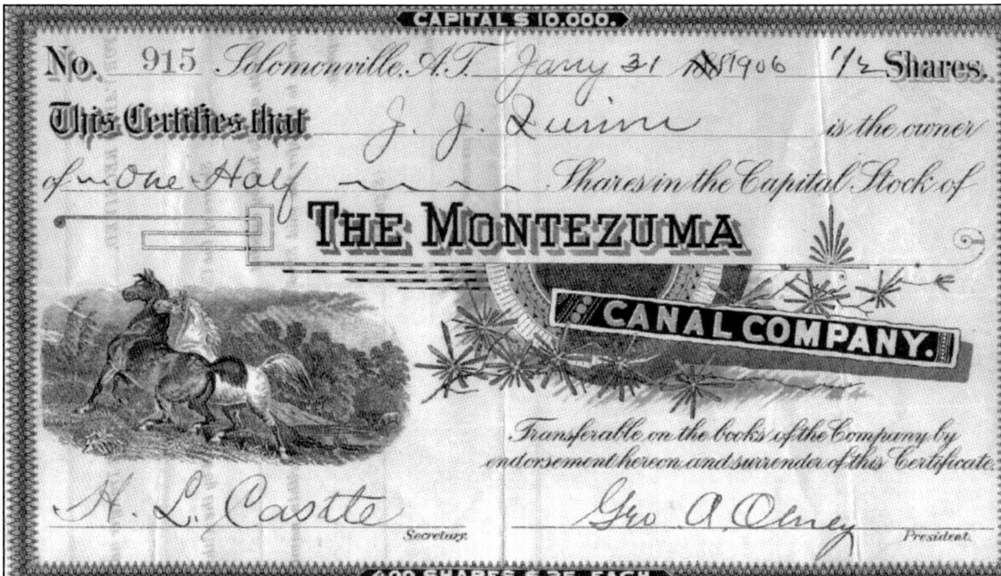

The first and longest continually operated canal in the valley was dug in 1874 by William Munson, Thomas McWilliams, and Tom McQuinn. In that same year, farmers in San Jose dug a ditch along an ancient system, setting a pattern for later development. About the same time, LDS farmers in the central part of the community started digging the Central Canal. Solomon incorporated the Union Canal in 1886.

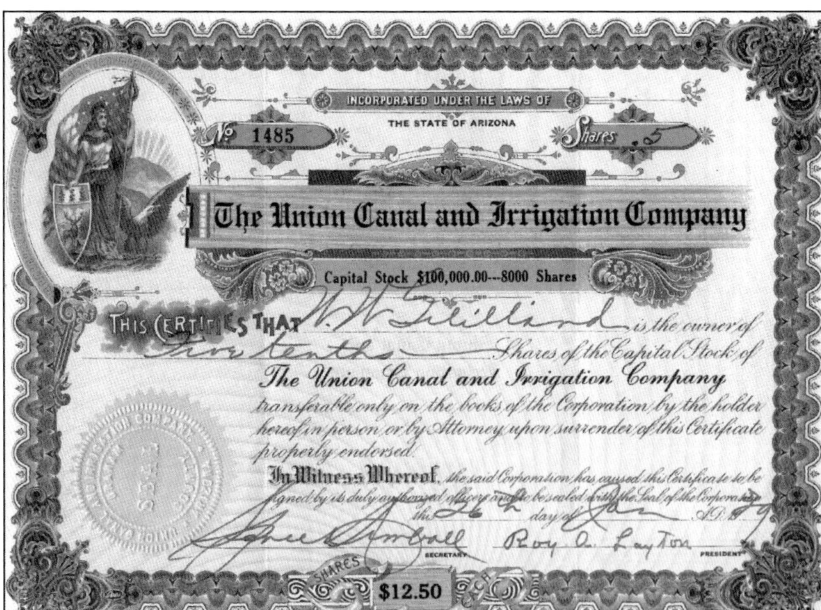

Solomon's Union Canal brought water to the farms south of the river between the already operating Montezuma and Central Canals. Two years later, Edward D. Tuttle, John Welker, Victorio Garcia, S. W. Pomeroy, some local farmers, and Solomon incorporated the Montezuma Extension Canal. By 1890, Solomon and his board of directors had incorporated the South Solomonville Canal with capital stock of $2,000. Like the Montezuma Canal, the South Solomonville Canal had its head in San Jose.

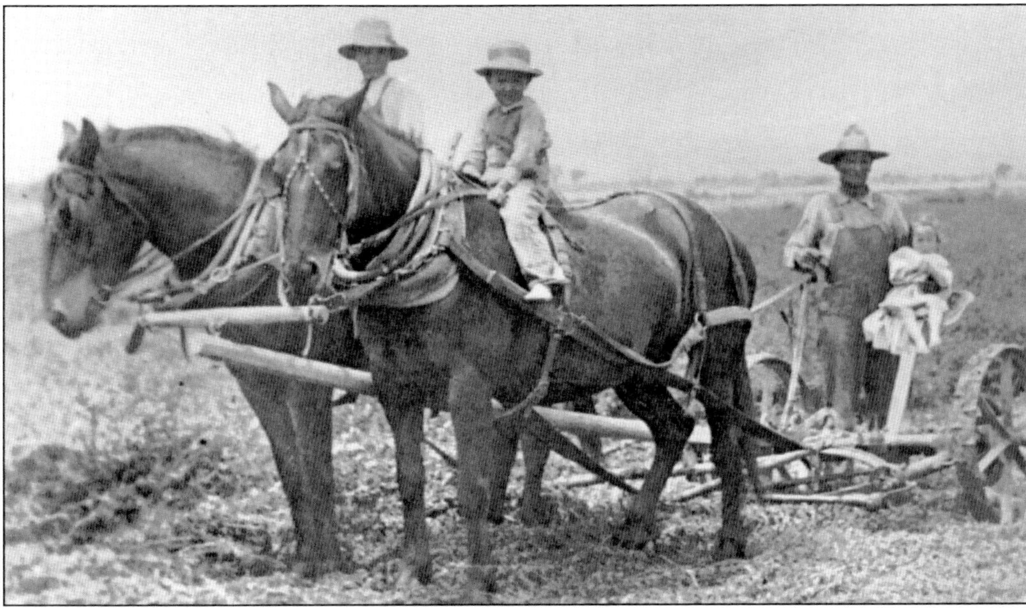

The use of gas-fired engines in tractors and as stationary machines came about slowly. In fact, it was not uncommon to see horse-powered farm implements working side by side with tractors throughout the Depression years. Farmers taught their children at a young age to handle the equipment and share in the responsibilities of running a farm.

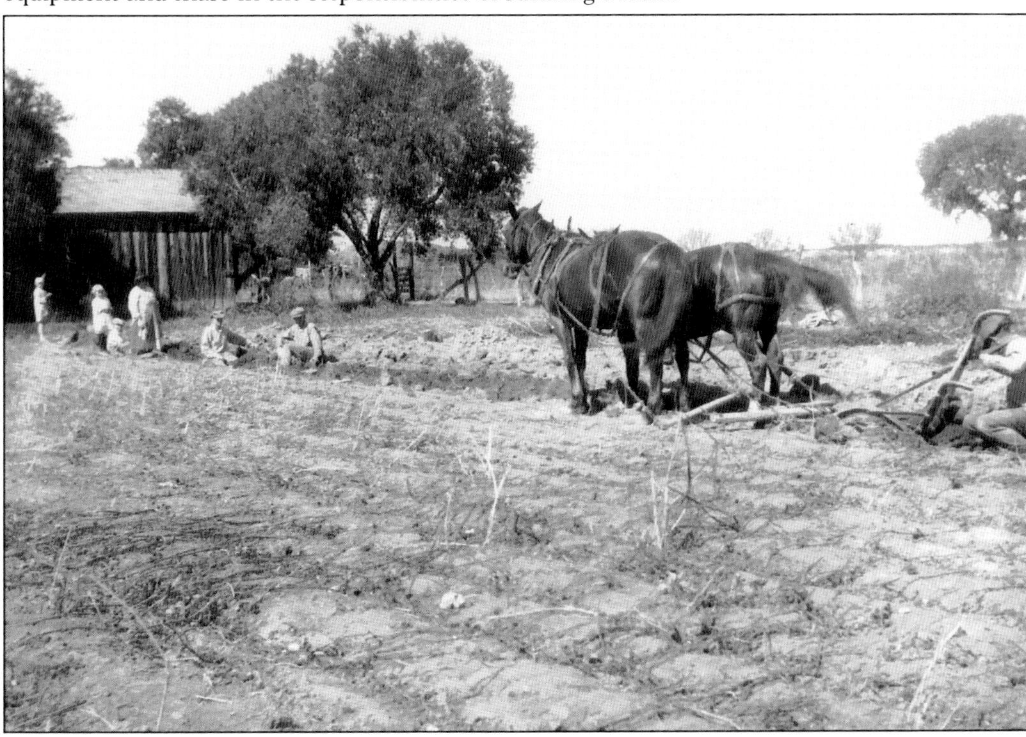

Ed McSweeny's farm in Central was one of many family farms in the area during the 1920s and 1930s. A team of horses and the entire family were all that was needed to put in a crop. The next photograph indicates that the McSweenys were harvesting sweet potatoes in the fall.

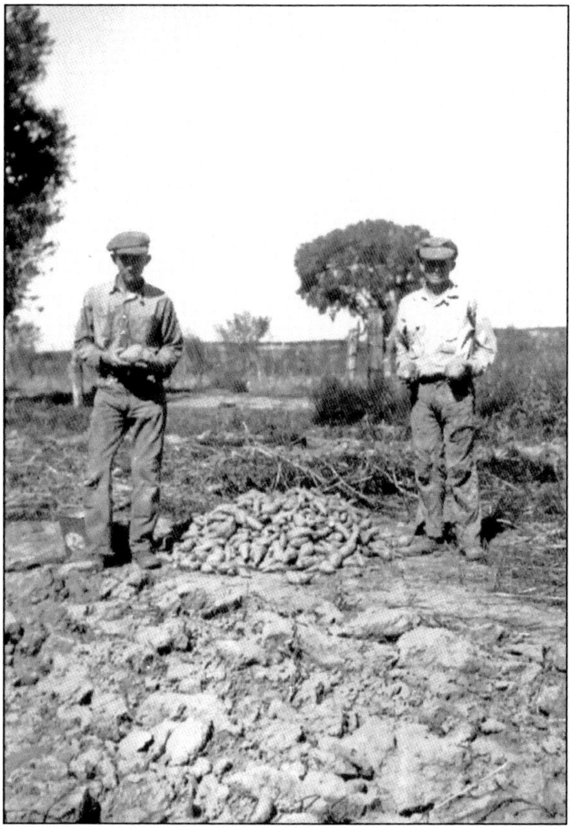

In the 1930s, sustenance farming helped valley residents survive the Great Depression. With cash scarce, a plentiful crop of sweet potatoes not only provided a sweet source of protein for the family, but also earned a penny apiece from local markets. Local farmers were very generous during hard times. Often, wagon loads of beef, fruits, and vegetables would show up unattended in poor neighborhoods. When the wagons were emptied, they would just disappear.

Unused flatlands attracted those who could buy the land, clear the desert flora, dig ditches connected to canals or other ditches, and cultivate the land. Christopher Layton (left) was a LDS church leader and founder of Thatcher. Here he and an unidentified friend stand near a roller used to level the land and to create the correct slope needed for irrigation and drainage.

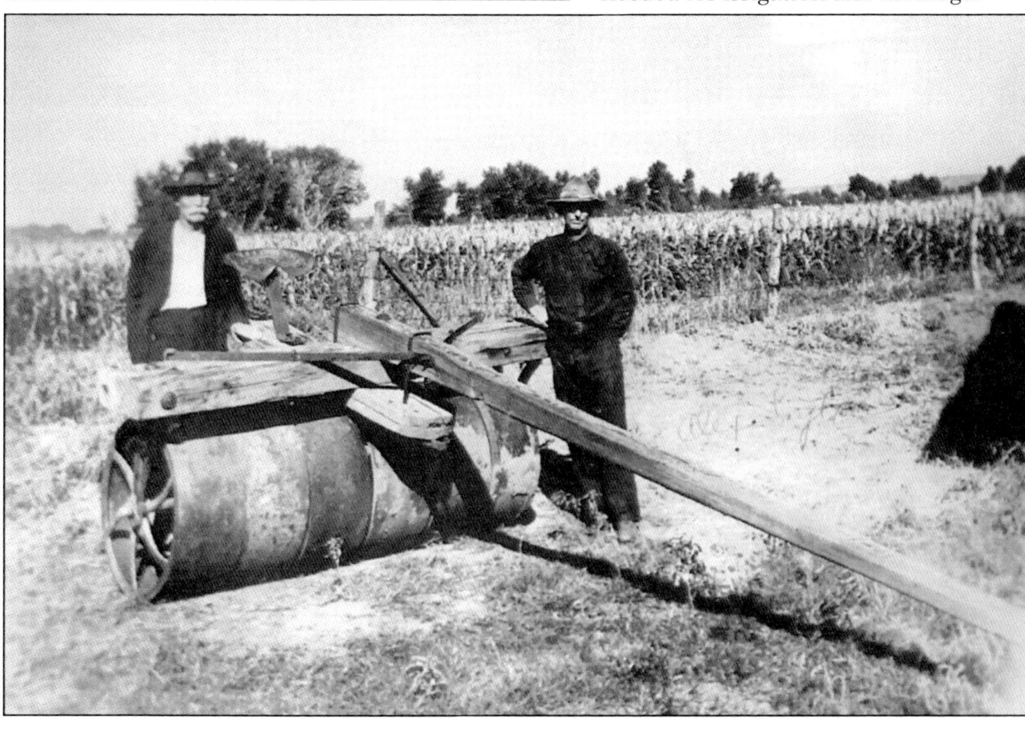

Andrew and Viola Angle were skilled farmers. Ed Moody, a veteran farmer in the Ashurst area, remembered when Andy dug up two humongous sweet potatoes. One weighed 28 pounds and the other 14 pounds. In 1925, the Angles moved to Jacobson Canyon on Mount Graham and planted an apple orchard, with neighbors willing to pay to pick the fruit right off the trees. Angle's Orchard continues to produce apples to this day.

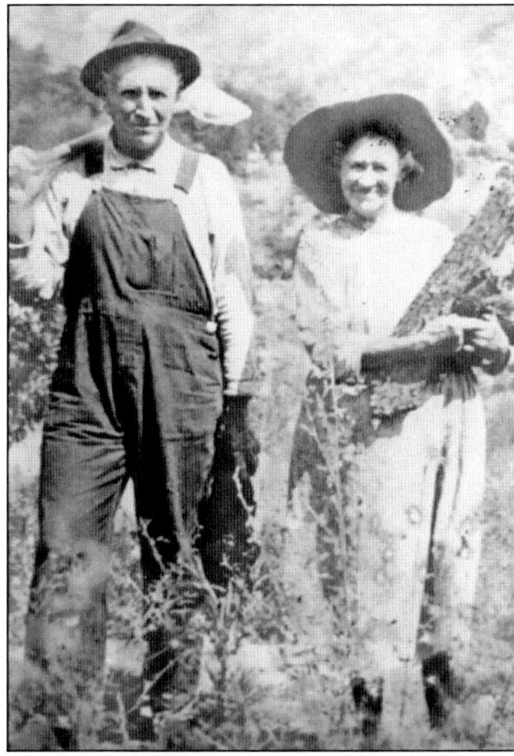

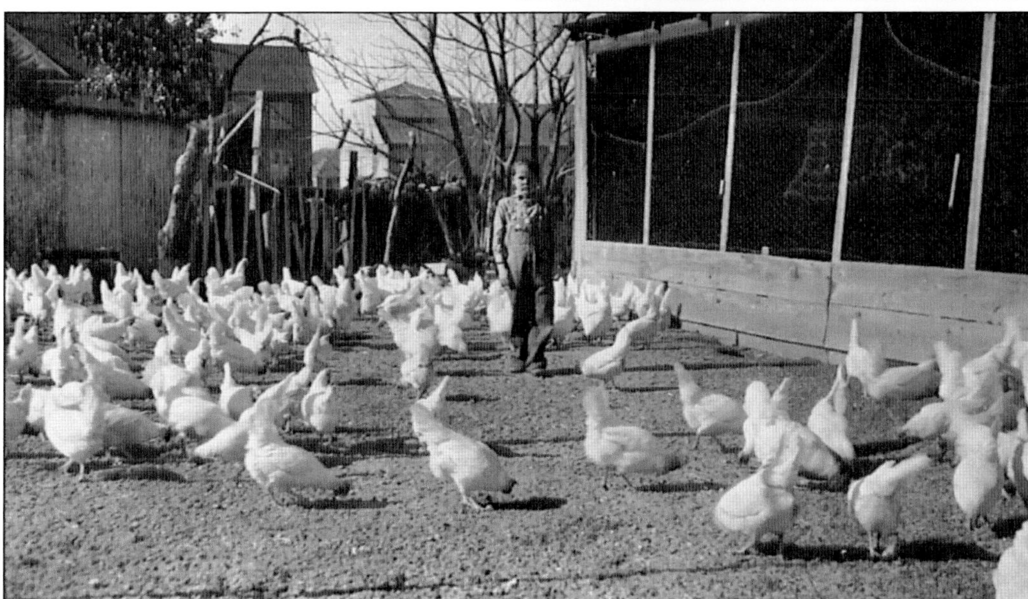

Another widespread activity was the raising of chickens for both meat and egg production. Some specialized in registered flocks like these white leghorns. It was easy to spot a farm with a large chicken-raising operation: the ubiquitous long chicken coops were usually accompanied by brood houses that contained heated incubators and sorting bins. Families often maintained a flock of laying hens. Each morning, a family member spread chicken feed across the backyard or collected eggs.

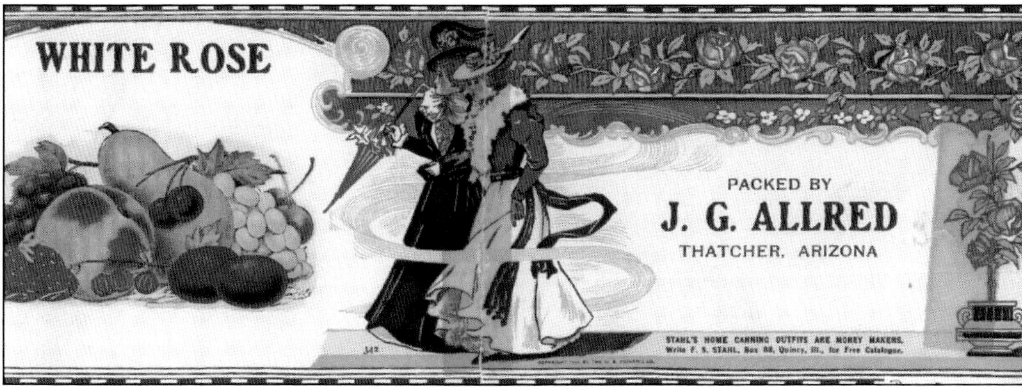

An ambitious young man and his wife, pictured below, expanded their fruit orchard and vegetable garden into a thriving canning company. This colorful label provides proof of production and marketing skills. Most households canned fruits and vegetables in the fall, while non-farming families appreciated ready-made products available in markets throughout the valley.

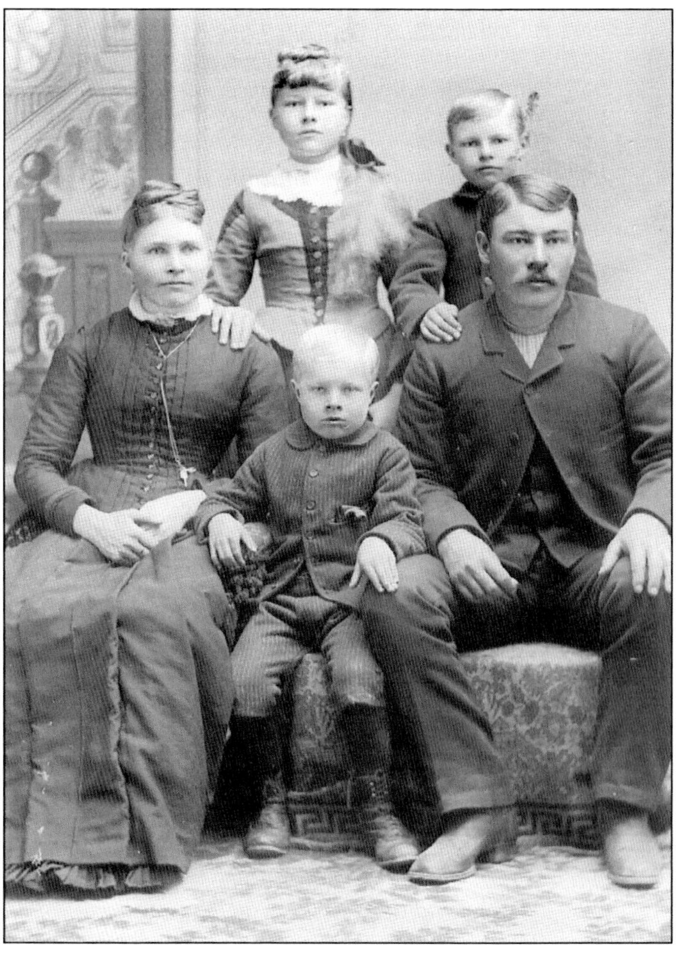

J. G. Allred and his family combined their efforts to produce a popular brand of canned fruits and vegetables. Josh, as he was known, was a clever young man with a great sense of humor. He was among a group of 14 seniors at the LDS Academy who were expelled in 1909 for ditching classes as an April Fool's Day prank.

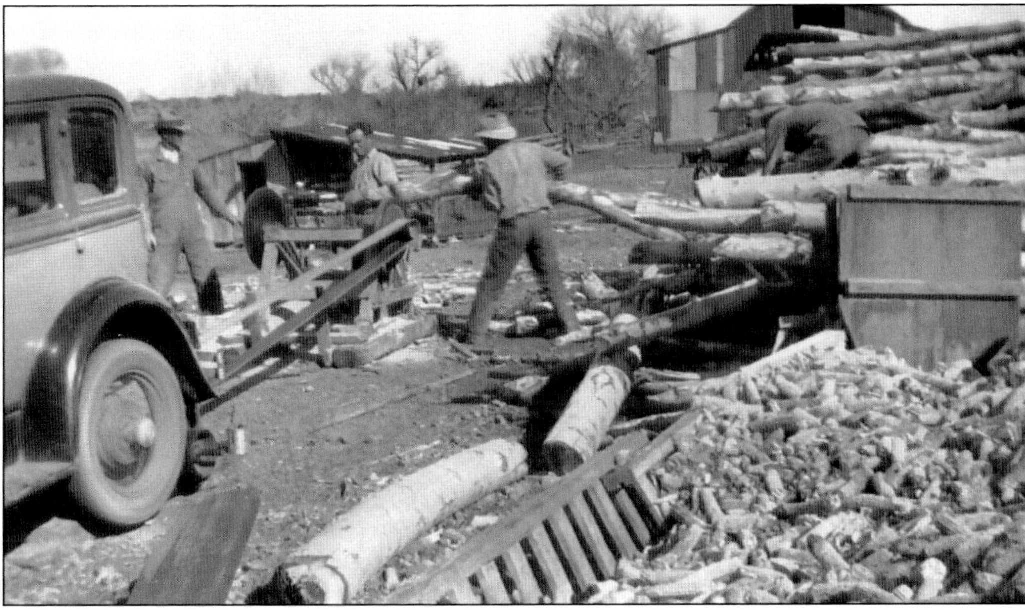

The use of automobiles to operate farm equipment was common during the 1930s. Here members of the Heaton and Lunt families cut up cottonwood trees that were cleared to create more tillable land. The Heaton Lunt operation in Duncan produced everything from alfalfa to onions, becoming one of the largest exporting operations in the area.

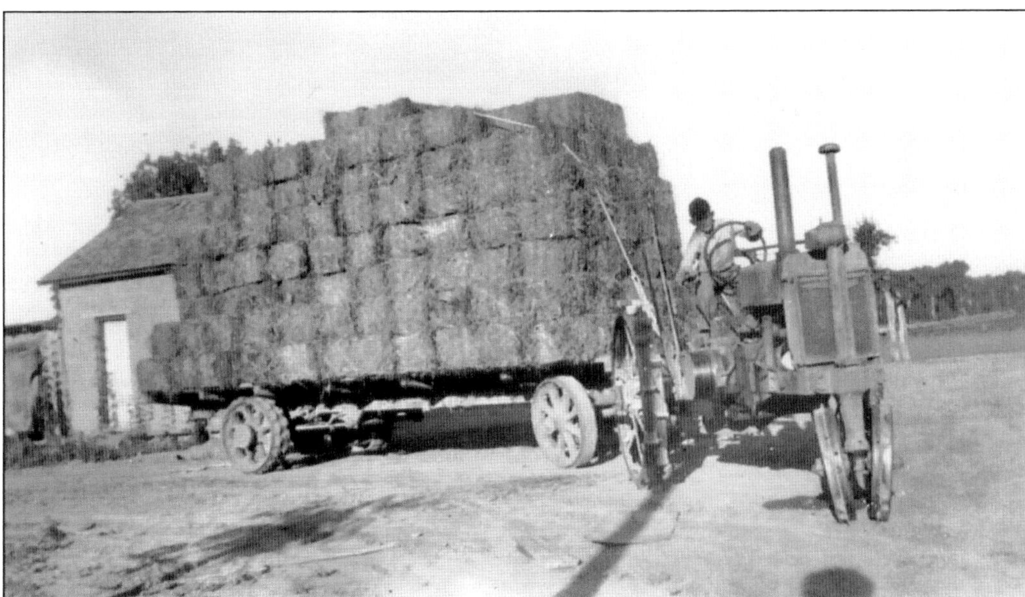

The first steel-wheeled tractor in the Gila Valley, this 1939 model provided years of service, and its engine is still being used today. Notice that the wagon also has steel wheels. This type was not any good on soft, muddy ground, but on well-worn roads it worked well and saved a lot of money in tire repair and replacement.

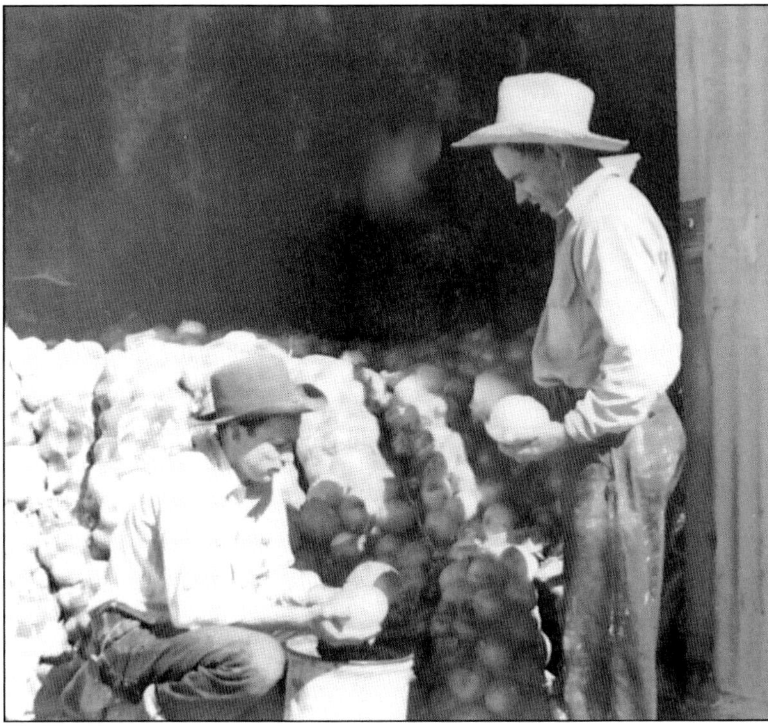

During the 1930s, onion production was a profitable business. Onions were harvested and sacked in the fields and then brought to warehouses in preparation for shipping. Truckloads left the Heaton Lunt Farm in Duncan and were shipped by rail to towns in California. Like cattle buyers, brokers would offer lot prices for truckloads of produce. Of all those who made profits off produce, farmers usually made the smallest.

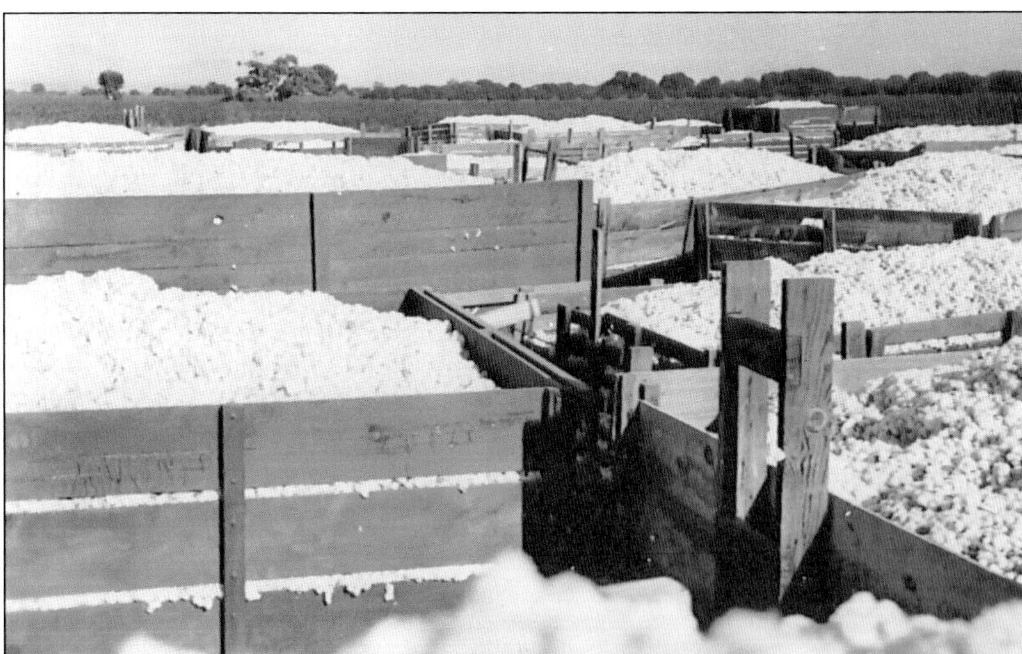

Clean, white cotton like this, waiting to be ginned in 1950, was all handpicked. The wagons parked near the rows being picked included two things: a scale where the filled cotton sacks would be weighed, and a table and chair with a farmer, his wife, or a cotton boss writing in a tablet the names and weights of each bag carried to the wagon. Paid 5¢ a pound, these seasonal employees would earn, on average, $10 to $20 per day.

Five

Cattle, Angora Goats, and Horses

Among the earliest ranchers in the area was Texas emigrant James Hinton. He befriended the Apaches at the San Carlos Sub-agency, married an Apache woman, and started raising cattle for the U.S. military. He was the first rancher to populate an area south of the reservation near Mount Turnbull. The demand for mining in the area resulted in the removal of the "Mineral Strip" from the reservation. Some 80 years later, the Mineral Strip was returned to the tribe, disrupting the lives of more than 20 ranching families.

Certainly the best-known early rancher in the area, even before Graham County was created, was George H. Stevens. Like James Hinton, Stevens married an Apache woman. But unlike Hinton's wife, Francesca Stevens lived with her husband in Solomonville until her death in 1882. Stevens bought the Eureka Springs Ranch and became the first elected Graham County sheriff in 1882. He served in the territorial legislature at the time Graham County was created. Additionally his Eagle Creek Ranch was the location of a horrendous murder that sparked a countywide search for the perpetrators.

Horses have been a source of pride and competition among Gila Valley ranching families. Around 1900, carriage horses and massive workhorses like Percherons were shown in competition. Thereafter, rodeo competition caught fire, and Graham County became the center for the early development of the Professional Rodeo Cowboy Association (PRCA). World champions and the PRCA presidency were bred and raised in the valley.

World War I increased the demand for mohair, causing the expansion of Angora goat ranching into all the foothills and the Mineral Strip. There was never a major conflict between traditional cattle ranchers and goat ranchers because they were often the same people. The end of Angora goat ranching came as a result of government regulations limiting the size of herds.

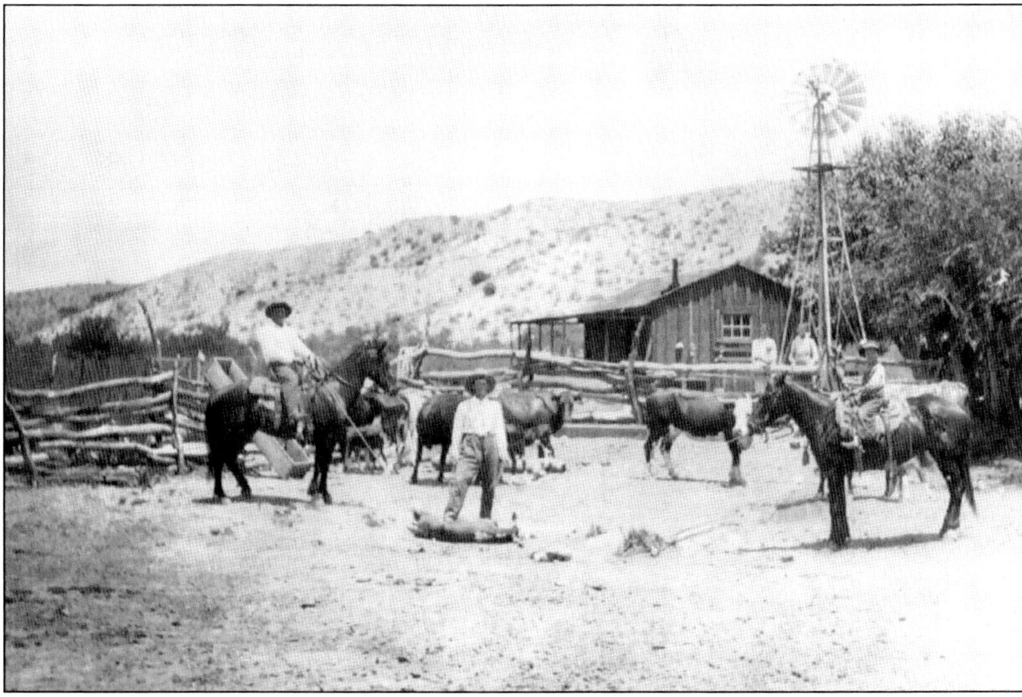

One of the earliest ranching families was the Hinton clan, who introduced cattle to the foothills of Mount Turnbull on what had been part of the San Carlos Apache Reservation. (Courtesy Sharon Hinton.)

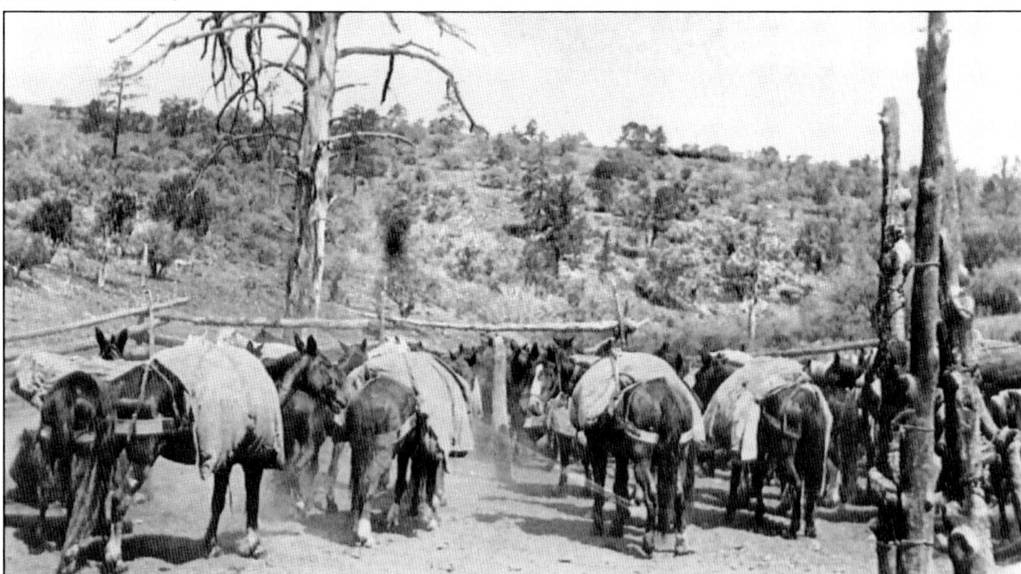

George Stevens's Eagle Creek Ranch was a popular location for mine speculators. The remoteness of the upper creek and the rugged nature of the area required fully equipped mule trains to sustain any serious operation. More money was actually made by the operators of mule trains, like the one pictured here, than by gold speculators. Years later, the area produced high-quality copper ore. (Courtesy Sharon Hinton.)

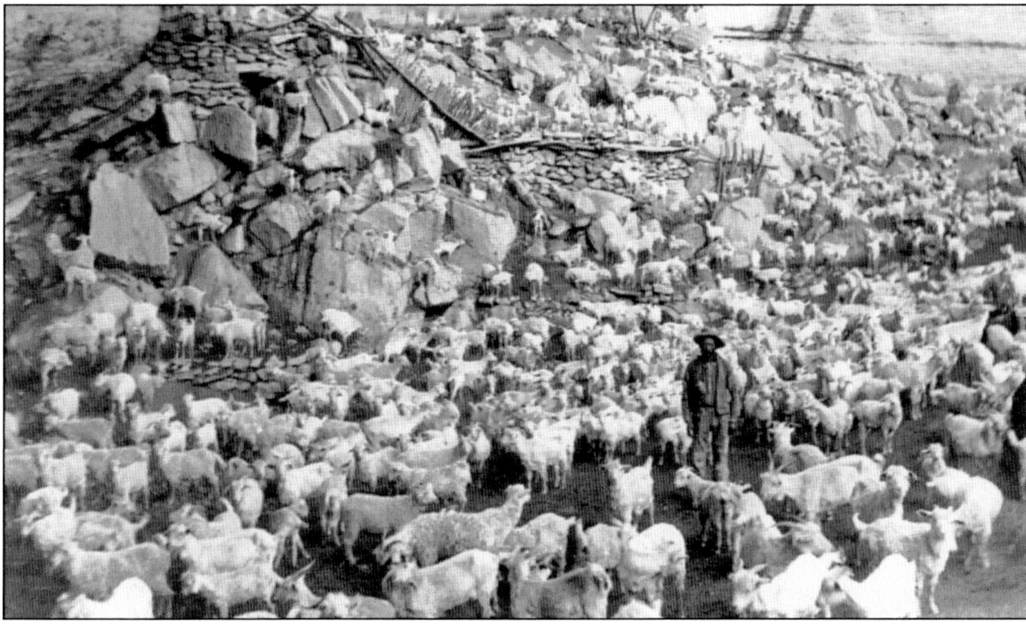

Angora goats such as these Alliburton goats in Turkey Creek provided a good source of cash both before and after World War I. Oscar Webster became a mohair broker and offered $4 per full gunnysack. The growth in the number of herds increased the demand for Mexican goat herders and shearers. Not all people got rich off goats, but the business spread across both sides of the Gila River and in the foothills surrounding Mount Graham, the Santa Teresas, and Mount Turnbull.

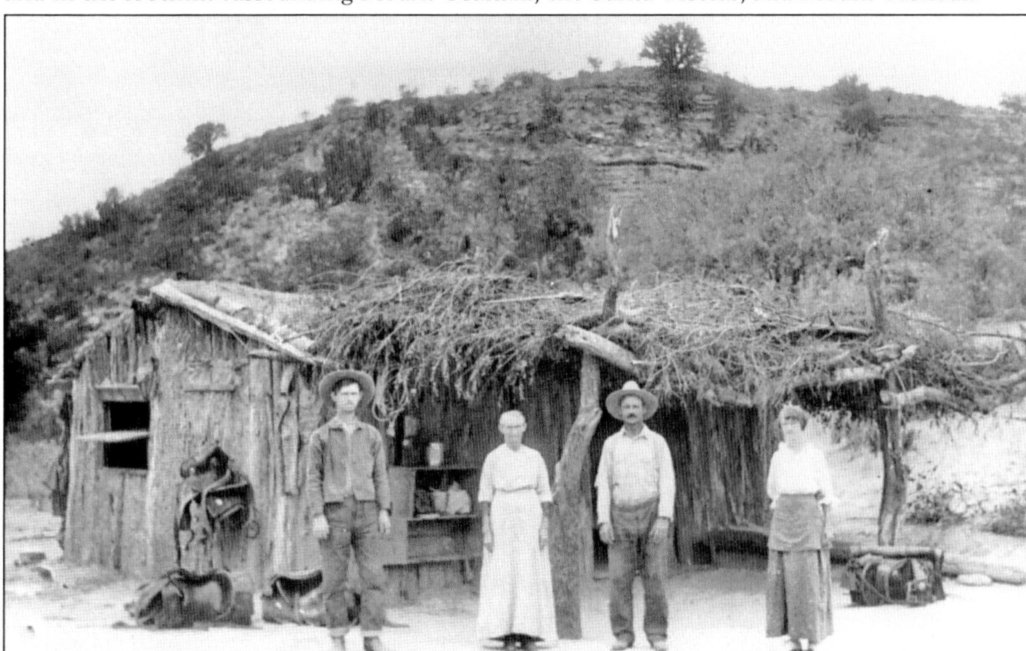

The Alliburtons lived in rustic surroundings while growing their Angora goat herd in Turkey Creek at the start of the 20th century. These isolated homes often survived to become line shacks after the construction of more comfortable ranch headquarters.

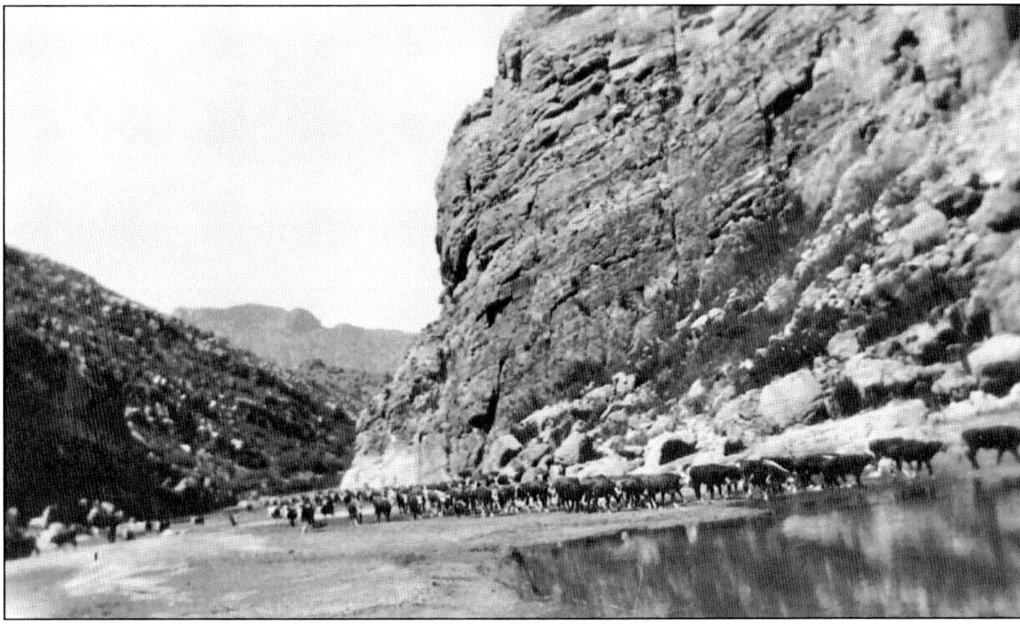

Roundups were important annual events on the ranches throughout Graham County. Here Marc Claridge and Ed Bowman combine their efforts to drive cattle up the Gila River at the site where the Coolidge Dam would be built in 1928. The two worked with Wheeler Reece and others in the area to develop sturdy stock that could survive in isolated canyons.

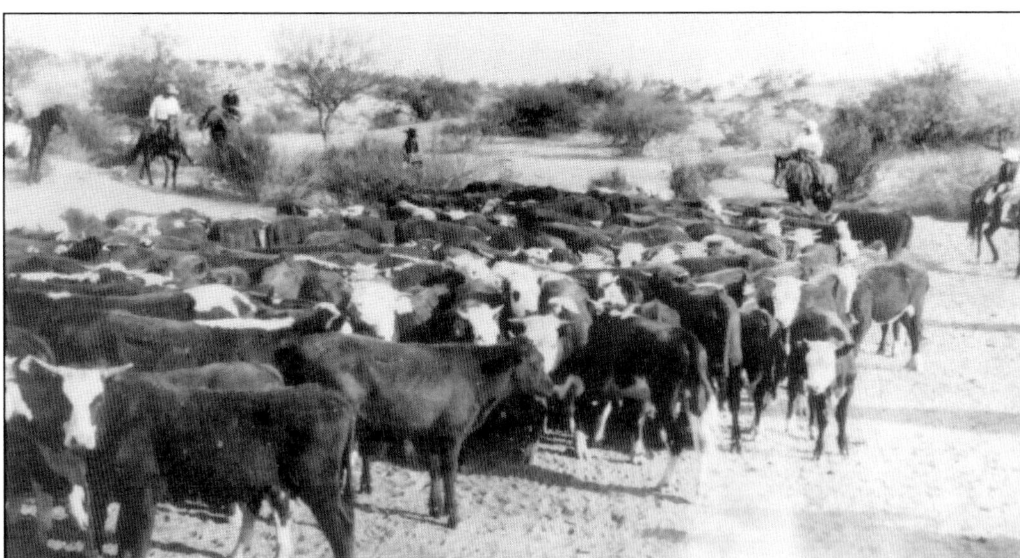

On the east slopes of the Mineral Strip, the Hinton roundups drove cattle eastward up the Gila River to the railhead at Geronimo. When the Geronimo depot closed, the cattle were driven three more miles east to Fort Thomas. Several members of the Hinton family developed ranches on and near the Mineral Strip and usually coordinated roundups. Traditional ranching was practiced on the Strip until all the ranchers were removed. (Courtesy Sharon Hinton.)

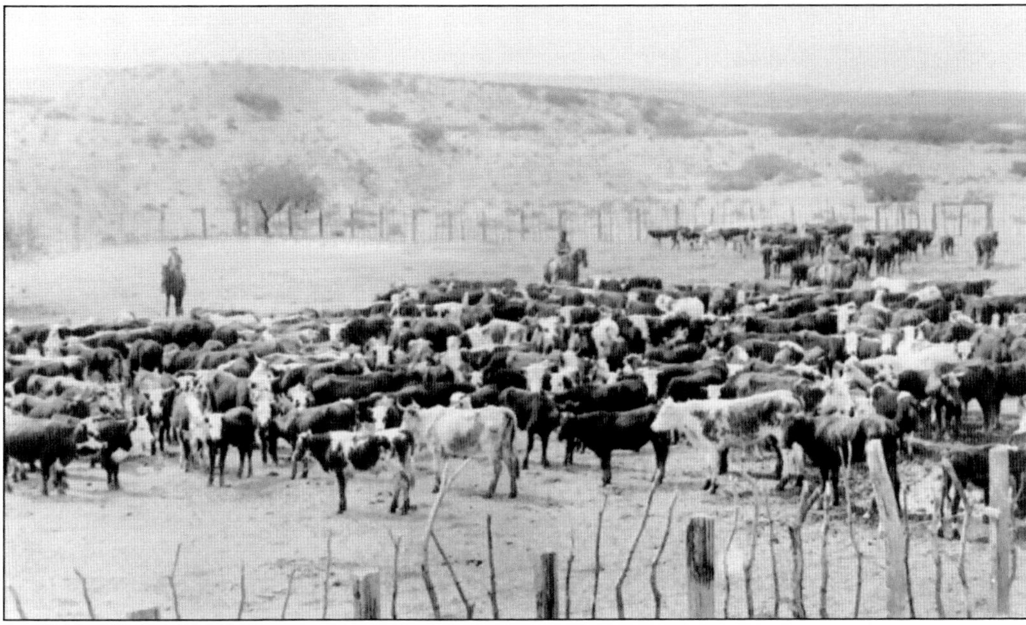

Hollis Holladay developed herds of sturdy cattle on Bear Flats, south of Pima. The steers were driven to railroad holding pens in Pima for shipment. It is apparent that these cowboys have corralled a herd to get the calves ready for branding. Branding was a tedious job that required skill and patience. The Holladay family moved its herd to the Black Rock Ranch, which survives today as both a working ranch and a guest ranch.

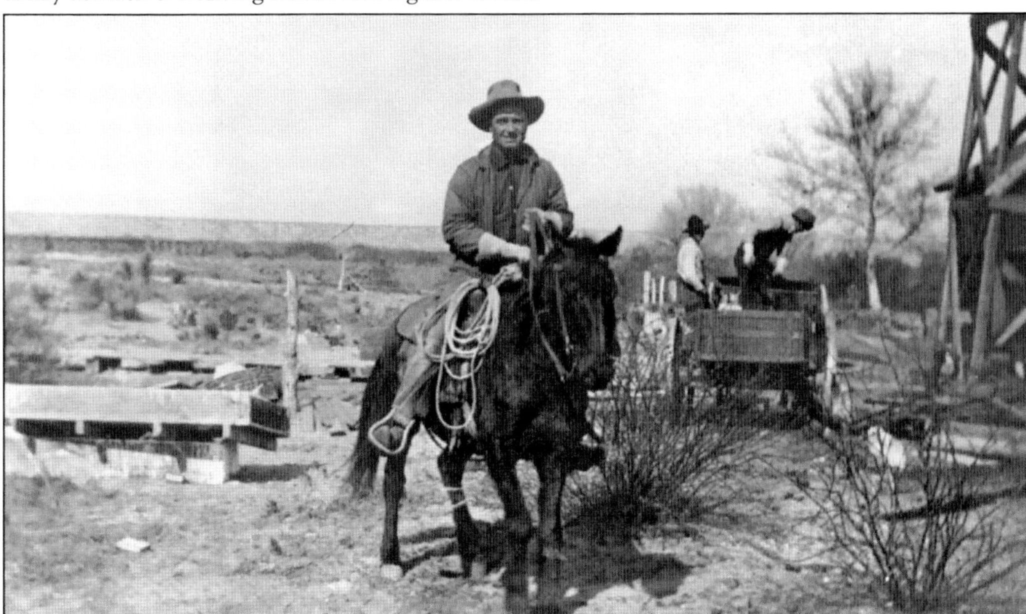

Near Black Rock, just off the reservation, Hollis Holladay (on horse) and Tee Hinton raised herds of Mexican longhorns and Herefords that developed an ability to thrive in the rugged terrain. Both ranchers leased numerous sections of land that required fencing and the establishment of water tanks and traps. Days were spent in the saddle tending to improvements on the land and taking care of injured and isolated cattle.

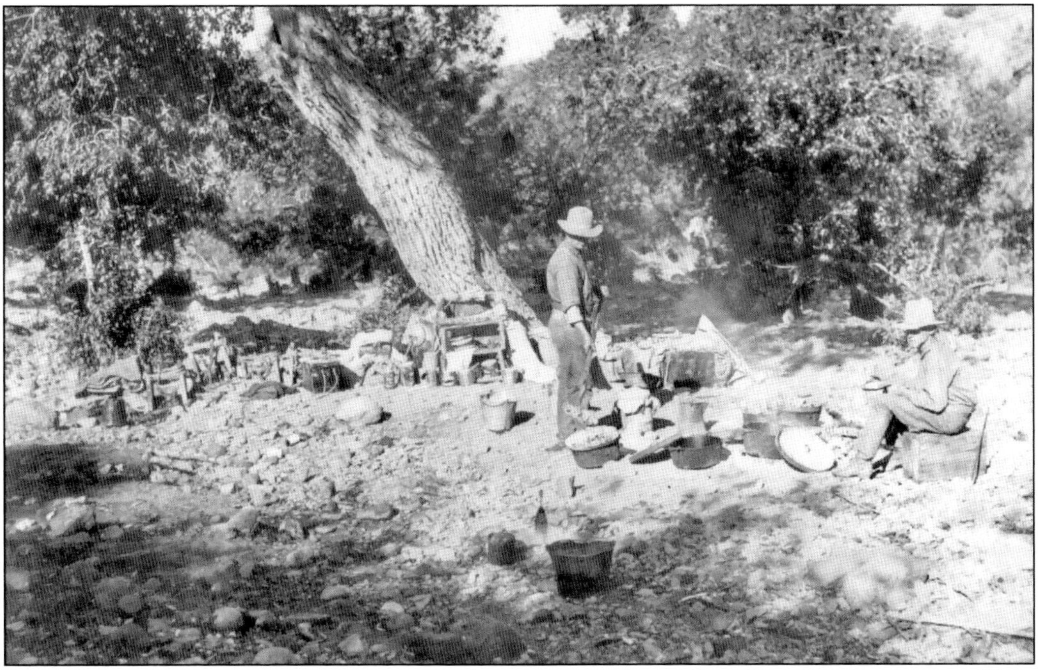

During roundups, it was necessary to provide cowboys with good meals and a place to rest. Here Tee Hinton grabs a bite while overseeing the cook, who has several Dutch ovens going at the same time. Cowboys demanded beans, biscuits, bacon, and chicken. They often complained when beef stew was served too often.

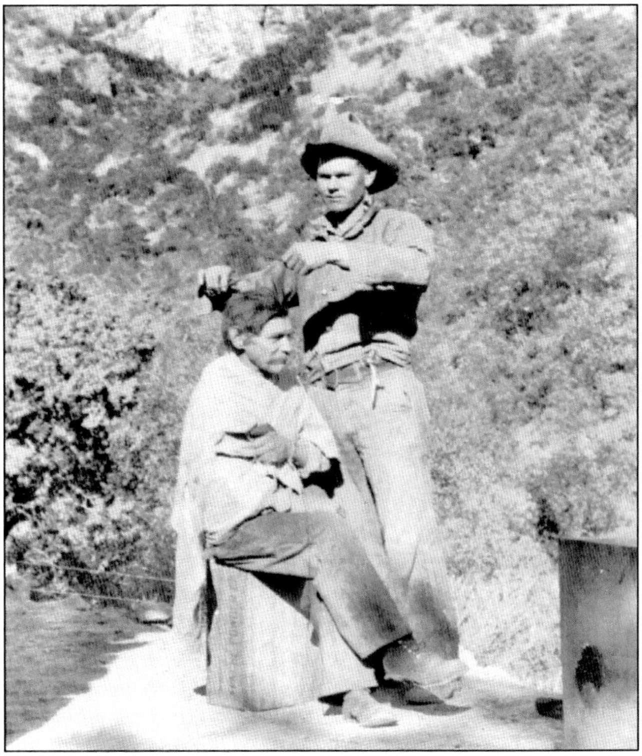

The life of a cowboy demanded a variety of skills, including that of a barber. In this photograph, Ed Cotter gives Buck Cosper a much-needed haircut. Since the distances were so great, trips to town were few and far between. Survival also required cowboys to take care of their own wounds, shoe their own horses, and apply stinky black ointment to the maggot-filled wounds on injured cattle.

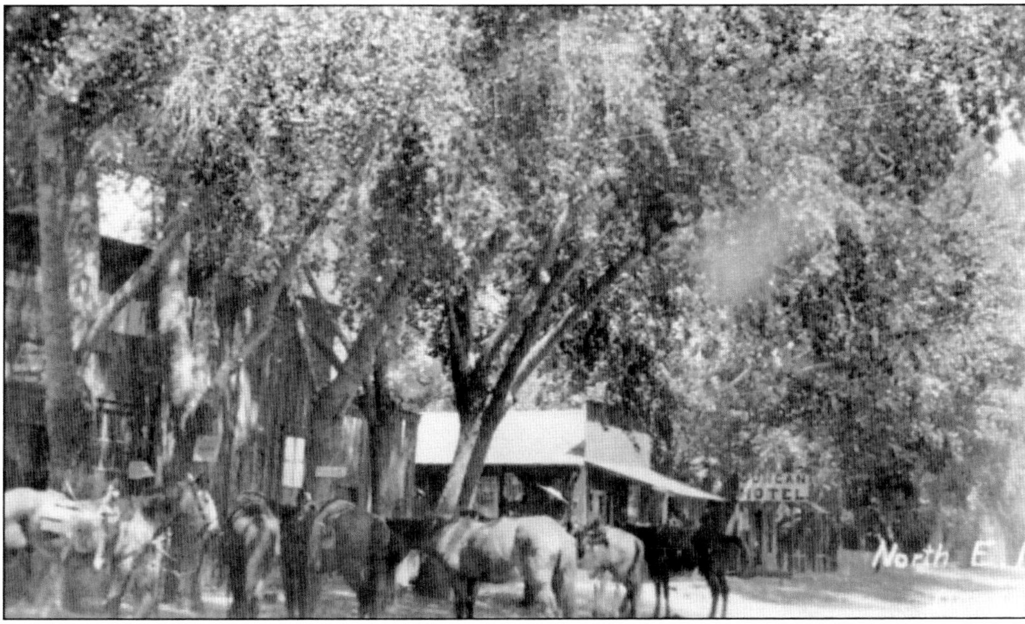

Located at the far eastern end of the valley, Duncan developed into a ranching center that attracted cowboys on their off days. On Saturday afternoons, the saloons were surrounded by horses and trouble. Lack of trust in the U.S. military to protect them from Apaches caused the citizens of Duncan to create their own militia. The Duncan Militia was a predecessor of the famed Arizona Rangers.

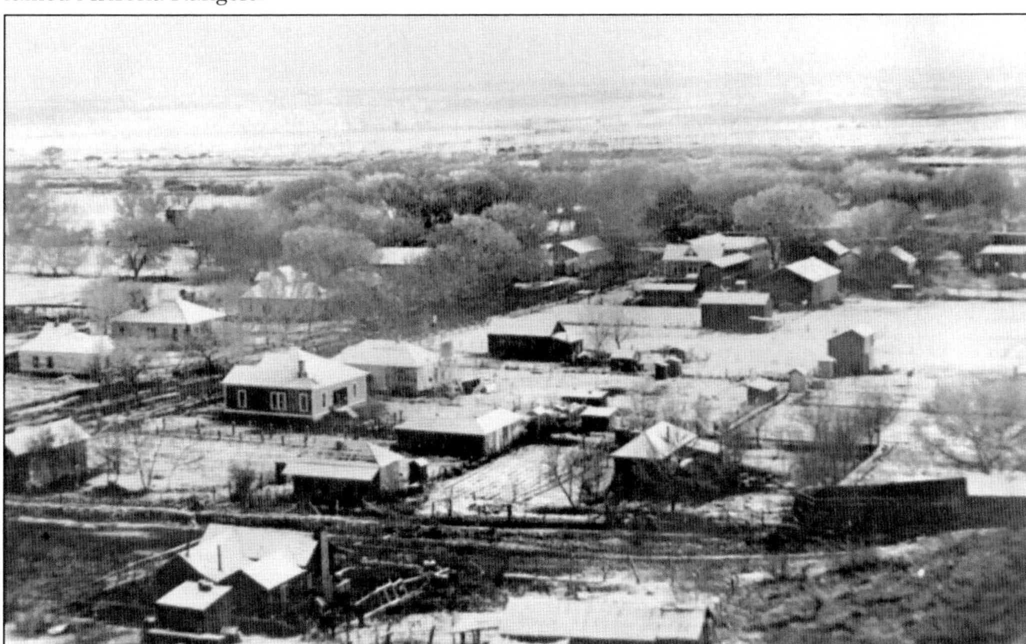

Duncan, Arizona, is seen at the beginning of the 20th century. Like Fort Thomas at the other end of the valley, ranchers built homes in town as well as ranch headquarters so that their children could attend school. The major town on the Gila River, Duncan served as a transportation center for the mines near Clifton and for the towns in nearby New Mexico.

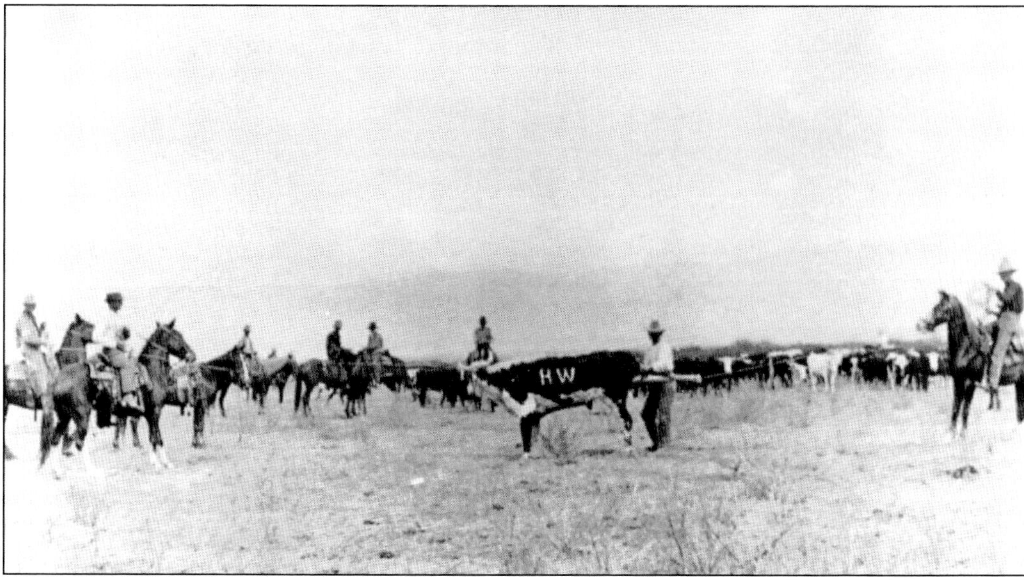

W. T. Webb, showing off a Hereford on his Bear Springs Ranch, was one of seven Pima residents who were arrested and charged with the Wham paymaster robbery. After being found not guilty, W. T., as he was known, went on to operate the 76 Ranch and run several successful businesses in Pima. As a member of the Arizona State Constitutional Convention, he was invited to travel to Washington, D.C., to participate in the statehood celebration.

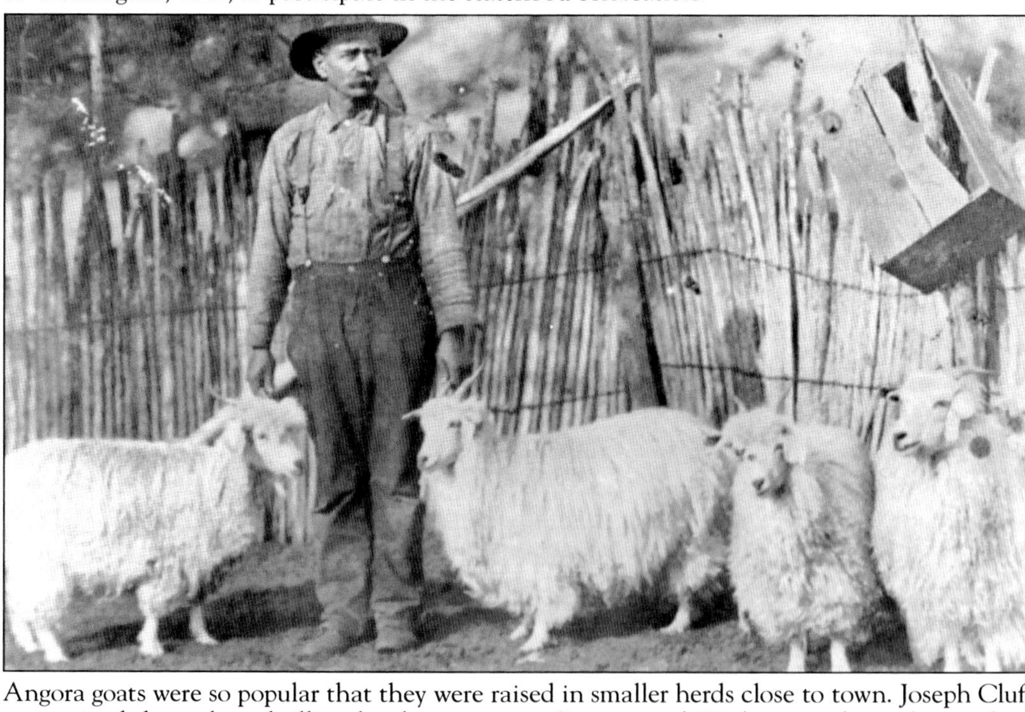

Angora goats were so popular that they were raised in smaller herds close to town. Joseph Cluff maintained these clean, brilliantly white goats on Cottonwood Wash, just a few miles south of Pima. It was not uncommon to see Angora goats being herded through downtown Pima and Thatcher. Since they were raised in such large numbers, goat meat was widely available and became a staple of the local economy.

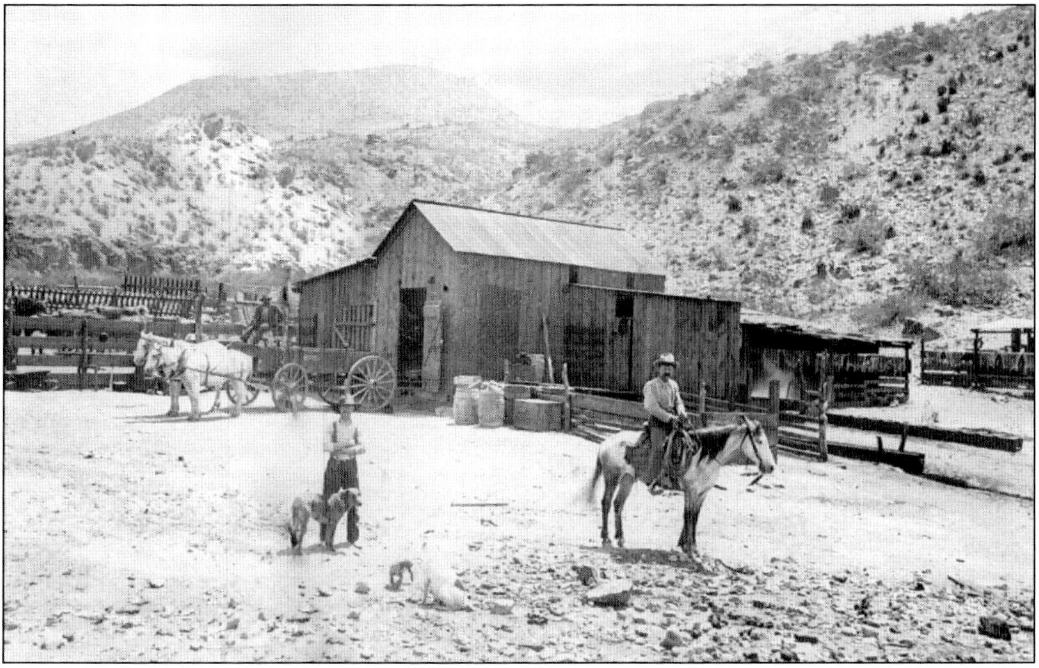

The area north of Safford was known for the San Juan gold mine and the ranches that had access to both Bonita Creek and the Gila River. This ranch was located on the site that is currently occupied by the Phelps Dodge Technical Center. The photograph demonstrates what was necessary to operate a large ranch: cattle, draft horses, saddle horses, and dogs.

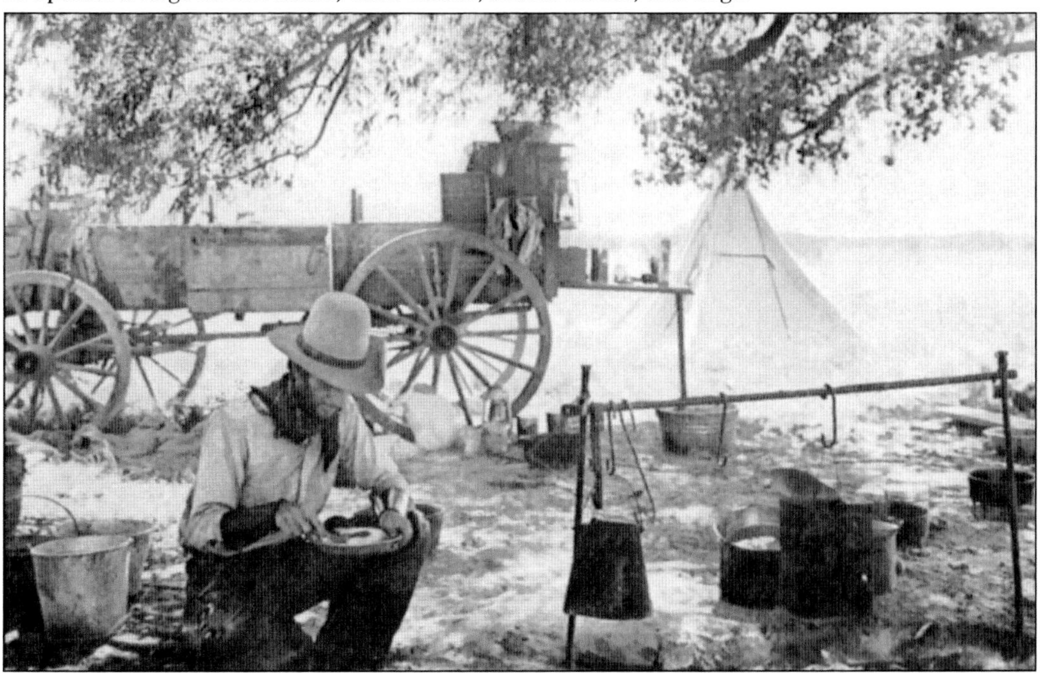

A ranching base camp was dusty and disorderly. Here a teepee, wagon, and cook camp provide temporary respite for tired cowboys. The hanging coffee pot and Dutch ovens had to be sturdy enough to survive the banging and bouncing of wagons traversing rough-hewn roads.

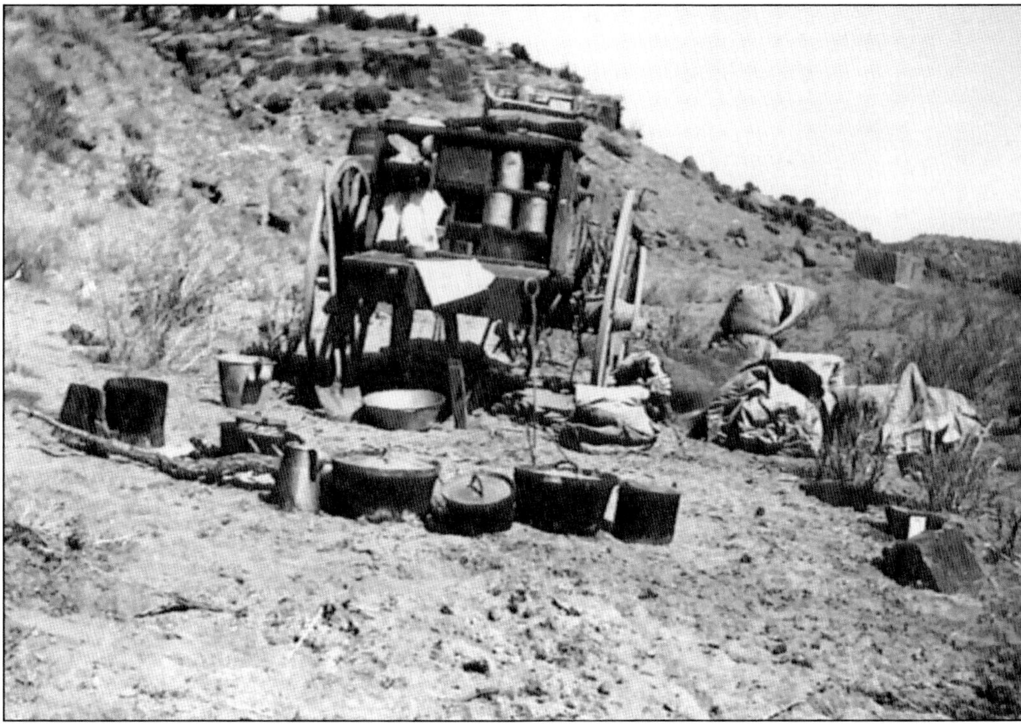

In 1902, a roundup cook proudly displays the tools of his trade. This image includes the rugged terrain of Gila Valley ranching, but it cannot be determined if the cook is setting up or dismantling his campsite.

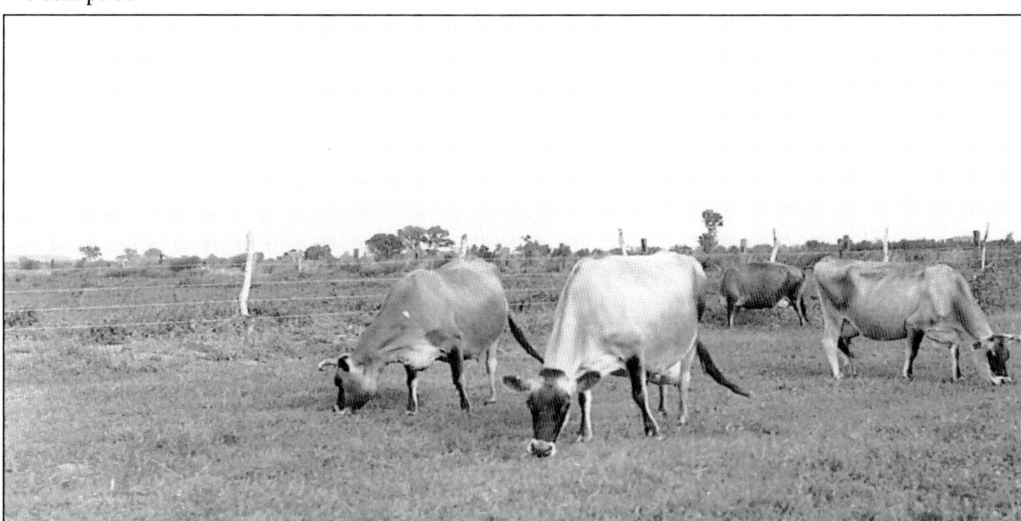

Robert Alan Smith started milking cows across the river from Safford around 1910. His son Ed Smith grew the business to a production facility of 450 cows, milking 200 head twice a day. University of Arizona agriculture professors often brought their students to the dairy to observe his operation. Ed was the first to develop a herd of Jersey cattle that produced high butter fat. He imported the first Jersey bull all the way from Jersey Island. Ed was also the first in the valley to use electric milking machines.

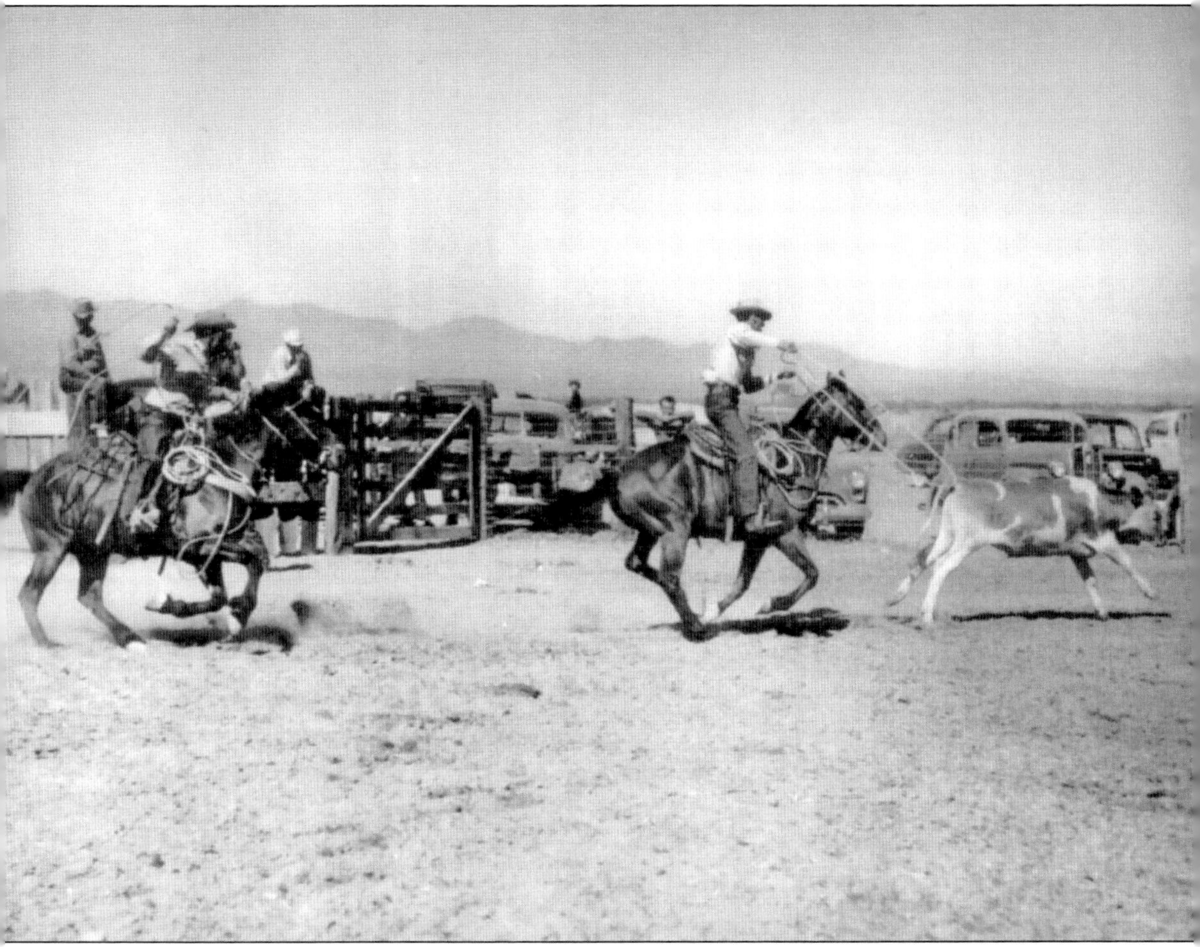

Buddy McEwen is in the lead, heading a calf, while Jack Hinton follows, ready to heal. Other roping duos included the father-and-son team of Wheeler and Duane Reece and later the championship team of Keith Smith and Duane Reece. Smith went on to become the first president of the Professional Rodeo Cowboys Association. Graham County produced three world champions: Breezy Cox, Hugh Bennett, and Everett Bowman. (Courtesy Sharon Hinton.)

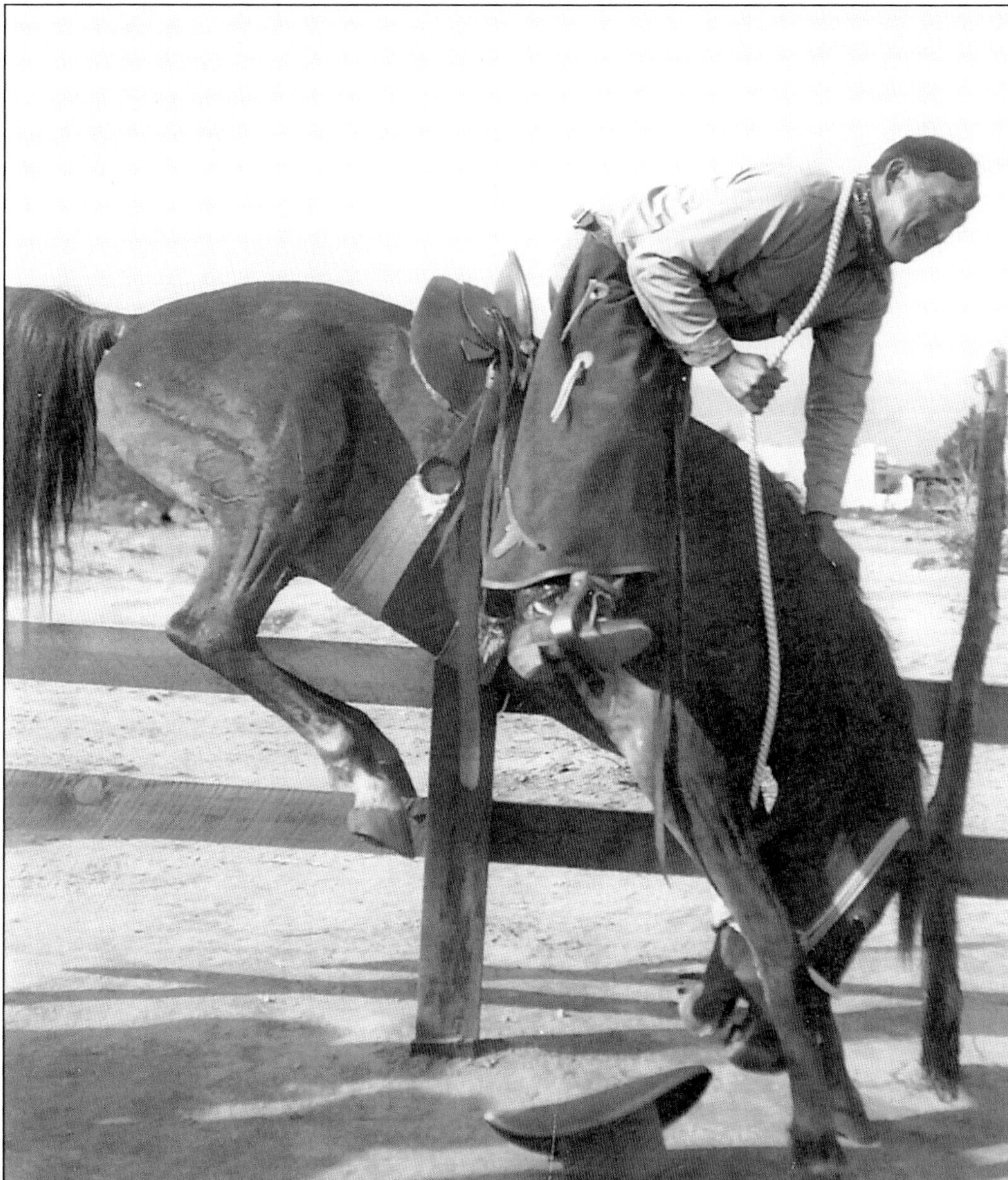

This bronco rider is Manny Hinton, the son of James and Kissie Hinton. Manny was raised on the reservation as an Apache; however, his half-breed heritage interfered with his desire to become a spiritual singer. When Manny was a young man, he would hide near sweat lodges to listen to and memorize spiritual songs. After years of rejection, Manny finally found a spiritual singer who agreed teach him. Today two Hinton descendants, Bert and Dory Hinton, practice that same art form. (Courtesy Sharon Hinton.)

Six

Transportation
From Horses to Railroads

Copper in the Globe area was the impetus for the building of a railroad through the Gila Valley. Between 1880 and 1890, tremendous growth and tenacious industry flourished within the valley. The so-called era of the Apache Wars demanded military forts between Fort Bowie in the south and Fort Apache in the north. A rugged and deadly military road was built connecting Willcox on the Southern Pacific Railroad line to Fort Grant on the southwest side of Mount Graham. The road continued northeastward past the Eureka Ranch, through Eagle Pass, and to Fort Thomas. There freighters and the military payroll wagon trains went on to the San Carlos Sub-agency and Fort Apache.

To transport copper ore to the railroad lines, part of the road was expanded northwestward from San Carlos to the mines around Globe. During the 1880s, thousands of tons were hauled south by huge wagons pulled by mules. On return trips, the freighters carried commercial goods and mining equipment. Life of a freighter was tough and deadly. Apache raids, bandits, and the physical dangers of weather and breakdowns cost the lives of Anglos and Mexicans alike.

During the late 1890s, the construction of the Gila Valley Globe & Northern Railway proceeded from Bowie Station on the Southern Pacific line to Safford and Globe. Even though freighters knew the dangers, they realized that it would bring new money and growth to the sleepy communities along it path.

Transportation demands were unique within the Gila Valley. Because of its isolation, Graham County often felt neglected by the state government. The railway was a one-way line, connecting the Southern Pacific Railroad to the copper mines near Globe. For five short decades, it provided passenger service, but that ceased when the agreement with the San Carlos Apache tribe ended. Until the middle of the 20th century, travel past Globe was a dangerous proposition. The next most popular routes in and out of the valley were either through El Paso, Texas, or Tucson, Arizona—both considerably distant.

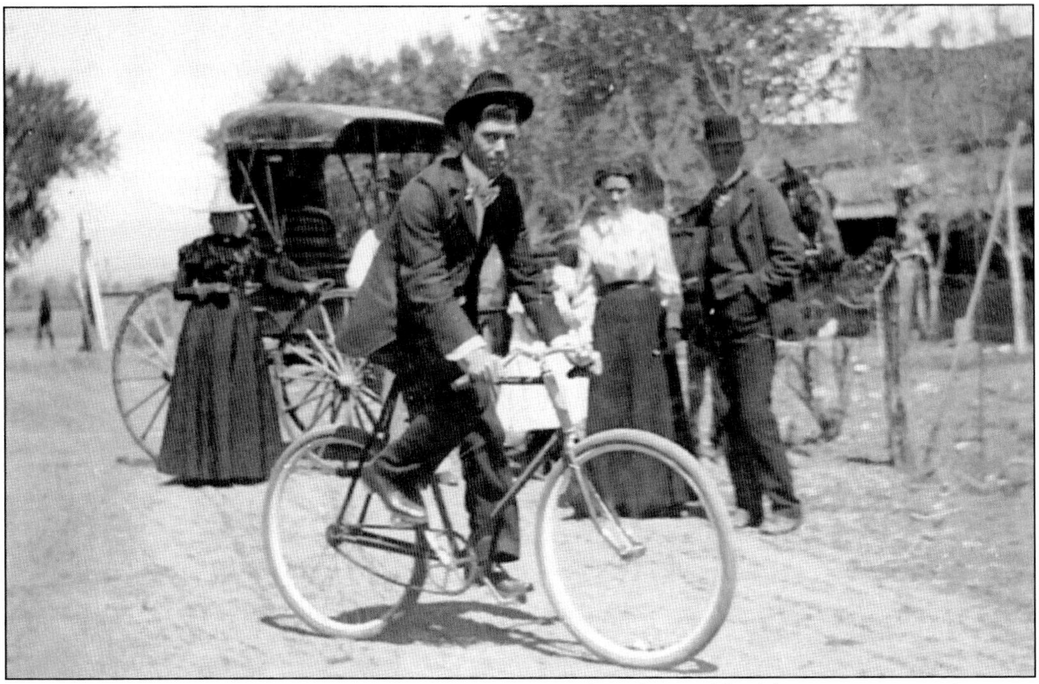

Early-20th-century newspapers support the contention that the road-building craze across America was instigated by bicyclists rather than automobile drivers. The demand for bicycles, like the one ridden here by a young Allred in Thatcher, almost outstripped production. Mail-order catalogs made it possible for buyers to get them shipped directly to their hometown post offices, and bicycle repair shops became as common as blacksmith shops.

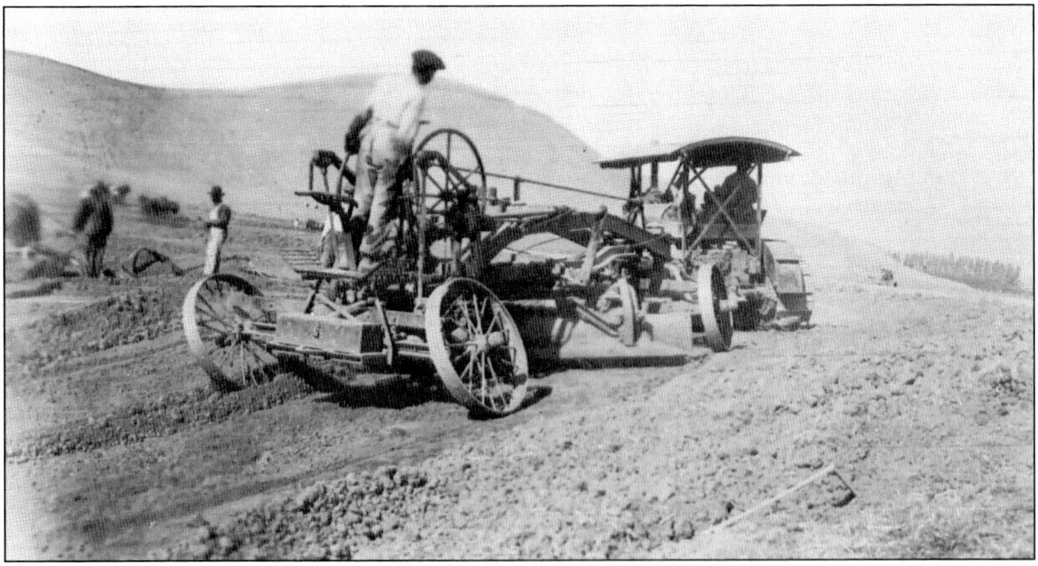

Road construction was much simpler during the early 1900s. Towns, cities, and counties contracted their local companies to build roads. Before her death, Hyrum Weech's granddaugter-in-law Mrs. Bertell (Cheryl) Weech told the author that Hyrum was commissioned to construct the Klondyke Road from Highway 70 to the Aravaipa Road in 1913. He supposedly completed the project for $800.

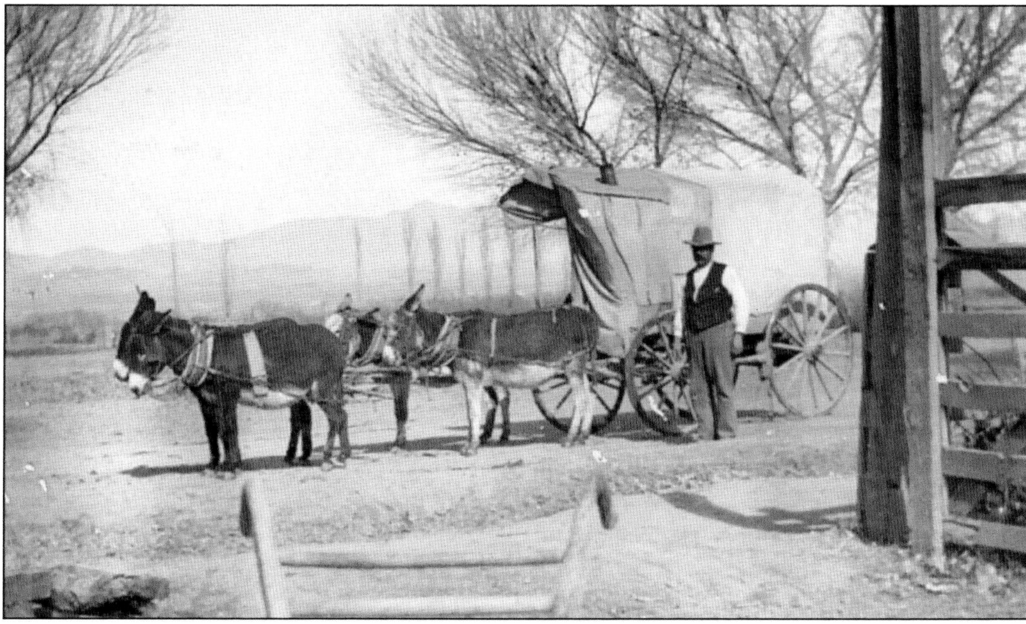

For years, donkeys transported people and goods across the valley. J. G. Allred would take supplies to his Angora goat ranch near Cottonwood Springs. A stove in the trailer could be used on cold winter nights. The lack of foliage on the trees in this image indicates that the stove would have come in handy this time of year.

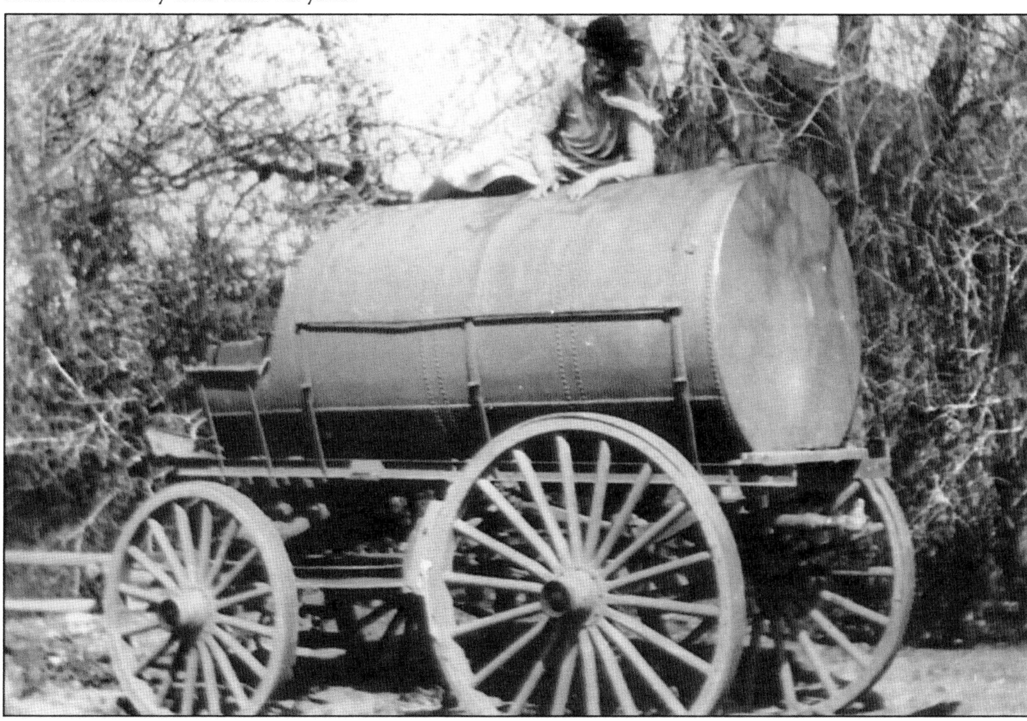

Because wells throughout the Gila Valley were often contaminated with alkali, many farmers and urban residents dug cisterns. They would haul drinking water in tanks, like the one pictured here, from "sweet water" wells, often miles away.

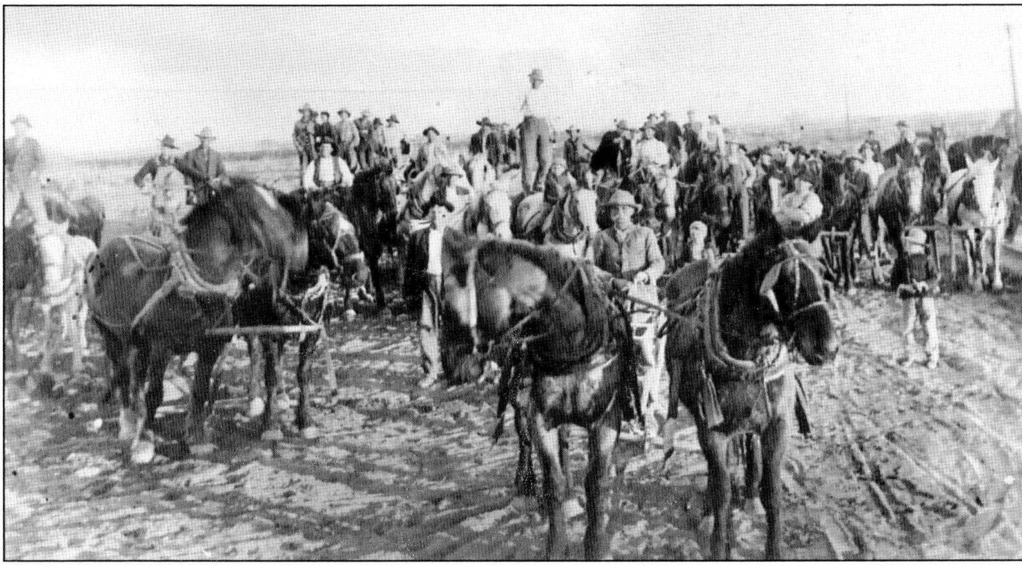

As the Gila Valley Globe & Northern Railway passed through the area, the citizens of Central decided to build a siding. Under the leadership of Oscar Webster, they gathered the community together to clear the land and lay the ties and tracks. Sidings were built in Safford, Pima, Fort Thomas, and Geronimo. At these sites, farmers and ranchers could load and unload produce and cattle.

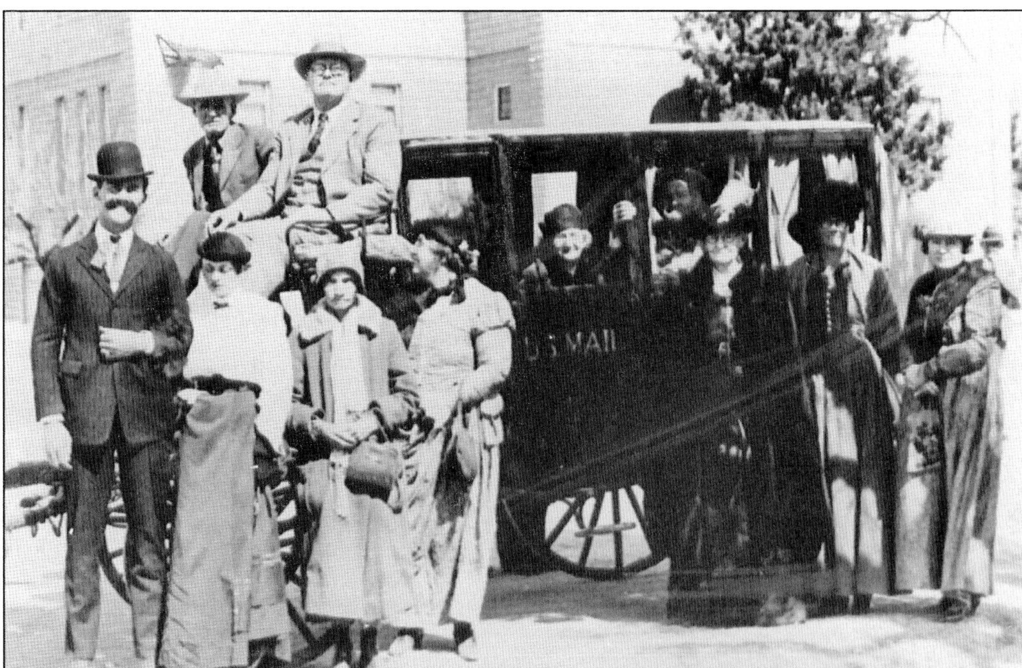

The use of local coaches as taxis was popular for social events at the LDS Academy in Thatcher. This jaunty group has met at the academy for an unidentified social occasion. Included here, from left to right, are Ferrell Layton, Charlotte DeSpain, unidentified, Elizabeth Layton, an unidentified lady in the coach, Lillian Claridge, and two more unidentified ladies. Driving the carriage are Rudd Phillips (left) and Heber Layton.

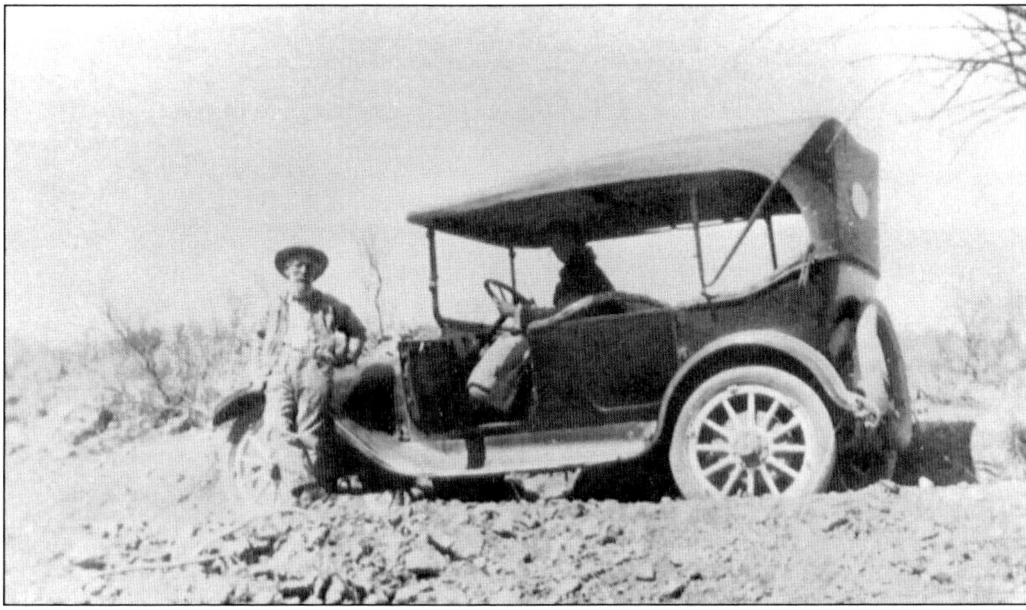

In 1917, a trek to Black Rock proved popular but difficult. The road from Fort Thomas to the picturesque camping site was only a dozen or so miles, but the hike took half a day. Here Mr. Wight (first name unknown), a Fort Thomas resident, takes a break to have his portrait taken.

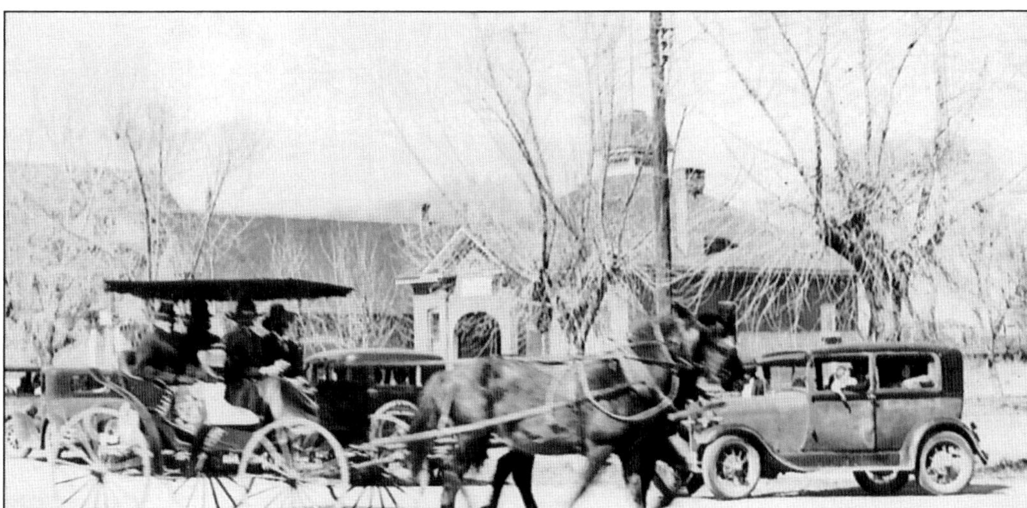

Automobiles and carriages shared the roads in Thatcher through the 1930s. This winter scene clearly shows the LDS Relief Society building on Church Street. The traffic indicates that the photograph was likely taken on a Sunday.

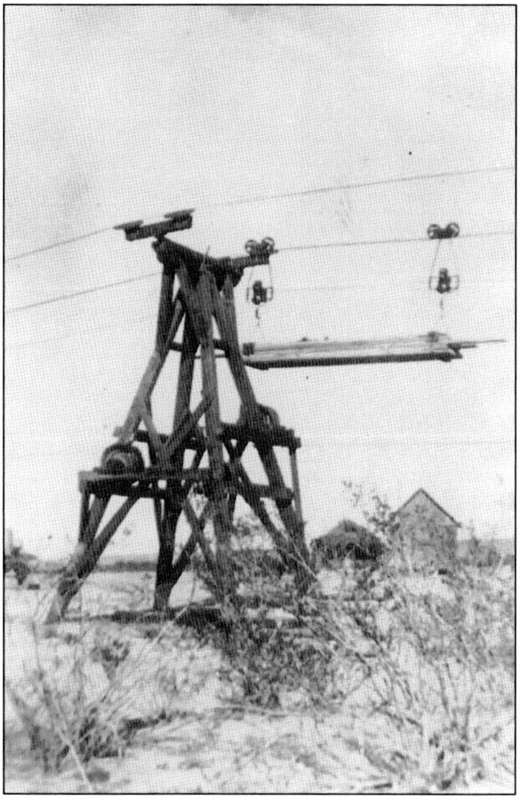

Early on, Pima residents worked hard to build sawmills on Mount Graham and were very creative in getting the logs off the mountain. They first built a water flume that floated the logs from the mills to the valley floor. Rot and wind damage destroyed that effort. Later they built a concrete and timber structure to ship the logs and rough-cut timber down by cable (pictured here). The so-called Tram was a greater physical success than financial, but it provided timber for the construction of homes and businesses all the way from Globe to Clifton.

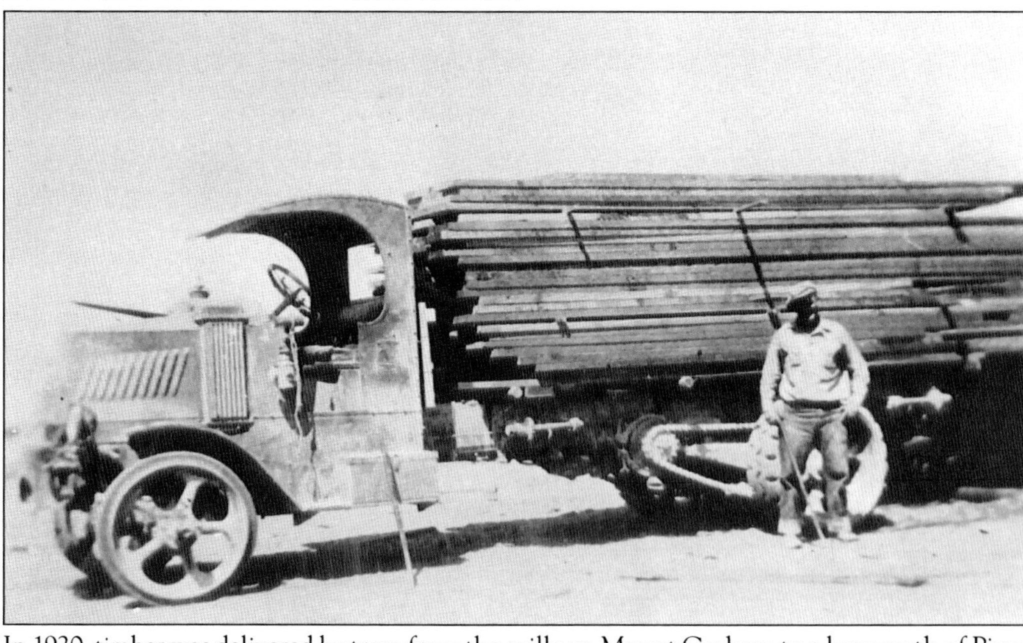

In 1920, timber was delivered by tram from the mills on Mount Graham to a base south of Pima. The lumber was then loaded onto these rugged trucks to be delivered to mining operations in Globe. Planks like those on this truck were more than 16 feet long, 8 to 12 inches wide, and 4 inches thick. Cut from virgin forests, they were in great demand.

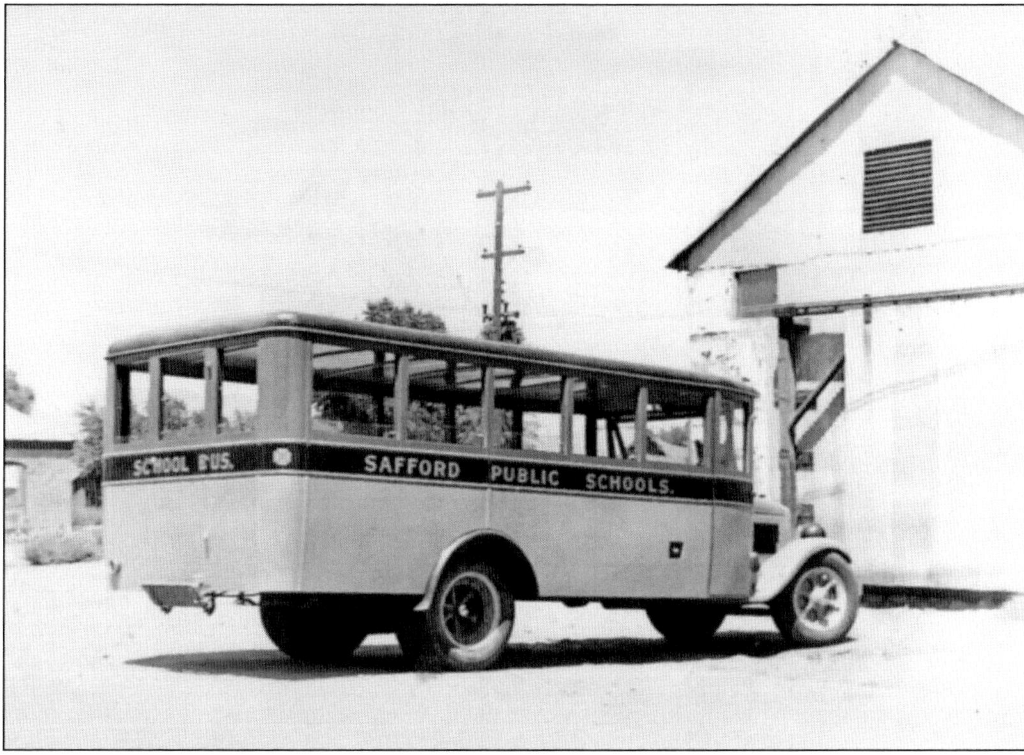

During the 1930s, Safford and Duncan were proud of their school buses. It was not unusual for seasonally employed farmers and ranchers to take up the duty of school bus driver.

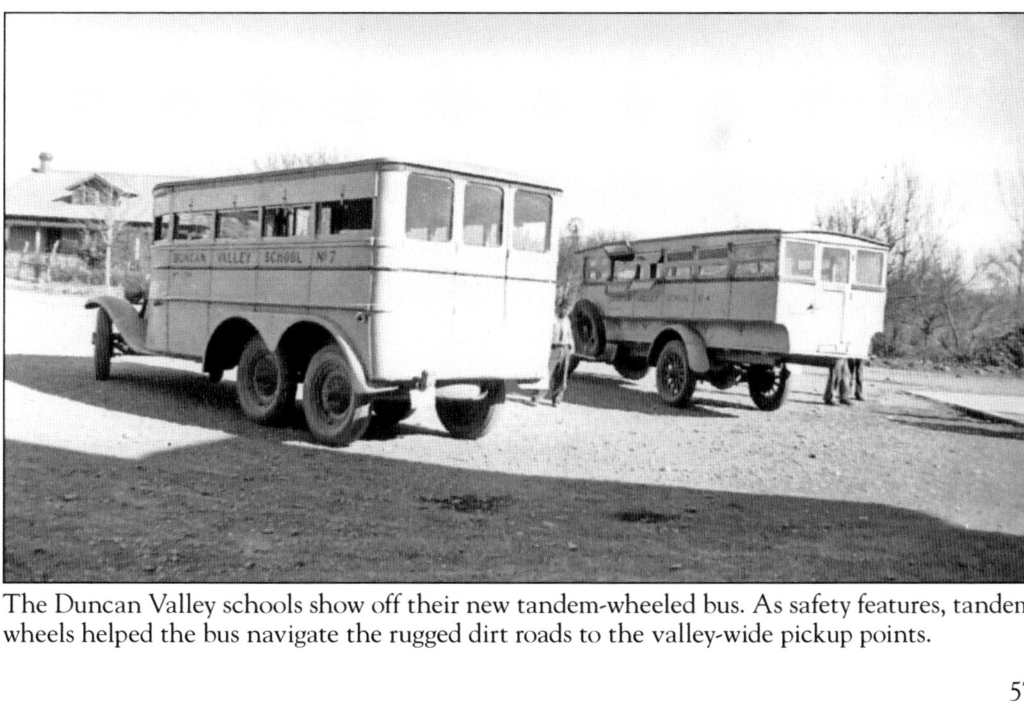

The Duncan Valley schools show off their new tandem-wheeled bus. As safety features, tandem wheels helped the bus navigate the rugged dirt roads to the valley-wide pickup points.

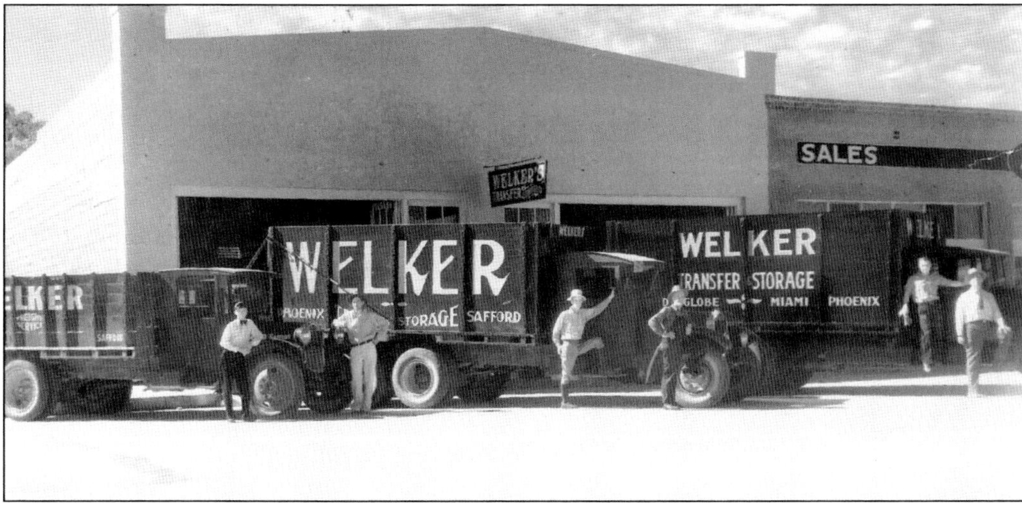

Welker Transfer and Storage was a successful business in great demand during the 1930s. Freight was delivered by train to depots throughout the valley, requiring firms such as Welker to retrieve the merchandise and deliver it to various enterprises across the county.

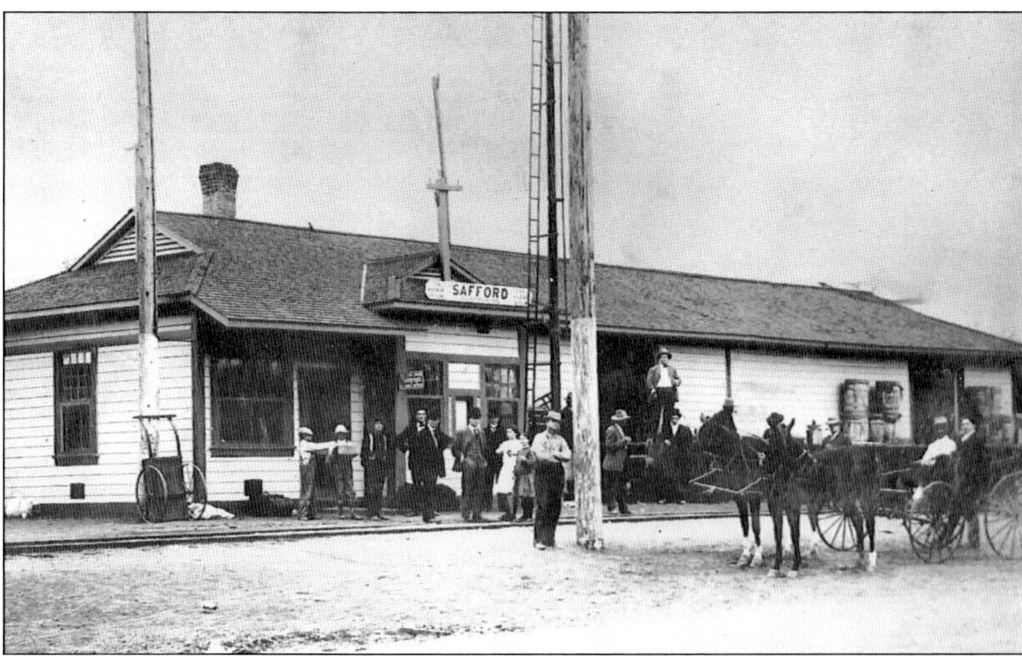

The Safford depot was a popular gathering place. This building was expanded and eventually replaced, and the one that stands today is a mute reminder of better times. Because of its location, the parallel street, Eighth, became a center for business, housing, stables, and hotels. Main Street runs three blocks to the north.

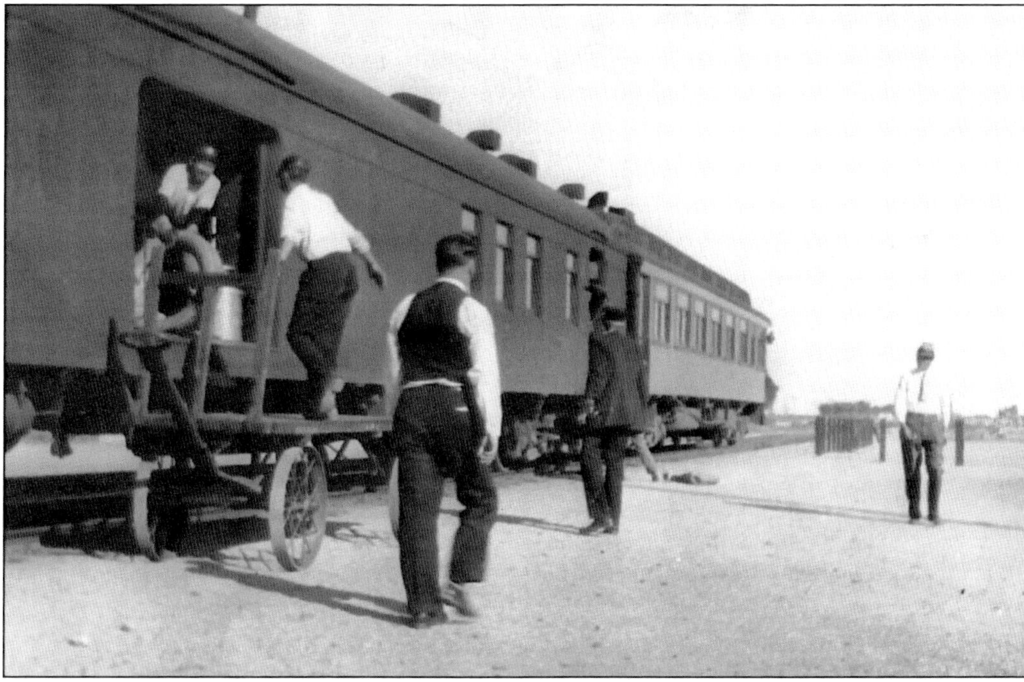

At a depot in the Gila Valley, workers unload five-gallon milk cans from one of the dairies near Globe and Safford. Milk delivery was prompt and continued daily for years.

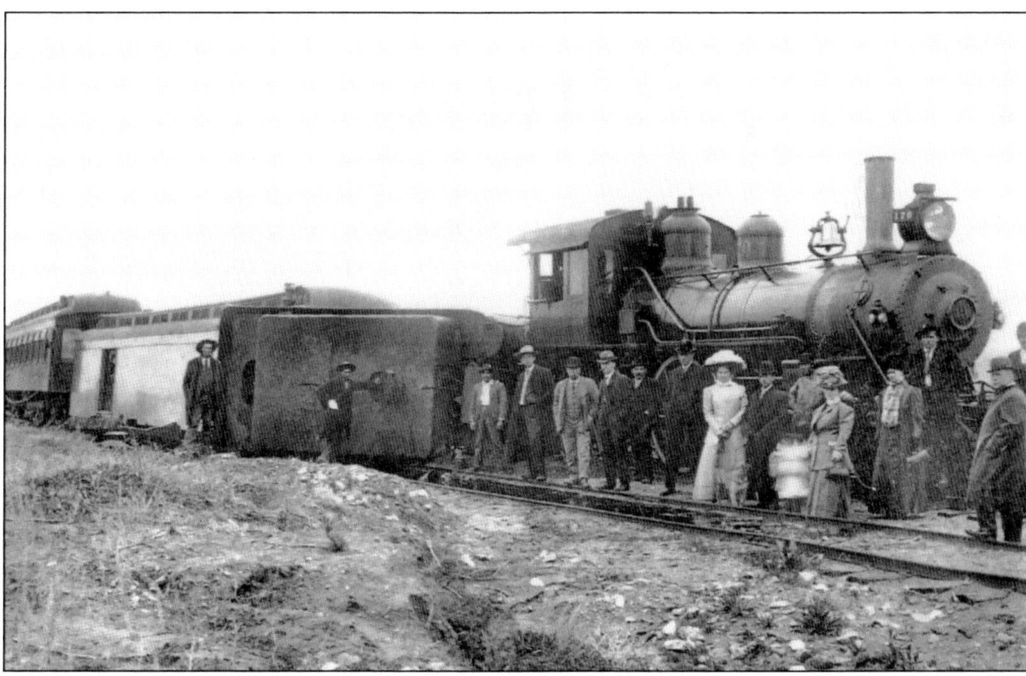

Passenger train derailments, like this one somewhere in the San Simon Valley, were not uncommon events. The tracks were laid directly on the valley floor. It was said that if a woman emptied her laundry water anywhere in the valley, three miles of track would be washed out.

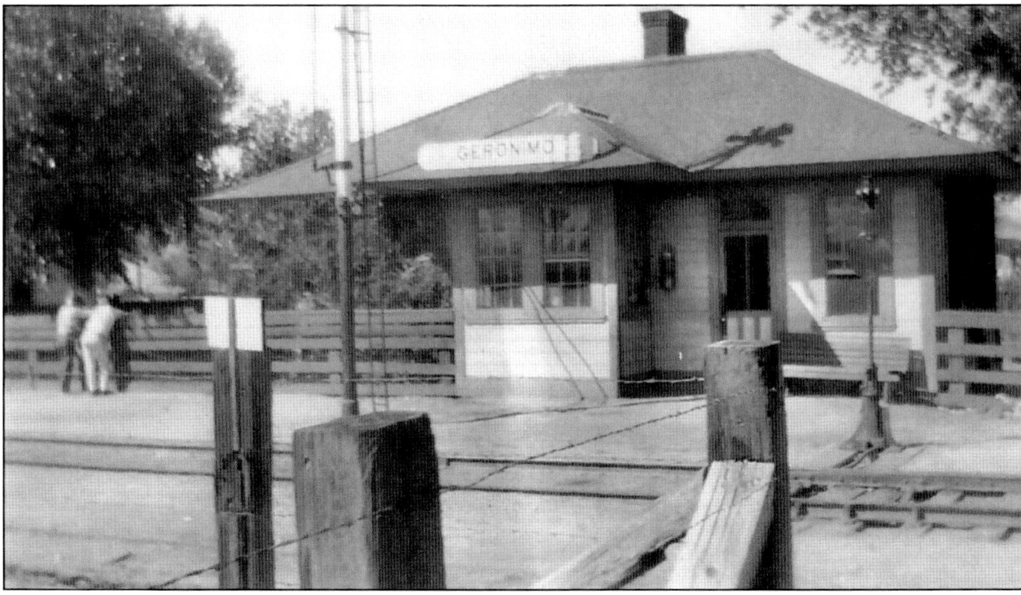

The Geronimo depot was unplanned. Railroad construction came to an abrupt stop at that location in 1896 when the San Carlos tribe unexpectedly refused to give William Garland, the owner of the company, permission to cross the reservation. It took three years for Garland to earn congressional and tribal approval. Meanwhile, Geronimo temporarily became an important trade center. For those three years, mule- and horse-drawn freighters delivered copper ore from Globe to Geronimo. Local ranchers built holding pens for cattle. The town developed stores, bars, restaurants, Chinese laundries, and even had a justice of the peace. It declined, however, after the railroad eventually reached Globe.

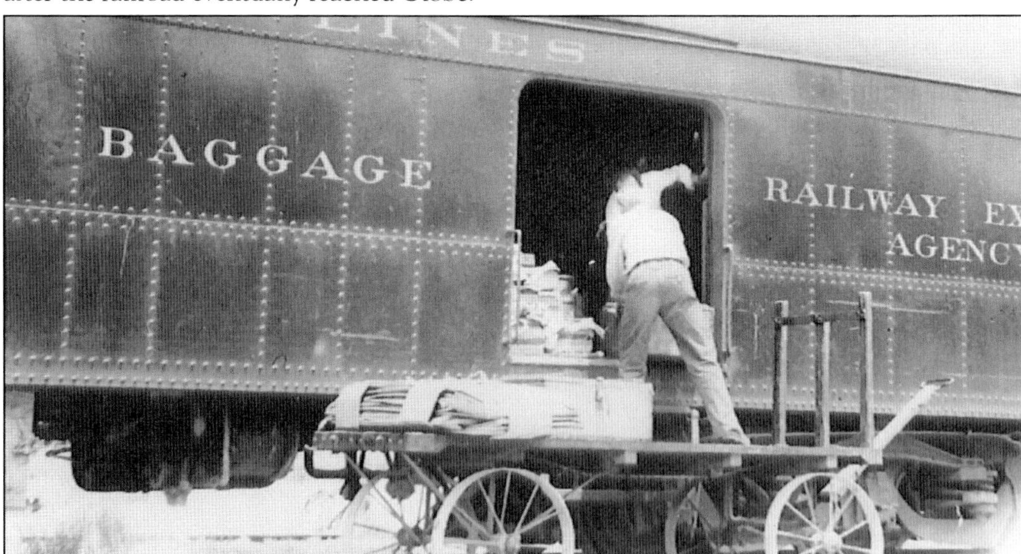

Mail delivery was one of the most important roles of the Gila Valley Globe & Northern Railway. Here the depot agent unloads mail with the help of the onboard agent. Often the train did not even have to stop; instead, the depot agent would place a canvas letter sack on a hook. The onboard agent would reach out with a long pole to snag the bag. Young kids usually gathered around to watch the bag magically disappear as the train passed.

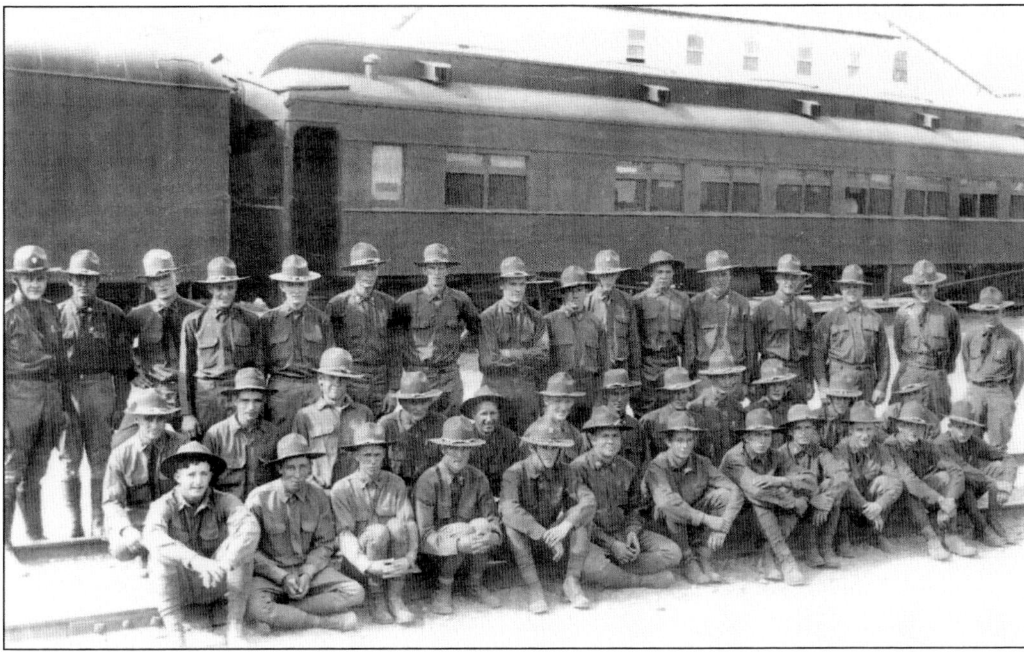

Passenger cars were put into great use in the Gila Valley both prior to and during World War II. Through the valley service, wives made connections with the Southern Pacific Railroad in Bowie in order to visit their husbands at various training bases before they were sent to war. Arizona National Guard Infantry Company G 158 poses before shipping off for training in 1940.

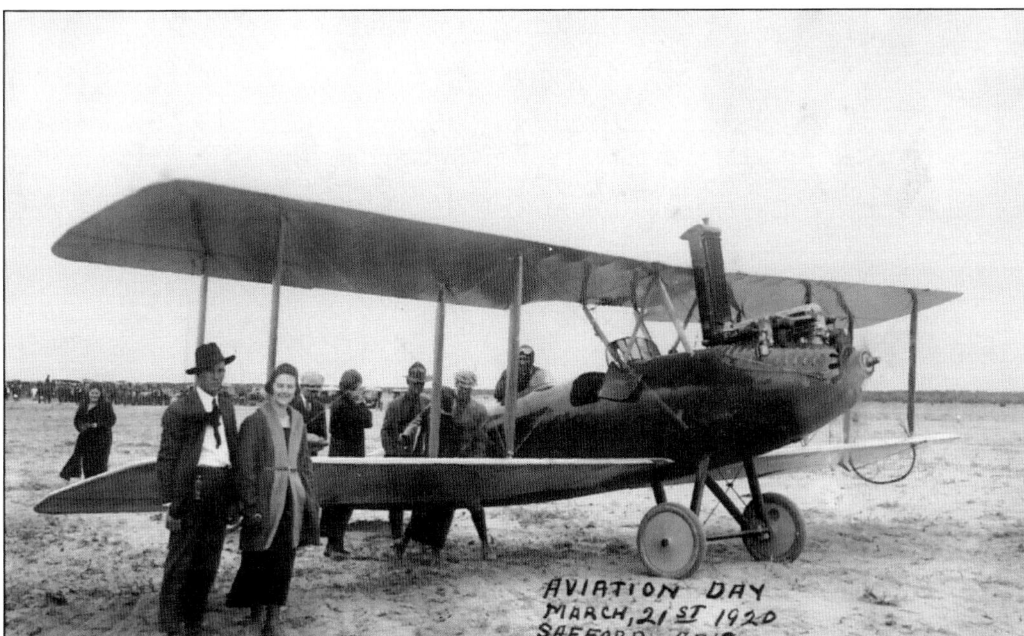

Aviation Day was celebrated in Graham County even before an airport was opened. Post–World War I barnstorming reached Safford early, and Aviation Day was created to attract paying audiences and to spread the popularity of flying.

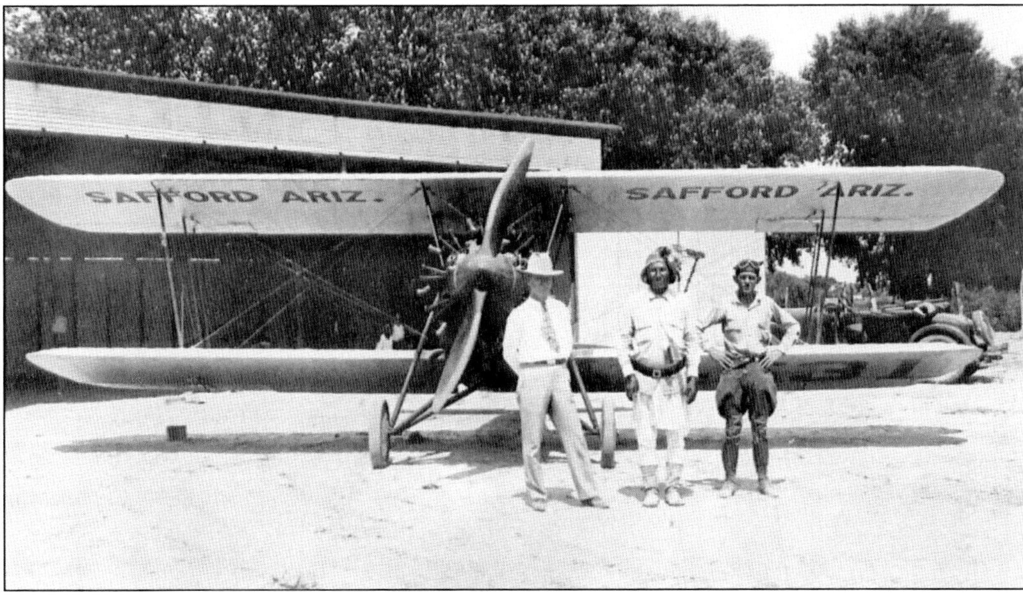

Graham County's first airport was developed by Ernest Wickersham, the son of a local merchant. Here an unidentified Apache has just returned from a flight piloted by Wickersham. The Safford, Arizona, insignia on the plane was a means of advertising the new airport, as were free flights for local political and social leaders.

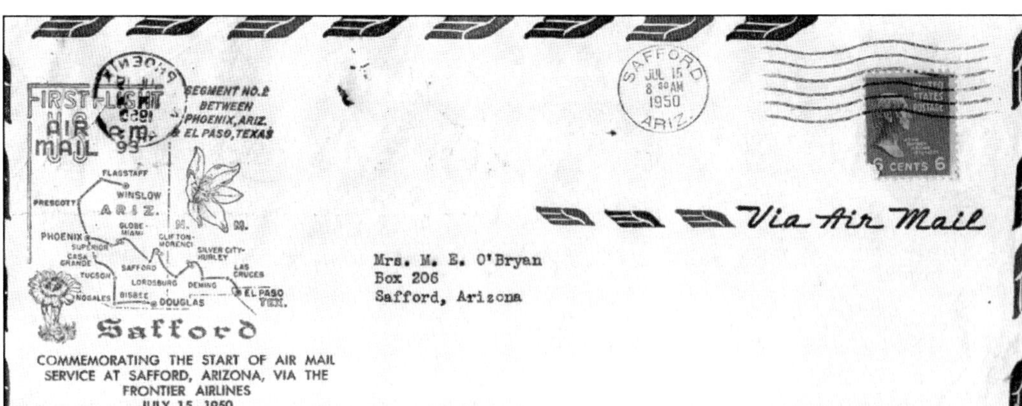

This envelope attests to the airmail service that existed for a short period of time in 1950. As the map shows, a private contractor delivered airmail from El Paso, Texas, through southern New Mexico and the populated cities of Arizona. From time to time, there has been airline passenger service at the Safford airport, but it has seldom lasted longer than a few months. The airport has served as a training center, the headquarters of the National Air Patrol, and a center for fighting wildfires in the area.

Seven

Mining, Milling, Fraud, and Copper

The lure of gold attracted prospectors to the perennial streams flowing from the foothills of the mountains surrounding the Gila Valley. Claims were recorded in almost every section of the county, but due to low yields, a rush never resulted. Copper, however, was plentiful, and large copper mining and milling operations sprang up to the north and east of the valley.

Copper mining demanded two investments: claiming thousands of acres of land and securing funds to hire an army of miners, carpenters, and mechanics. Both required contacts in the east, where investors were available and lawyers could be enticed to travel to this rugged territory.

Mines developed in Globe before there were safe roads to the area and around the Clifton-Morenci-Metcalf communities before there were population centers large enough to support the industry. The Gila Valley became the supply center for both operations, as well as the transport provider for Globe (roads to and from Clifton went into New Mexico). Employees came from the valley, Mexico, and points eastward.

By the 1890s, the convergence of mining wealth, increased numbers of potential investors, and vast expanses of unexplored lands led, inevitably, to mining fraud. Graham County was the site of one of the most ambitious and successful scams ever carried out. Known as the Spenazuma Gold Mining Fraud, it was created by a con man in New York City. With funds from his marks, Dr. Richard C. Flower invested in claims near Black Rock, a beautifully remote area south of Fort Thomas. Dozens of locals were employed, and immediate progress was reported.

Flower's efforts were supported by valley residents because of employment opportunities and the rise in property values. John Birdno, publisher of the *Graham County Guardian* and a real estate investor, did a great deal to legitimatize the operation. Much of our understanding of the growth and development of the valley comes from the numerous publications of John Birdno.

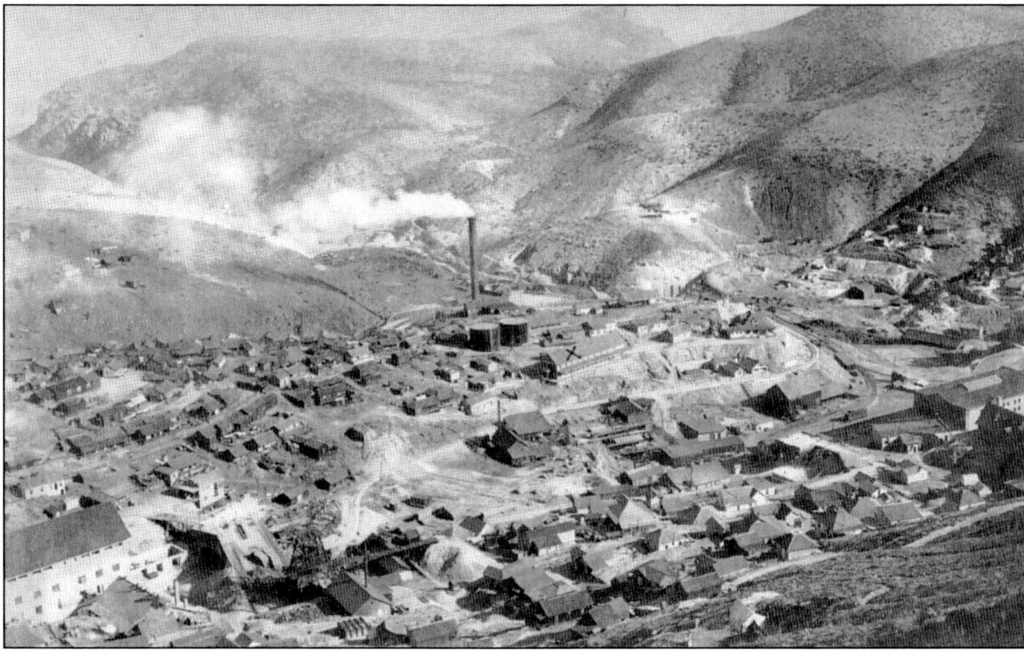

The Gila Valley lies about halfway between two major mining districts: Morenci and Globe. This 1900 photograph of Morenci shows a town built around an underground copper mine. The mine entrance is located in the large building in the center. The copper ore was delivered to the crusher mill and smelter, near the smokestack in the background.

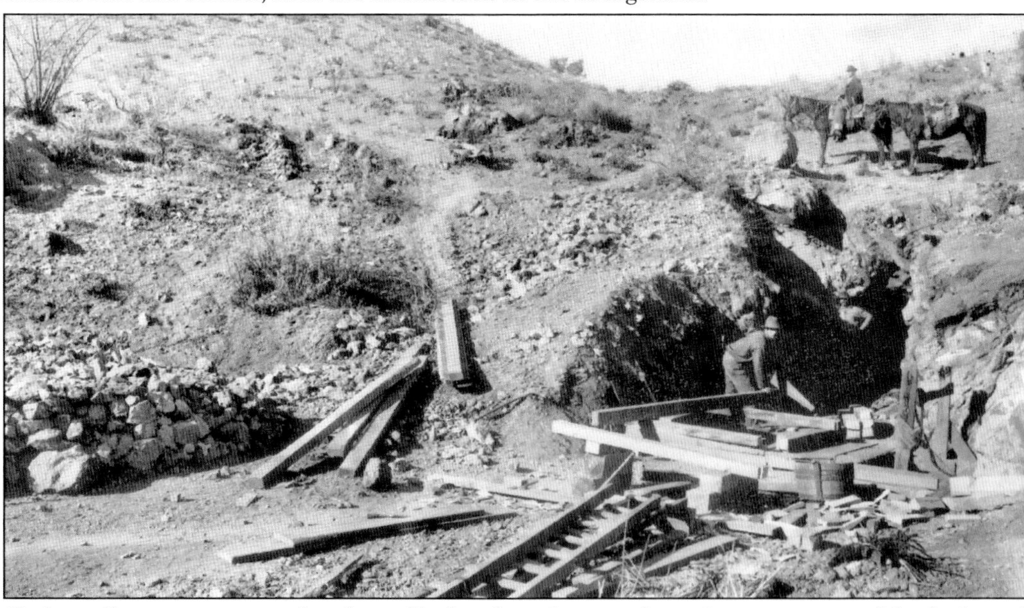

Graham County is peppered with small, abandoned mines that, when constructed, looked much like this adit (horizontal tunnel). Gold, silver, and copper attracted prospectors who often worked as hard at getting investors as they did digging shafts. The successful copper strikes in Globe and Morenci attracted new prospectors to the county and even encouraged well-established businessmen, ranchers, and farmers to spend countless days and weeks wandering across the foothills looking for telltale signs of precious ore.

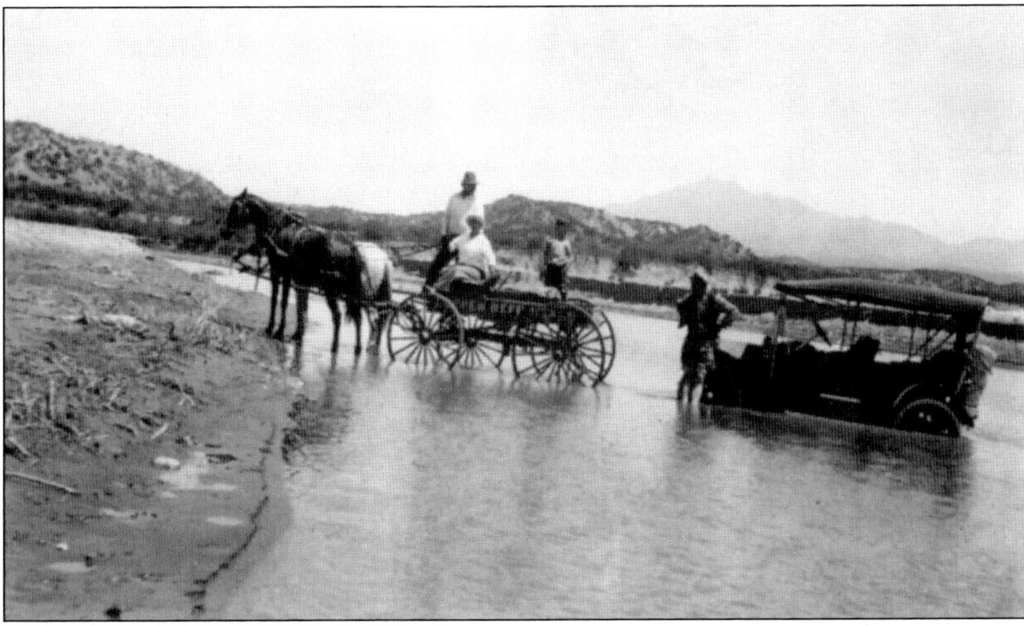

One of the most active prospecting areas was Mount Turnbull. In 1896, the 232,000-acre region, called the Mineral Strip, was removed from the San Carlos Apache Reservation. No mine on the Strip ever produced profitable ore bodies. However, the surrounding mines between Superior and Globe were lucrative. Here the Mineral Strip Copper Reef Mine "taxi" helps a stranded motorist stuck in the Gila River near San Carlos.

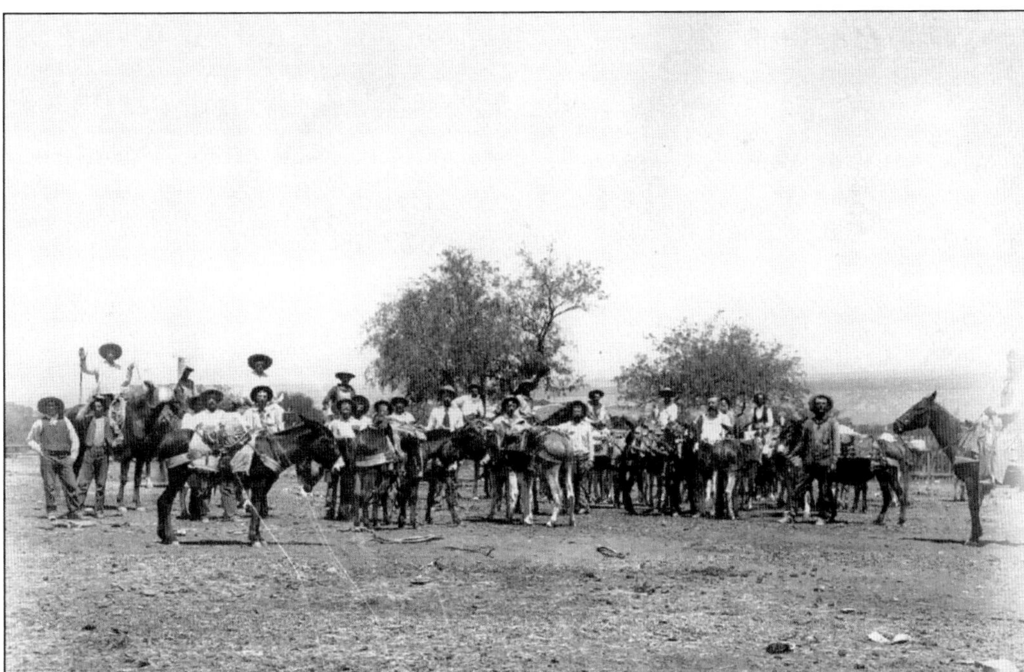

Mining was a labor-intensive operation. Pictured is the Geronimo mine outfit in 1901. These men prospected and supplied mines in the Santa Teresa range, including Mount Turnbull.

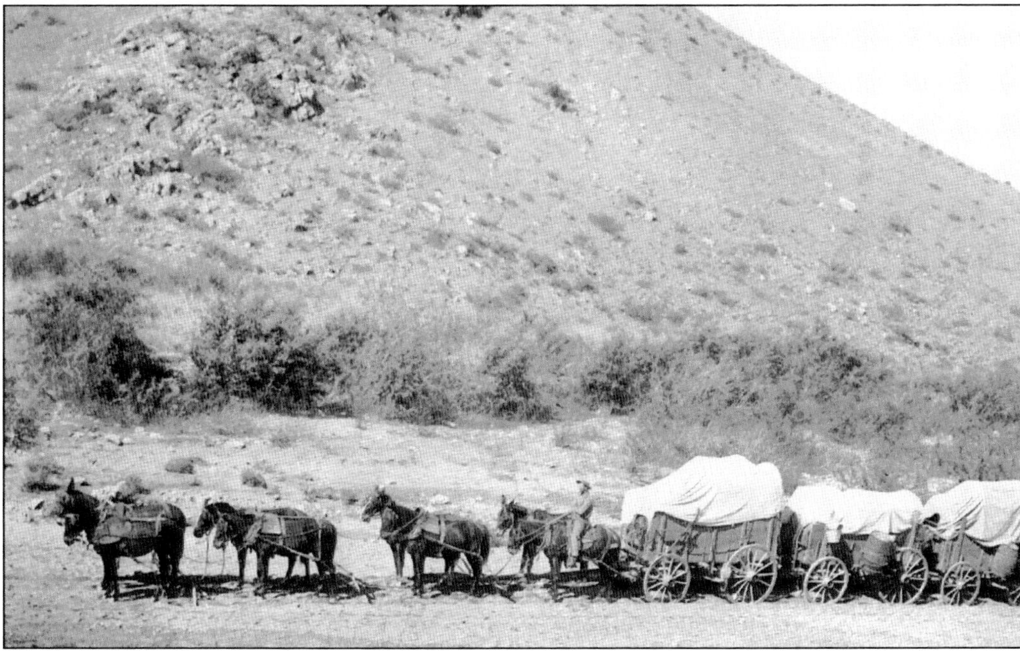

Freighting to and from Globe was a treacherous occupation. Multiple wagons pulled by sturdy mules were commonplace, and yet it was well known that, on average, a breakdown or delay occurred every three miles. The most common delays were caused by washed-out roads and land falls.

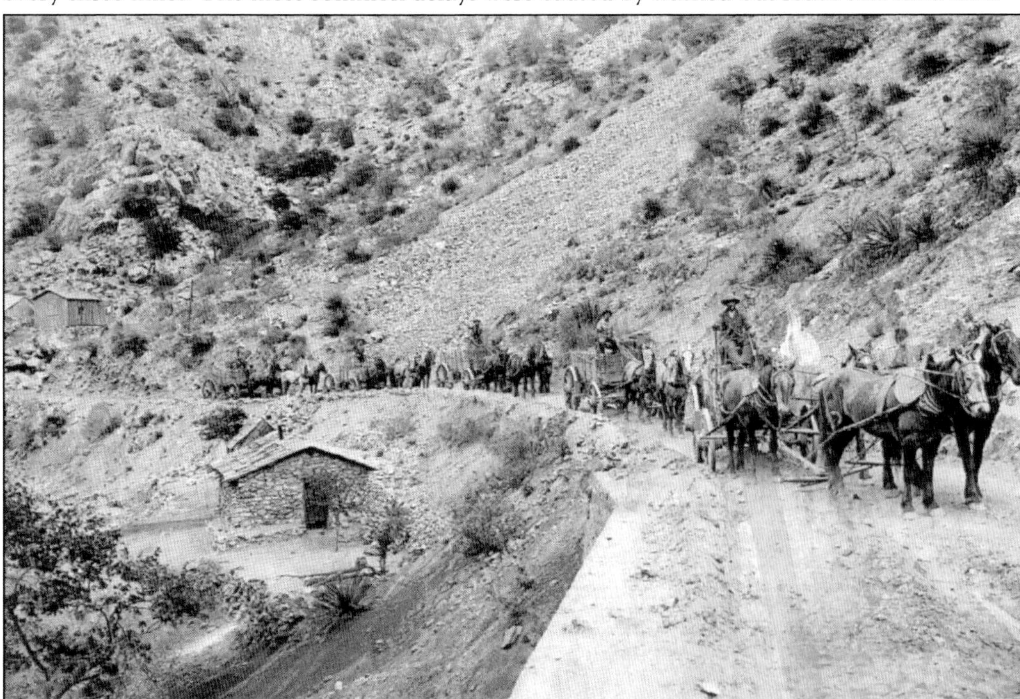

Frank Webster operated this freighting enterprise, which transported supplies from Clifton to the mines at Morenci and Metcalf. Independent contractors provided much of the equipment and labor needed in both mining and railroad construction.

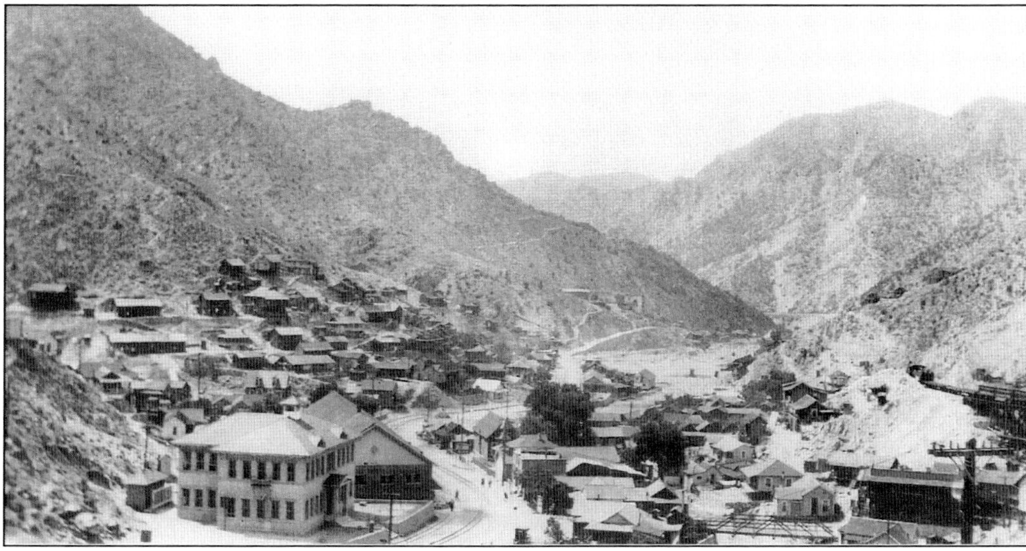

The mining community of Metcalf, built around the Longfellow mine, took pride in the stylish Longfellow Hotel in the forefront of this photograph. Today Metcalf no longer exists, having been demolished and replaced with the huge Phelps Dodge open-pit mine.

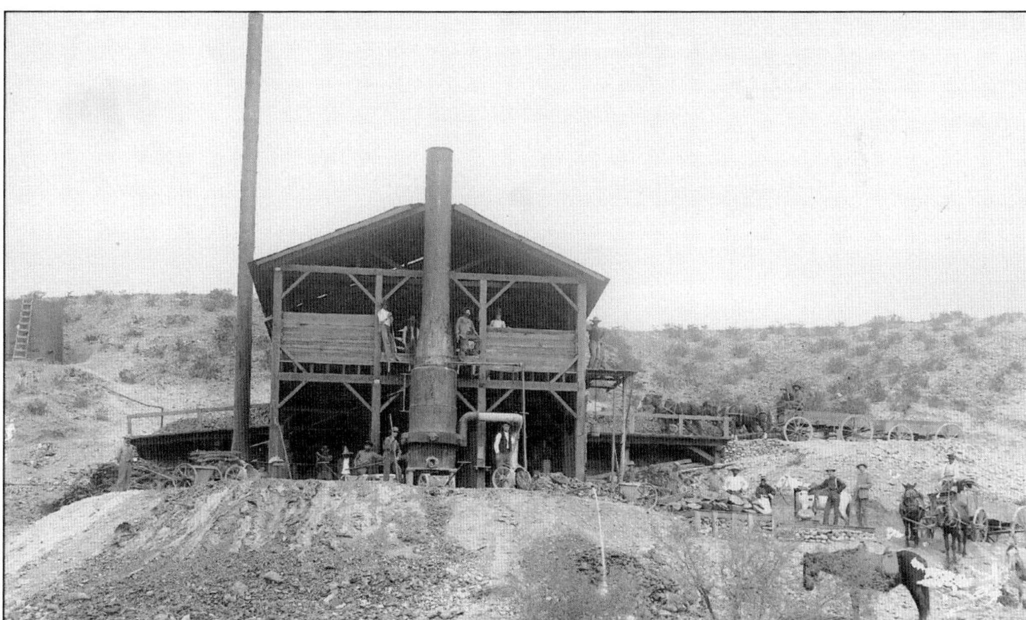

North of Safford, near the confluence of Bonita Creek and the Gila River, the San Juan gold mine owners invested a lot of money, as pictured here, but never produced enough profitable ore to continue.

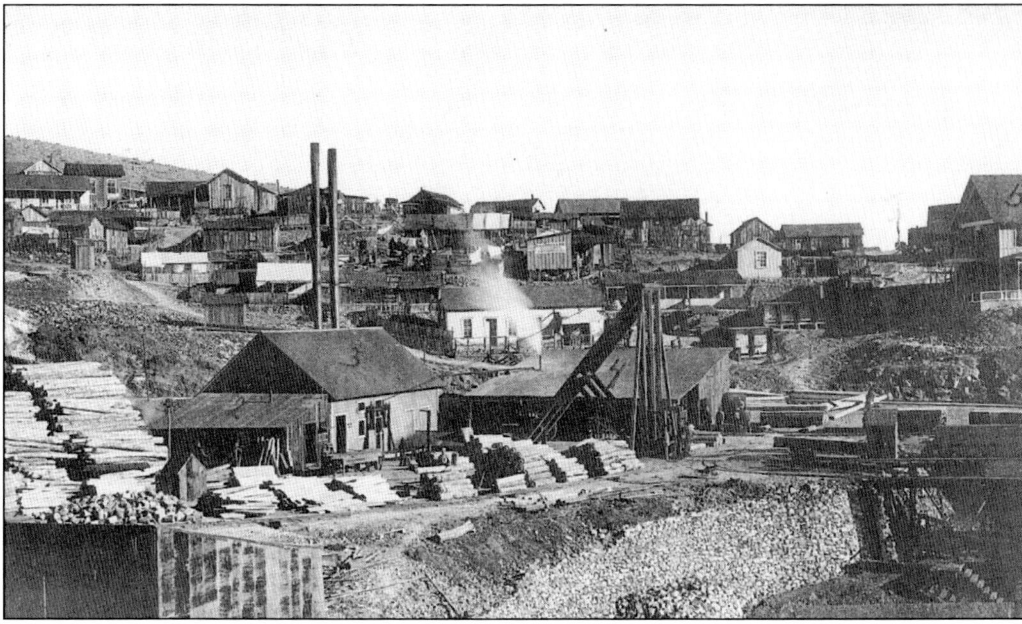

Surrounding the entrance to this copper mine in Morenci are thousands of feet of timbers used to shore up the shafts. The hoist (marked as building No. 4) delivered men and equipment hundreds of feet beneath the surface.

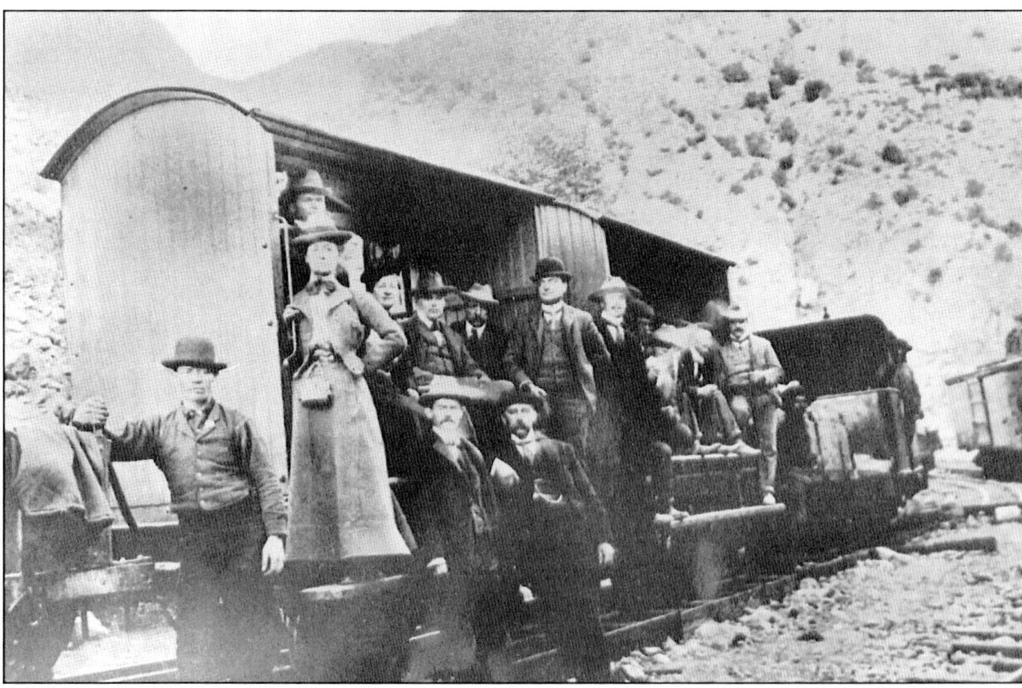

Visitors often took this 22-inch, narrow-gauge railroad from Clifton to the mines in Morenci and Metcalf. A popular attraction, the engine was eventually immortalized by becoming a monument in Clifton.

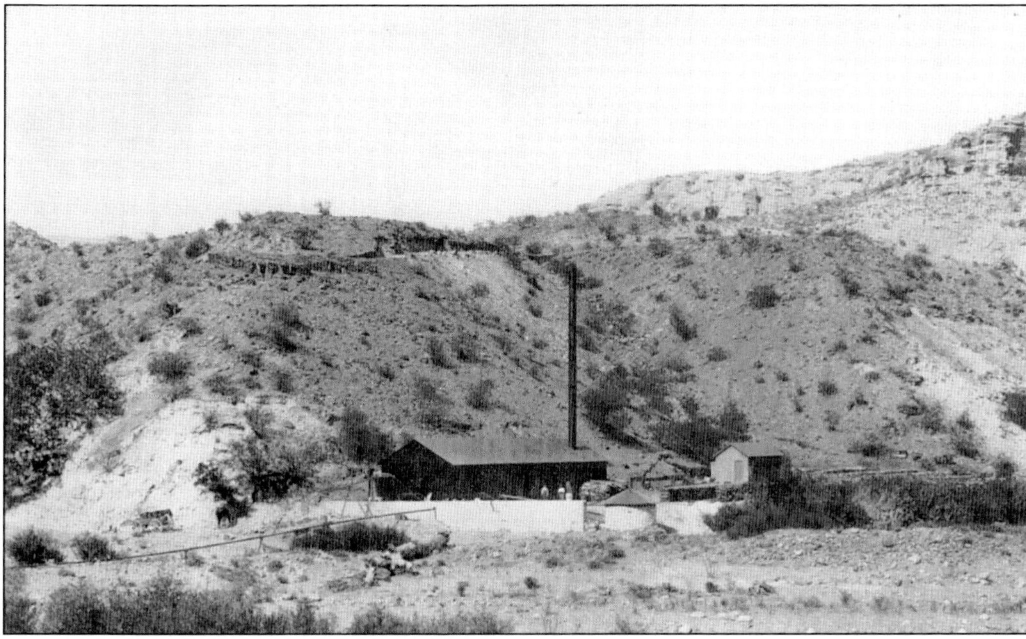

One of the most famous sites in the Clifton area was the pumping station. The steam-powered plant extracted water from Eagle Creek to supply the towns and mines in the area.

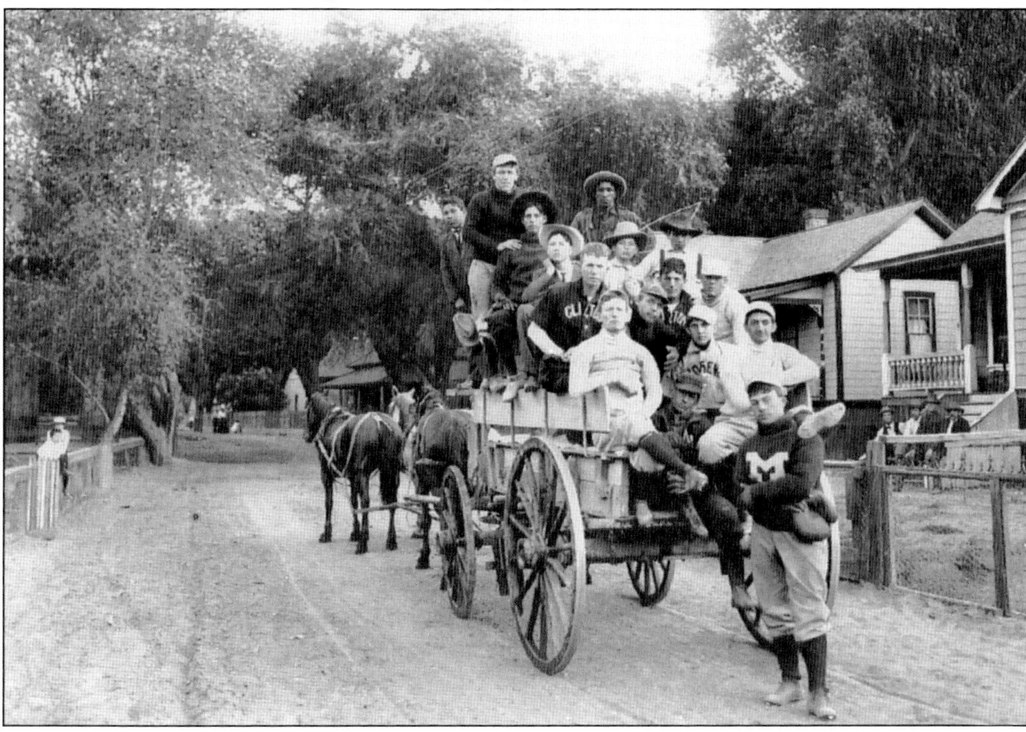

Life in the mining community of Clifton did include some play. The most popular sport at the start of the 20th century was baseball, with community and school teams traveling throughout the county to compete. This jaunty group of ballplayers represented the best skills and the pride of the community.

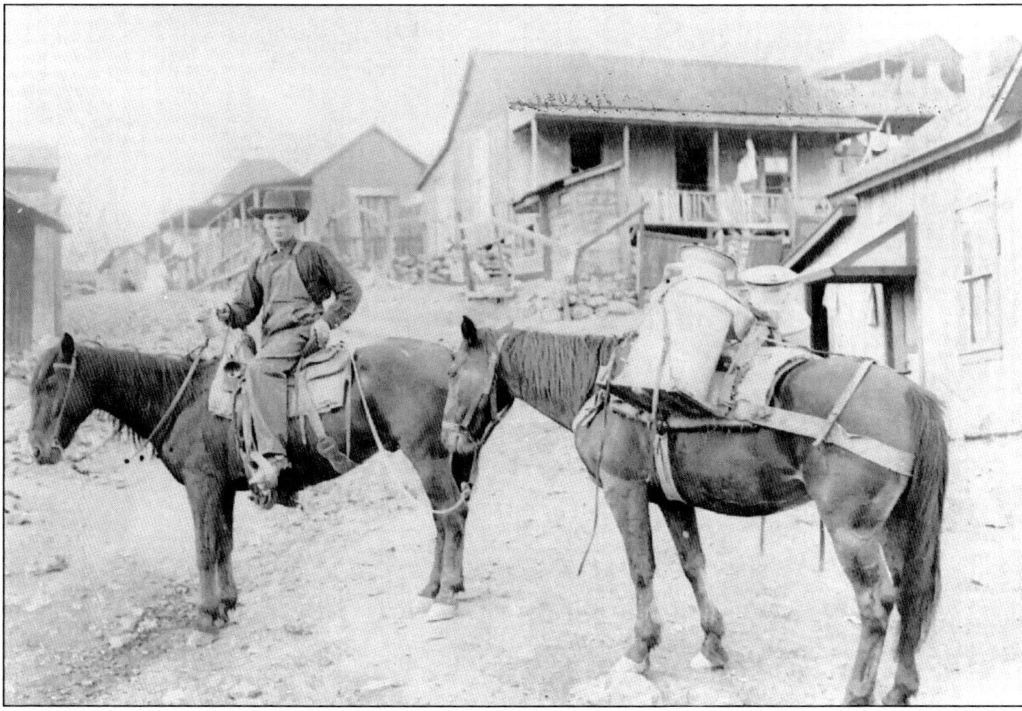

As pictured here, the rugged hillside residences of Clifton required sturdy horses to deliver supplies, including milk. Two five-gallon cans of milk required a strong horse and a strong-backed man to load and unload.

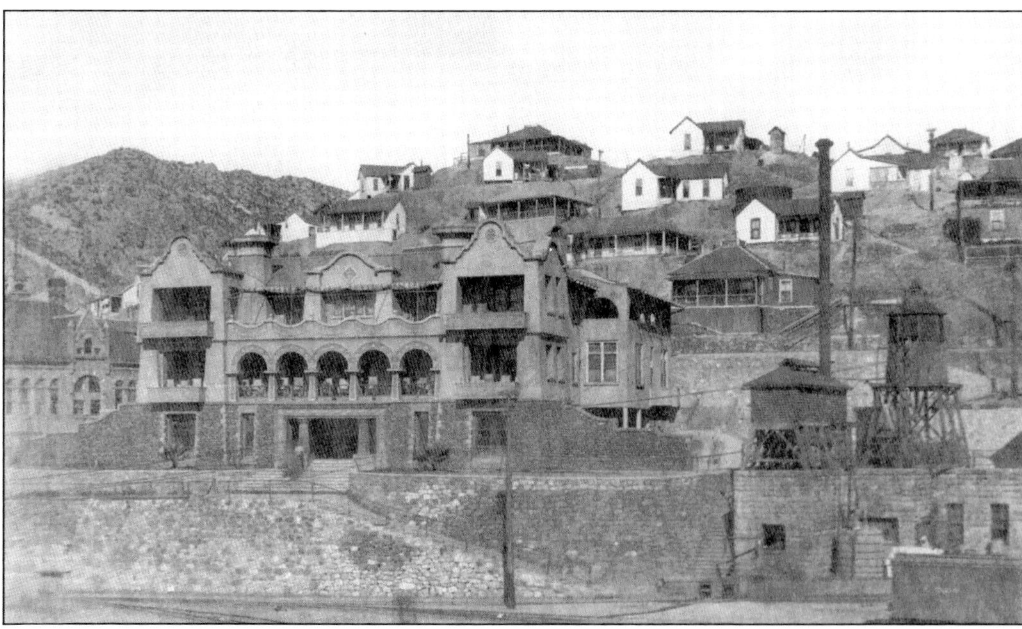

In 1906, Morenci was proud to showcase this hotel, which stood at the bottom of a hill covered with the homes of miners. The Morenci Hotel provided rooms for mining executives, drummers, contractors, and tourists. The *Clifton Clarion* reported a dizzying array of visitors who were anxious to see what was happening in the mining community.

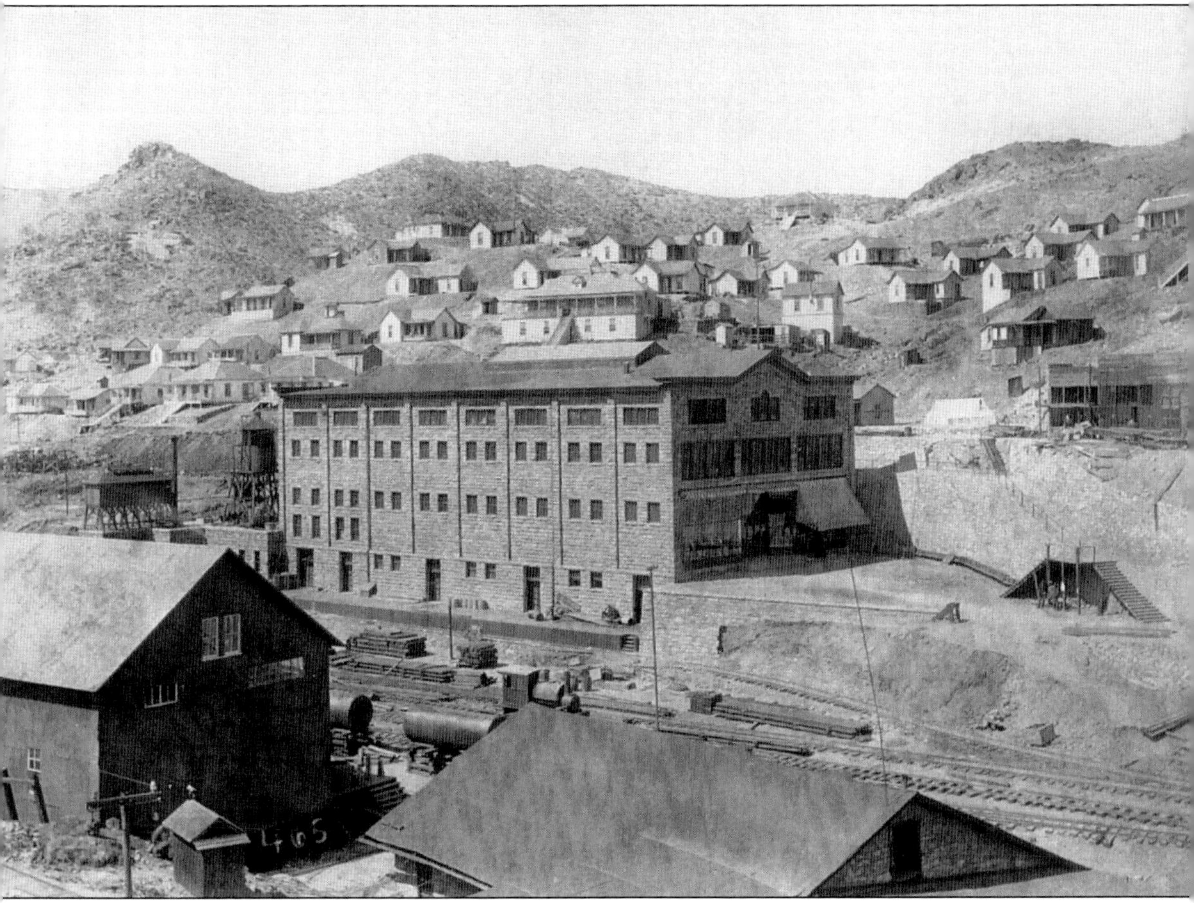

Morenci took on the role of company town. The DC Store, the largest mercantile in the mining district, stood next to the railroad yard, where mining equipment, copper ingots, ore, and goods were constantly being loaded and unloaded. The company town allowed its members to take advantage of low rent but forego owning property. Unless community members traveled to Clifton or Safford, they depended upon the company. For that reason, among others, employees chose to live in the surrounding communities of Clifton, York Valley, Duncan, or Safford.

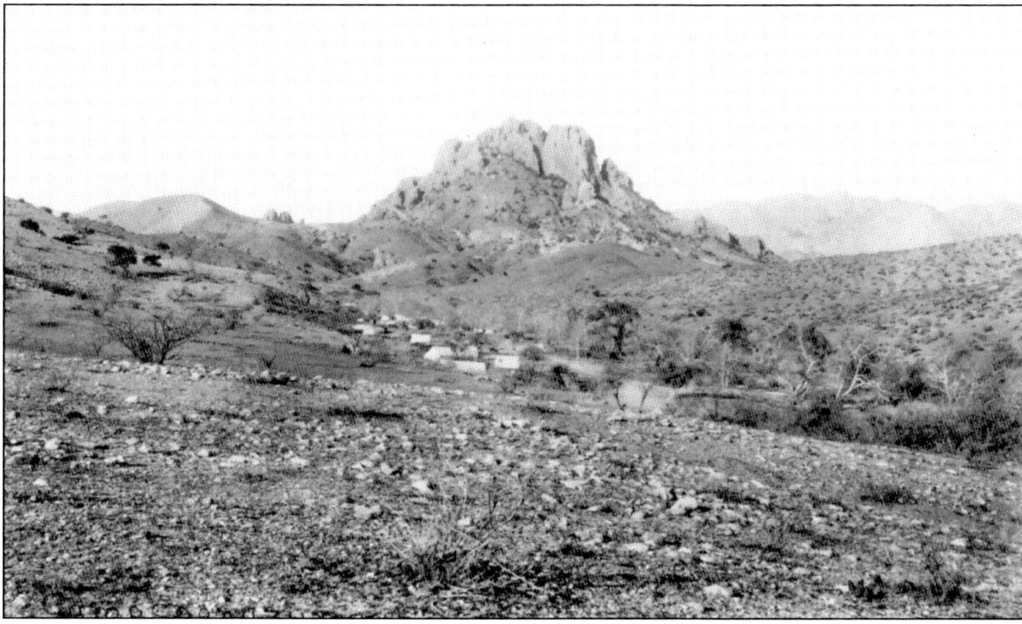

Along with successful mining came fraud. The rocky hill in the background of this photograph cradles the tent community of Spenazuma, a fraudulent mining business. Few locals were involved in the deception, but sought employment and promoted the mining operation. Stocks were sold in New York and New Jersey. The fraud was eventually exposed by George Smalley, a journalist from the *Arizona Republican*.

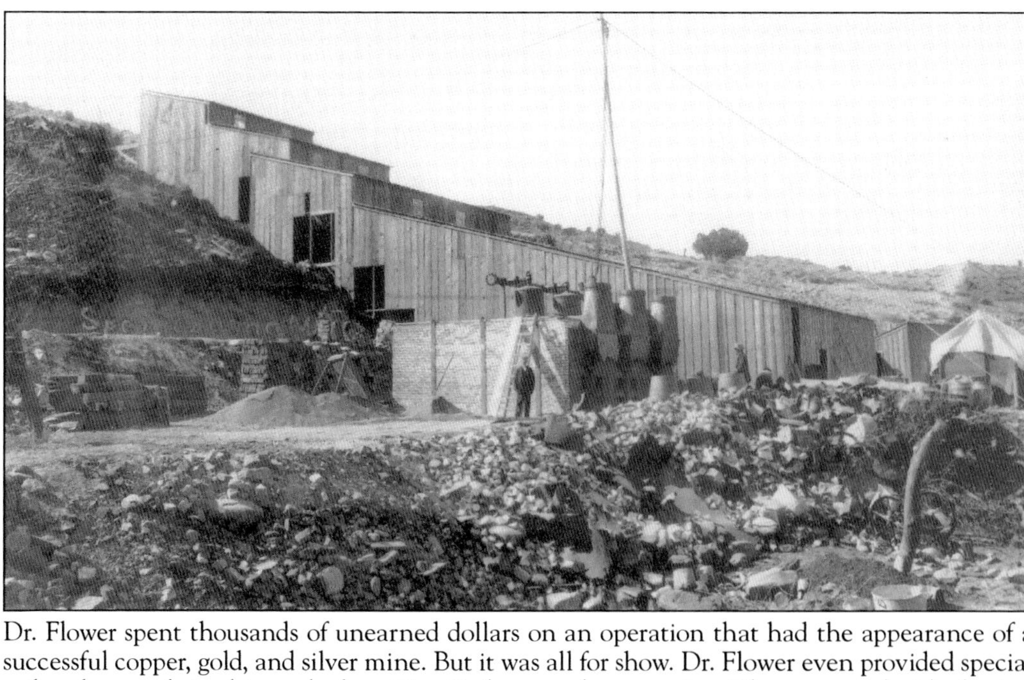

Dr. Flower spent thousands of unearned dollars on an operation that had the appearance of a successful copper, gold, and silver mine. But it was all for show. Dr. Flower even provided special railroad cars to bring his marks from New York to see the operation. They returned with glowing reports of the profitable business.

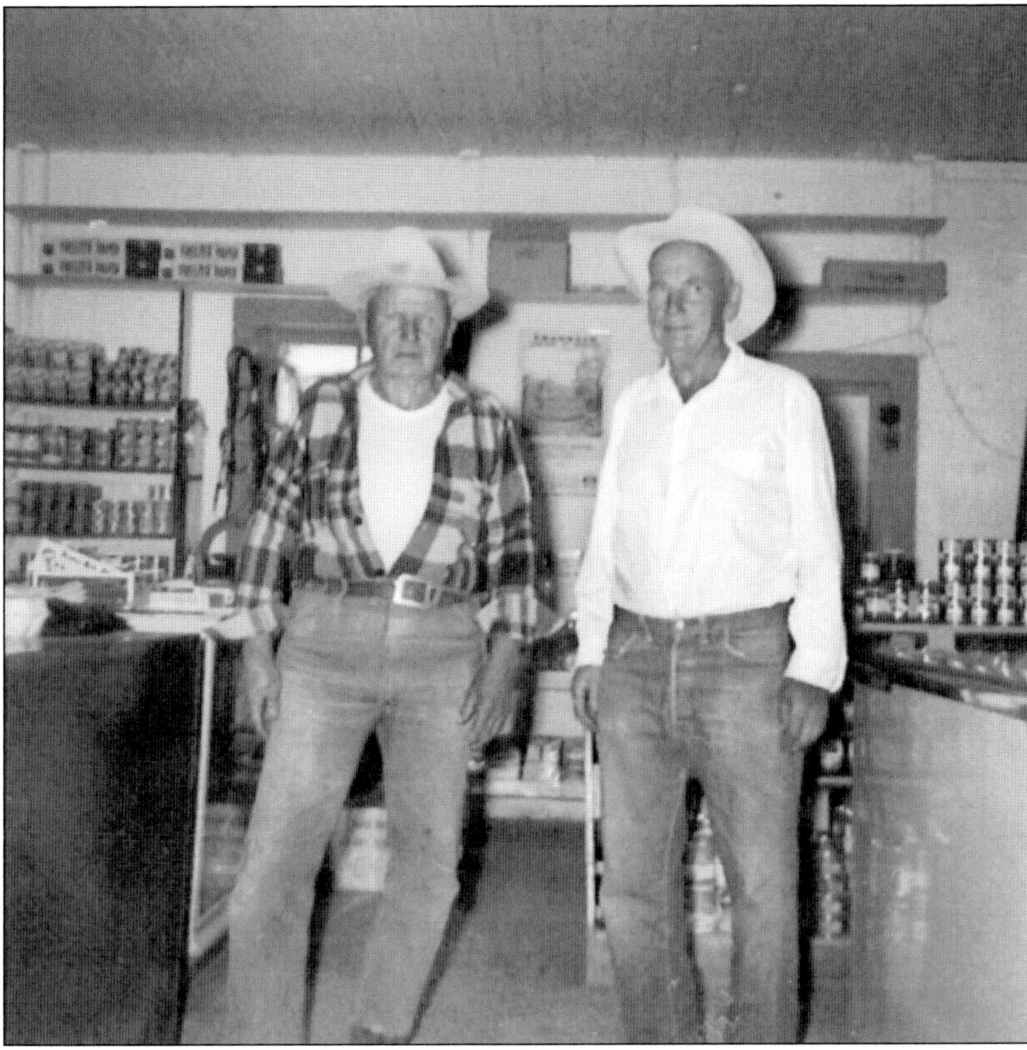

After their family staked claims in the remote Galiuro Mountains near Aravaipa Canyon, brothers John and Tom Power failed to register for the draft in World War I. Consequently, Graham County sheriff Frank McBride and three men set out to arrest the boys. Three of the four arresting officers were killed (including Sheriff McBride) in an alleged shoot-out. John and Tom were sentenced to life in prison. To this day, some believe that the shoot-out occurred between draft evaders and properly commissioned officers, while others believe the Power boys' story that the sheriff was in on a scheme to steal their mining claims. After their pardon in 1960, the elderly brothers lived out their lives in and around Graham County.

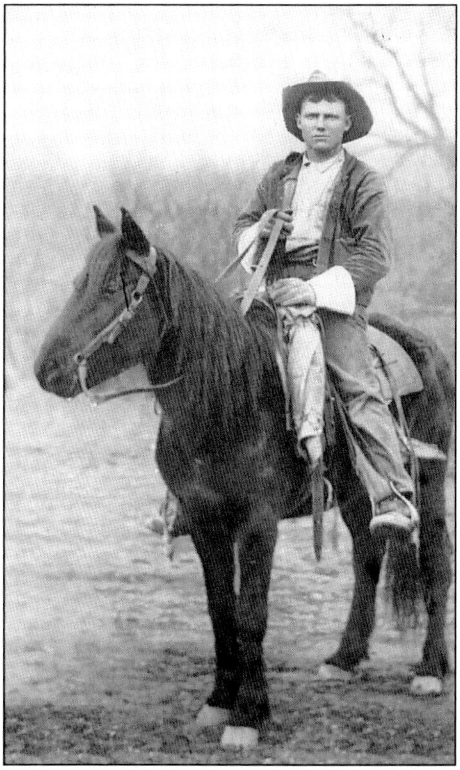

Young Tom Power is pictured just before the shoot-out that would change his life forever. Both Tom and John Power were strong men in the prime of their lives when the raid took place. The shoot-out resulted in the death of their father as well as the three lawmen. The brothers fled to Mexico and were captured after returning to the United States a short time later. Along with their handyman, Tom Sisson, they were sentenced to prison, serving time in Arizona State Prison at Florence.

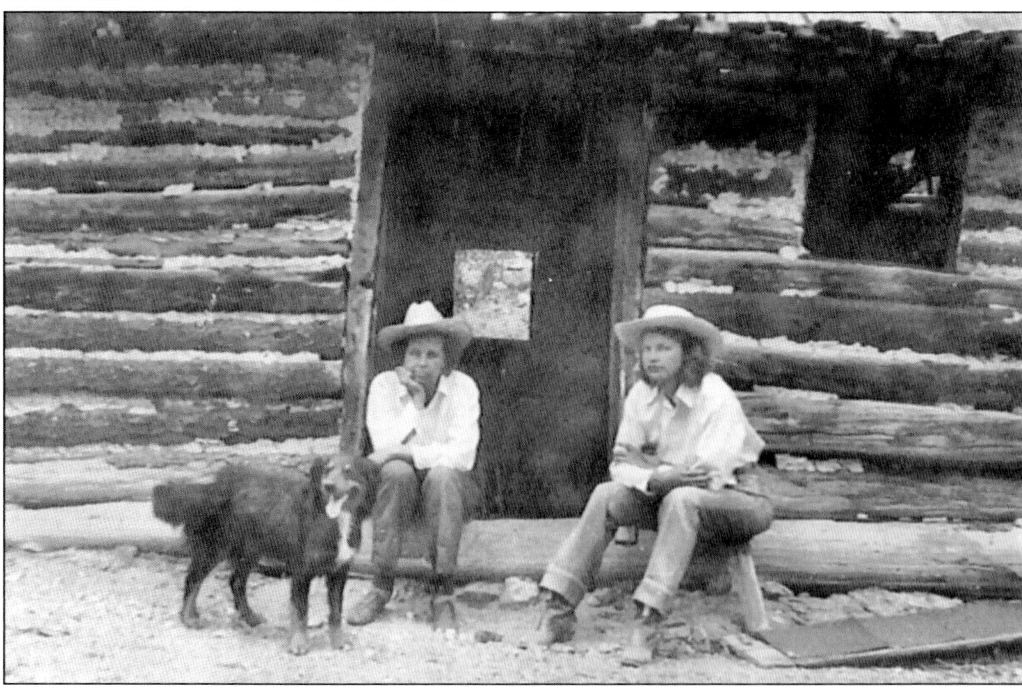

For decades, the Power cabin has been a popular destination for adventurous tourists. Here Babe and Hope McNair visit the cabin during the 1930s, the heyday of guest ranches in Graham County. Today the cabin can only be reached by a relatively long hike or by horseback.

Eight

PIMA

PIONEERS, FARMING, AND RANCHING

The westernmost of the three largest communities, Pima was the most fully developed at birth and the quickest to establish a sense of community and identity. However, for some reason it grew the slowest and never developed as a heavyweight in commerce and communication. An early-20th-century traveler through the community saw well-tended yards, sturdy and beautiful homes, plentiful gardens and orchards, a busy downtown: a community modeled after Salt Lake City.

In the fall of 1889, about 15 miles west of Pima, a well-planned attack was carried out against the army paymaster. (The event became known as the "Wham Paymaster Robbery" and has been thoroughly researched.) Paymaster Joseph Wham and his guards were traveling from Fort Grant to Fort Thomas and Fort Apache. The attackers got away with $28,345. Thereafter, seven locals were arrested and taken to Tucson for trial. Because of conflicting eyewitness testimony and broader state politics, the men were found not guilty. The memory of this incident and its unanswered questions were a source of embarrassment to much of the community.

Pima grew to be an attractive community, anchoring the west end of the valley as Solomonville anchored the east end. After statehood, a competition occurred between Safford and Pima to garner the title of county seat. When Safford prevailed, Pima settled into its identity as a bedroom community that maintained its sense of pride and reverence for its pioneer founders.

From the time of its very founding, the remembrance and celebration of the town's 28 founding families has been an important fact in the lives of new residents and descendants. That tradition has continued to this day.

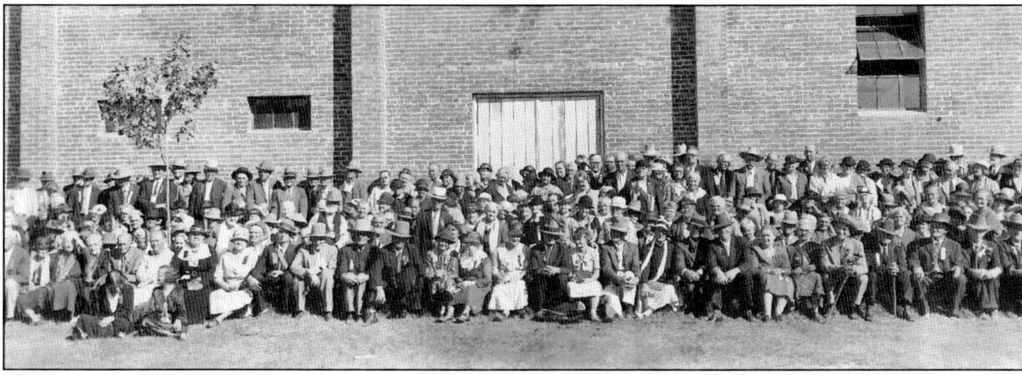

Pioneer reunions are part of the psyche of Pima. By the start of the 20th century, there were dozens of descendants of the original pioneers, all proud to pose for this photograph. Pima was founded in 1879 as Smithville (named for Jesse N. Smith, president of the Eastern Arizona Stake, but not a resident of the valley).

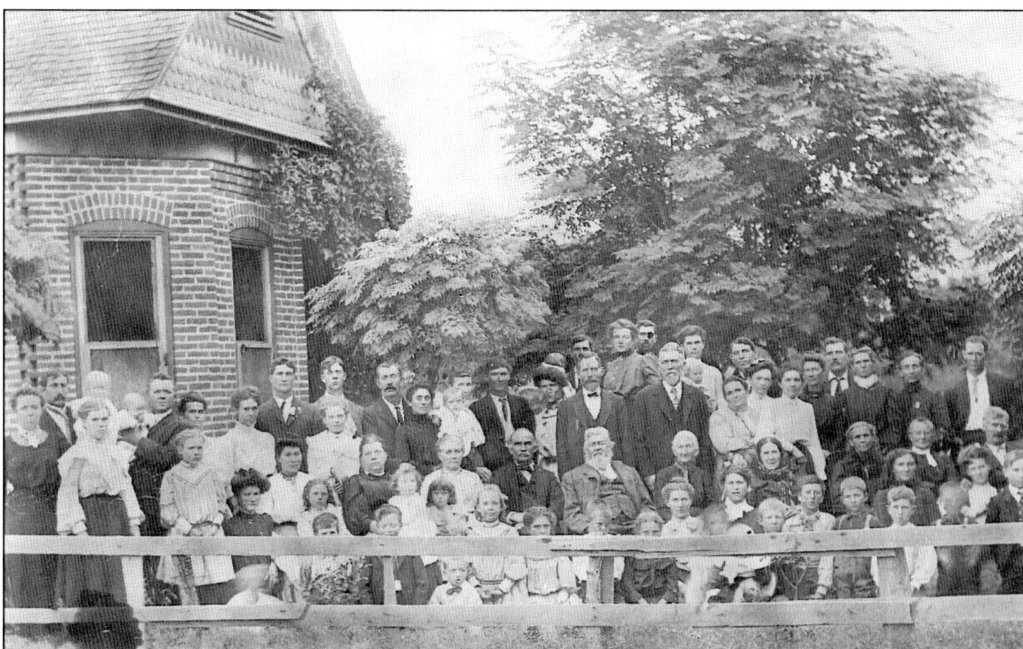

The Williams-Allen reunion is celebrated annually. Throughout the years, family reunions, such as this one, have been held in homes, at schools, and at popular gathering sites like Mount Graham and Cottonwood Wash.

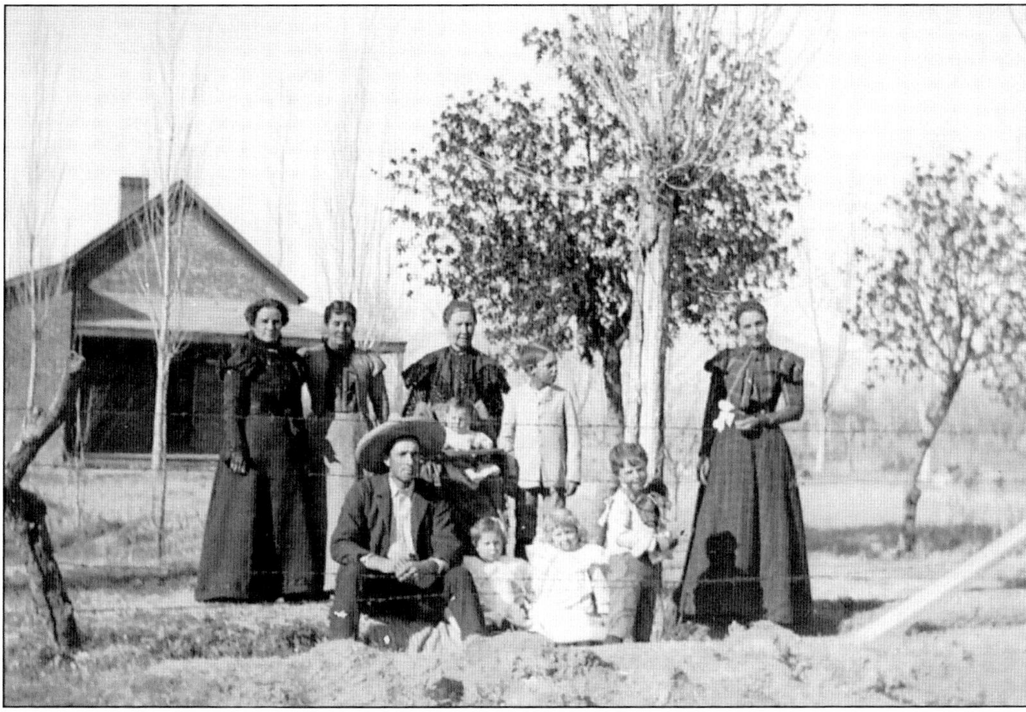

Early Pima homes were simple affairs usually surrounded by vegetable gardens and orchards. The George Cluff family is shown in front of the family's modest home. The young man wearing the sombrero is Foster Cluff.

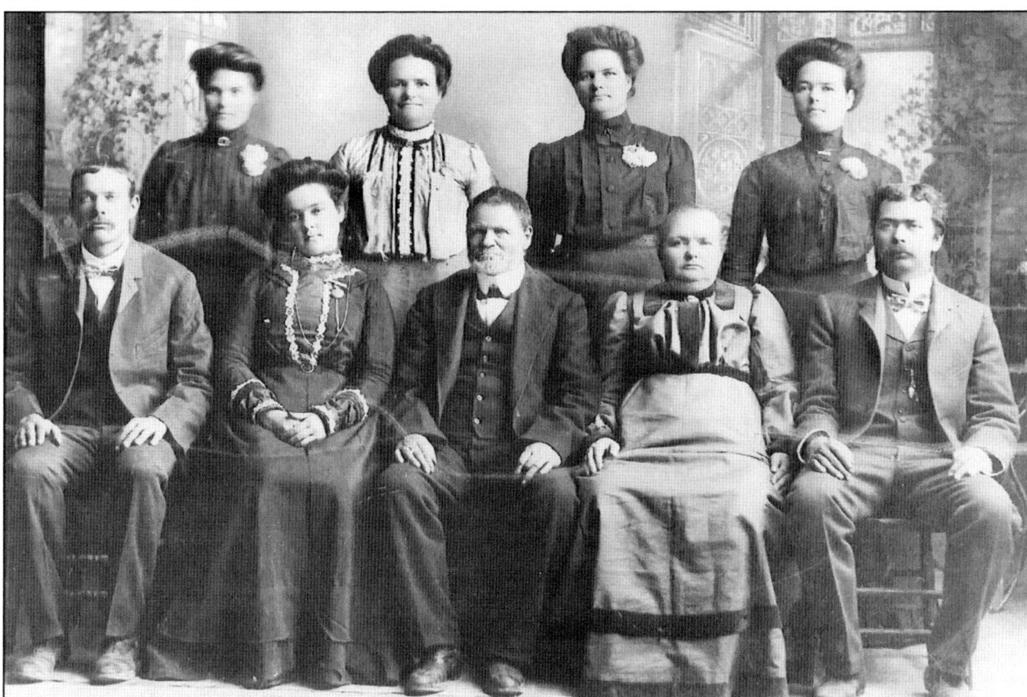

The Walter Barney family still has descendants in the area, much like many Pima families.

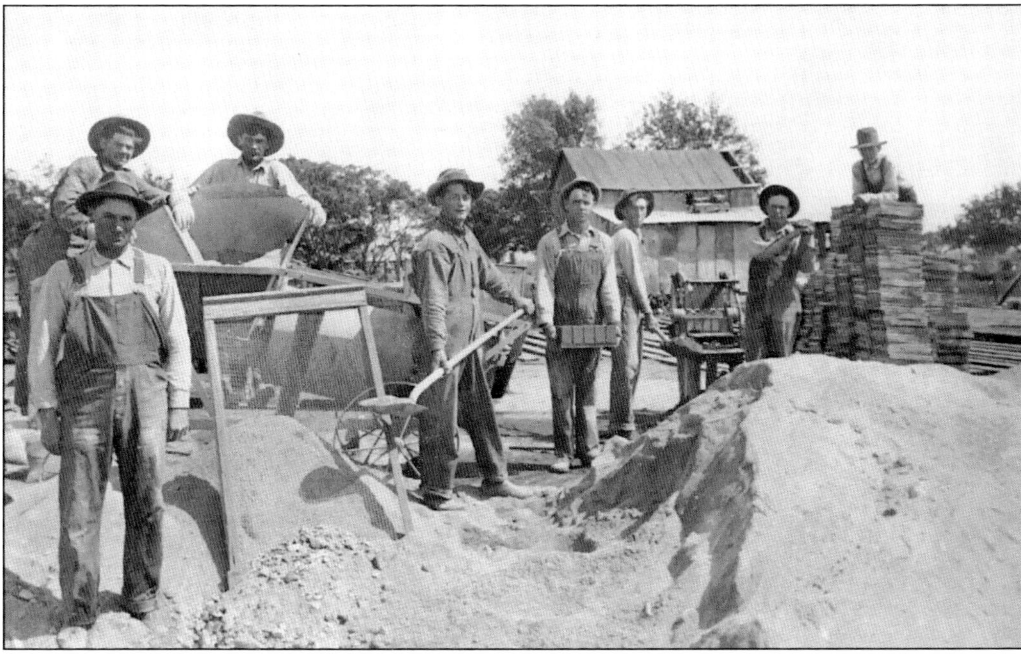

George "Brick" Williams developed a manufacturing company that produced brick in a kiln south of Pima. He delivered his product from Globe to Clifton. Known as the best quality, Williams's bricks were used in homes and businesses throughout the valley. Ebenezer Bryce was the first to build a brick house, across the river from Pima. It survives to this day.

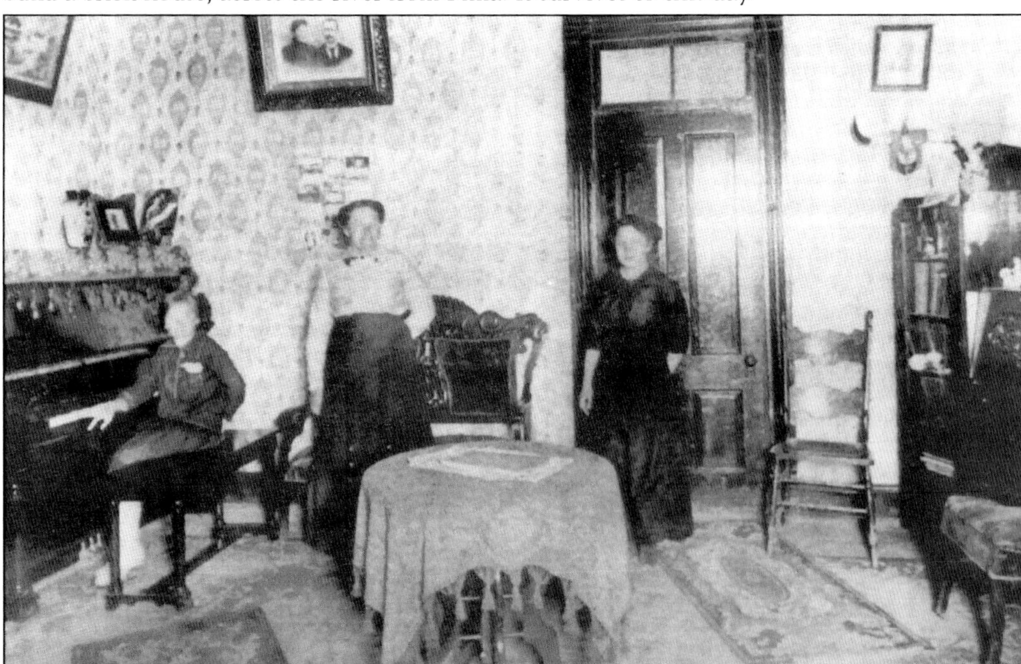

Hotels sprang up in all the communities in the Gila Valley. Pictured here is the Victorian interior of the Pima Hotel. Most of the residents of early hotels were "drummers," traveling salesmen who needed space to display their wares.

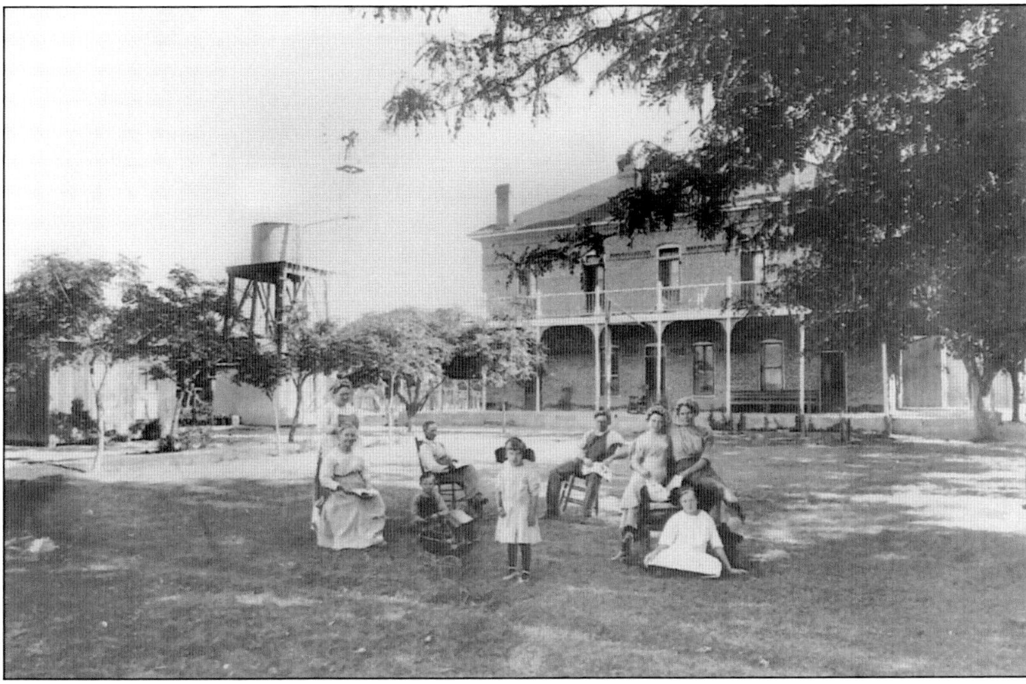

The 1912 Cluff Hotel in Pima provided a broad, shaded lawn and plenty of freshwater for its kitchen and guest rooms. The water tower and windmill in the background guaranteed a good supply of water.

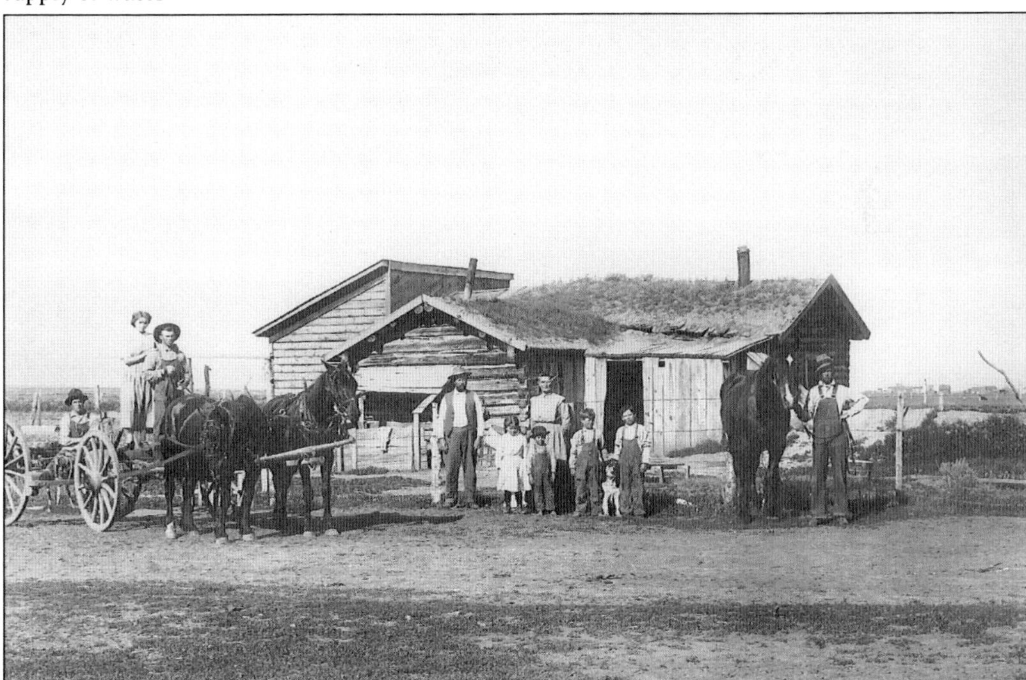

Early homes were crude affairs, as demonstrated by this photograph of a house with a unique sod roof. The exact location in Pima has been lost to history.

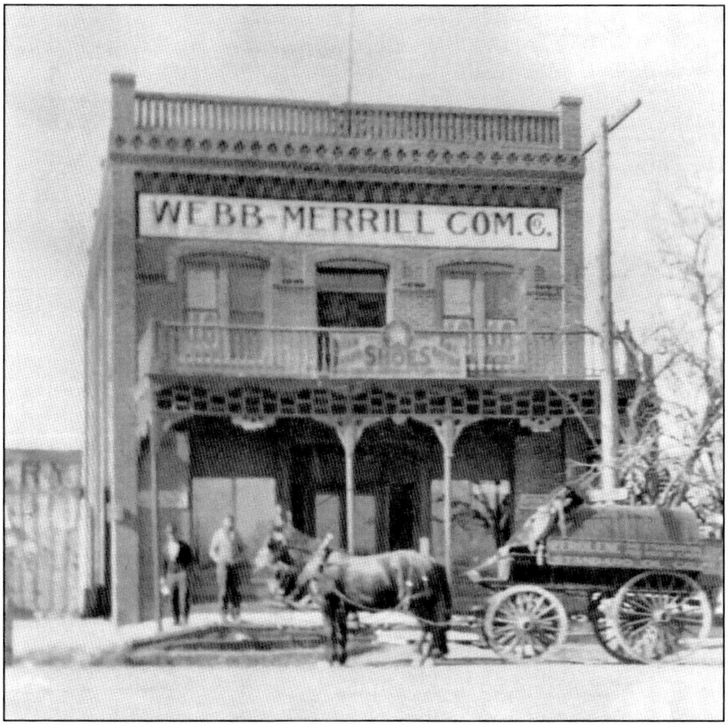

The popular Webb-Merrill building housed a mercantile and the offices for an enterprise that included freighting, farming, ranching, and the brokering of cash crops of fruits, vegetables, and grains. It was owned and operated by W. T. Webb of Wham Robbery fame.

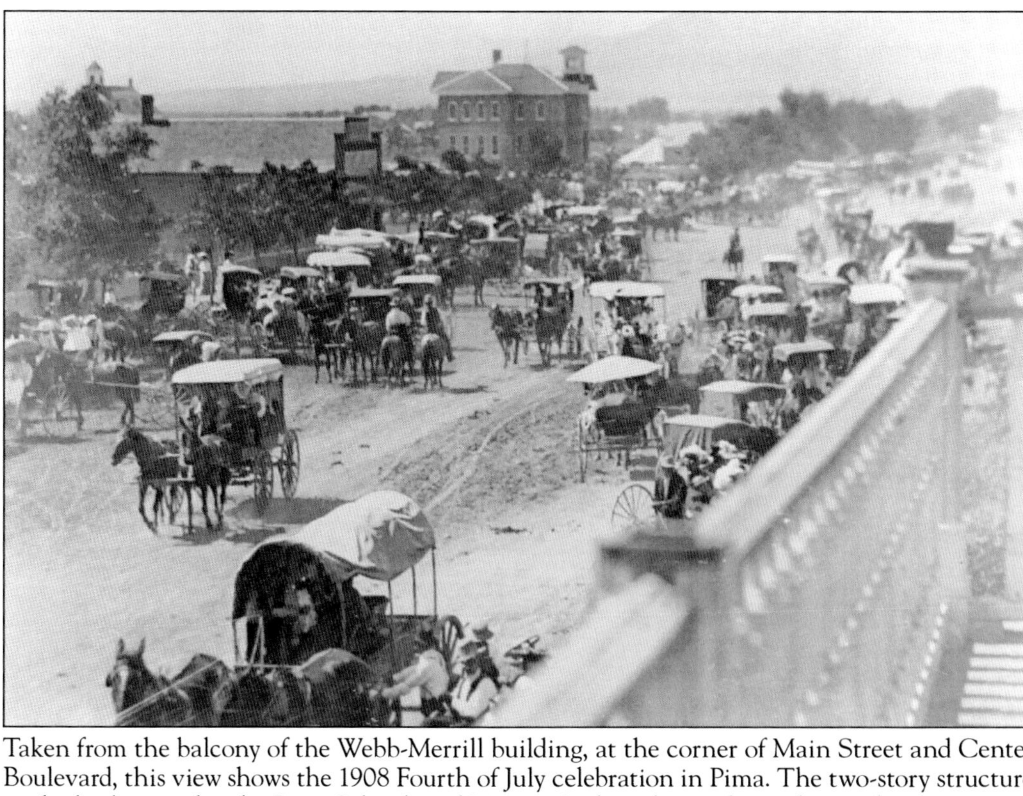

Taken from the balcony of the Webb-Merrill building, at the corner of Main Street and Center Boulevard, this view shows the 1908 Fourth of July celebration in Pima. The two-story structure in the background is the Pima School, and Mount Graham looms far to the south.

This incarnation of the Pima School stood for decades. Early Pima residents built four schools by 1892, more than any other early community in Arizona. Ryder Ridgway helped settle an argument over the oldest extant school building in Arizona by proving it to be in Pima. The building, constructed in 1882, is the Cluff Hall (currently housing the Eastern Arizona Historical Society Museum), which preceded all other school structures by at least three years.

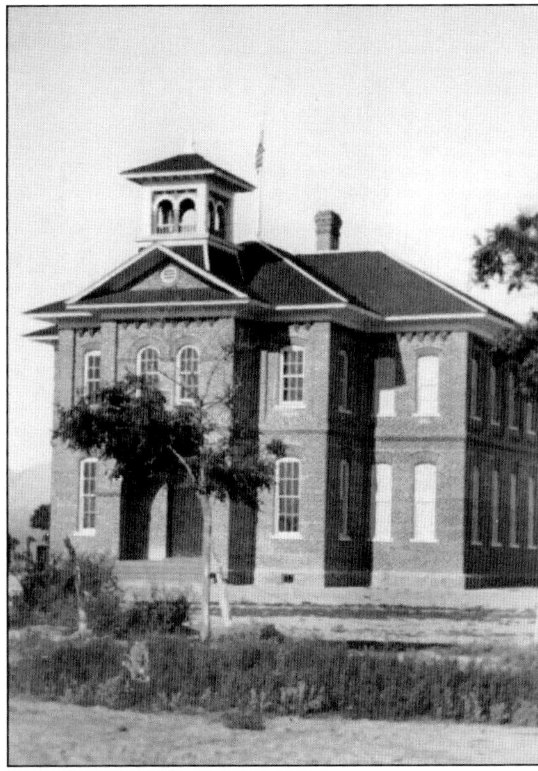

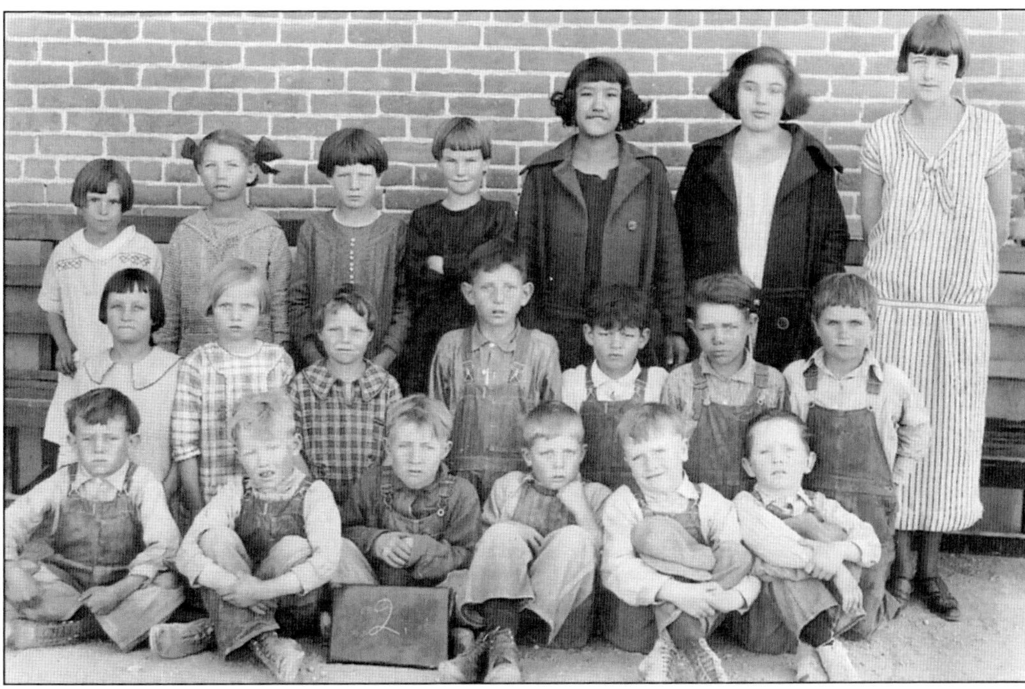

Hazel O'Bryan proudly stands with her students in Pima in the early 1920s. The handwritten caption on this old photograph indicates that this is a second-grade class, but some of the children in the back row are obviously too old for that grade.

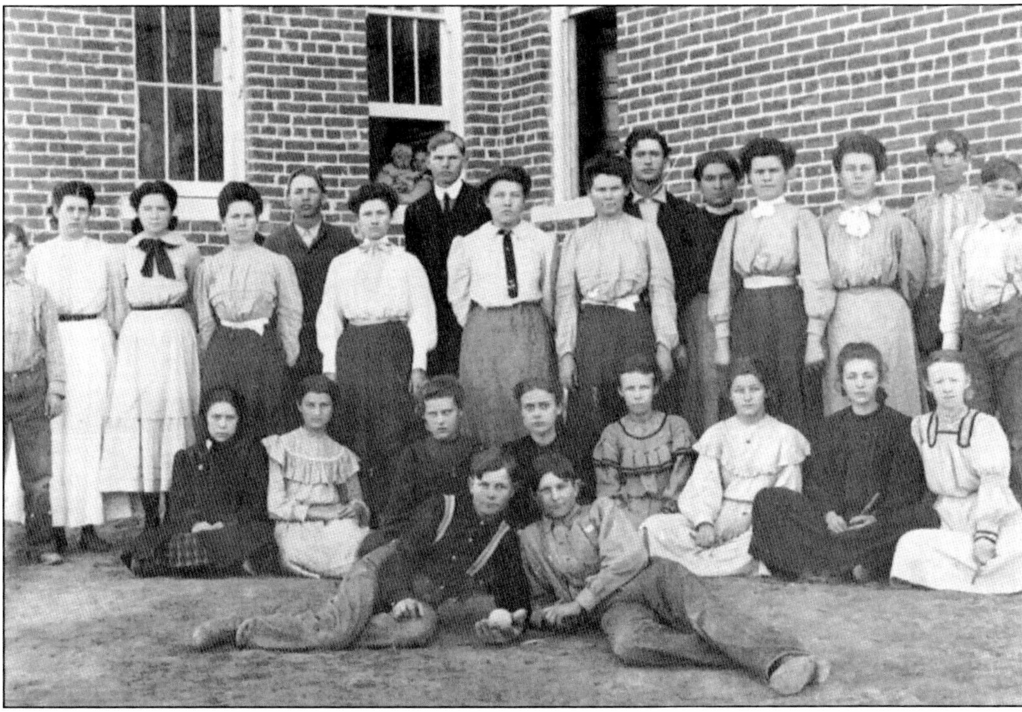

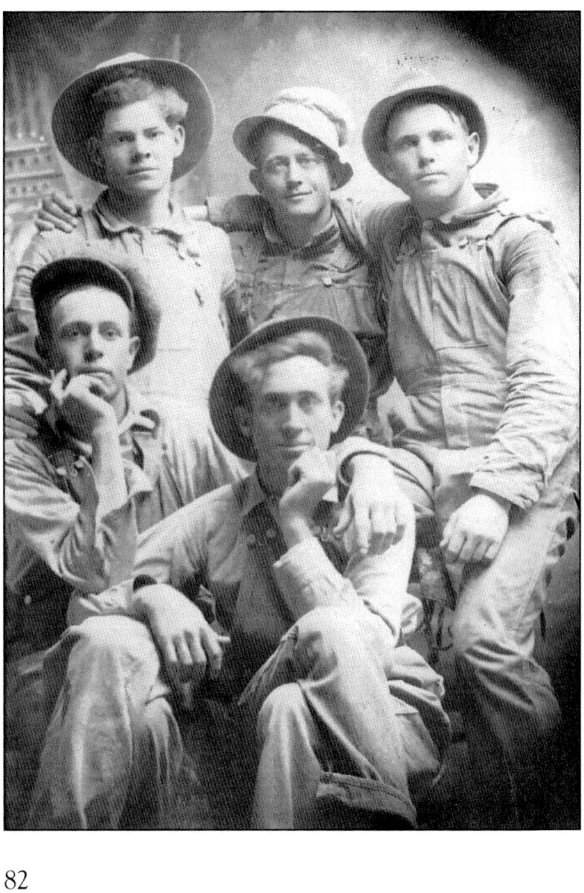

In 1906, eighth-grade graduation marked the end of formal education. Few students went on to attend local high schools or academies. The Pima School faculty poses with the seventh- and eighth-grade students of that year. All but two of the students have been identified.

Pima's eligible young men pose for posterity in 1912. Pictured from left to right are the following: (first row) Don McFate and Eric Hundley; (second row) Oscar "Curly" Taylor, Henry Haynie, and Loran Holladay.

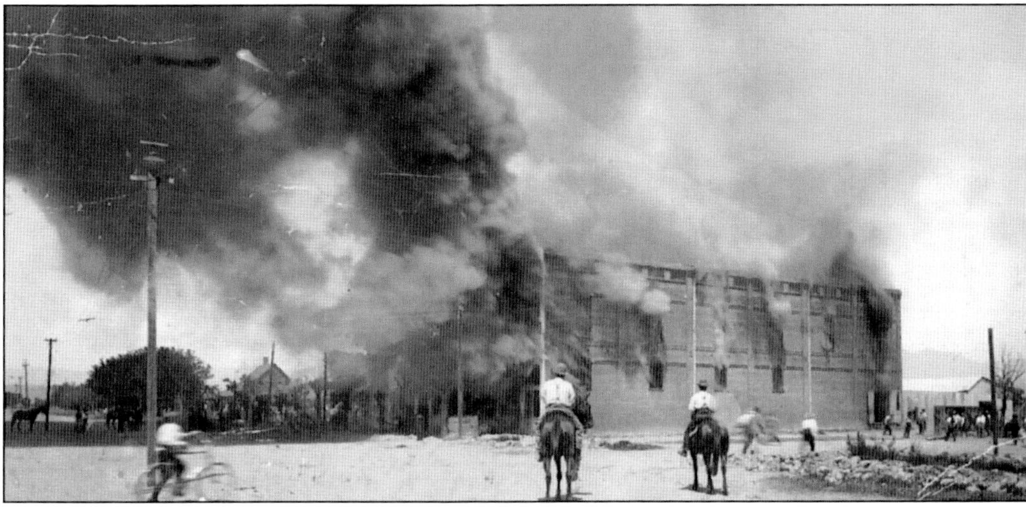

On Easter Sunday, April 13, 1914, the largest building in Pima, the Lines Hall, burned to the ground. Even though built of brick, the interior was devoured by the fire. Nothing could be done to save it, so onlookers just stood in awe.

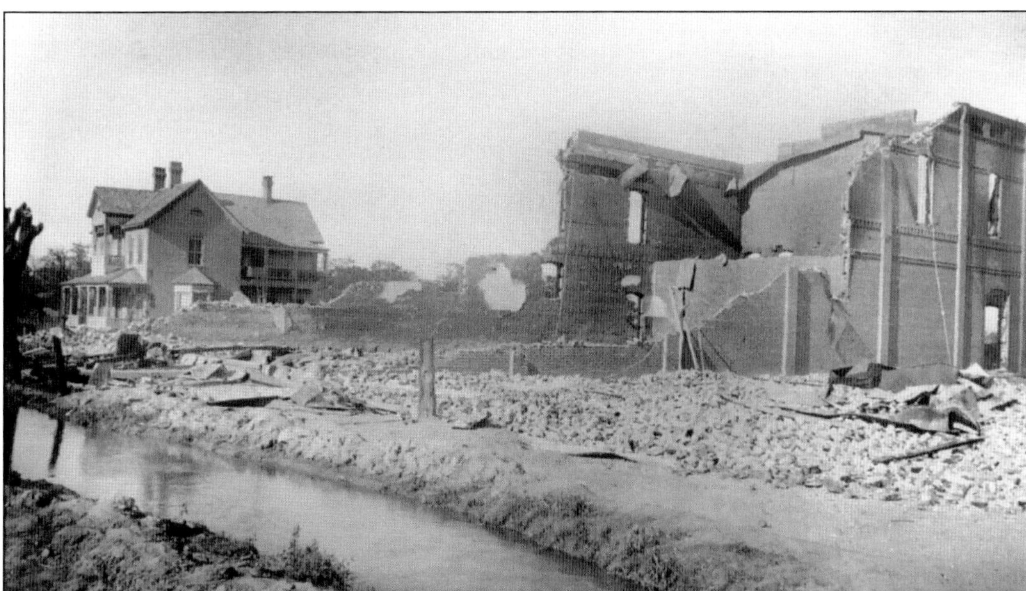

Brick recovery from the Lines Hall took days. The dance hall was not rebuilt, but the bricks were used in construction projects across the valley.

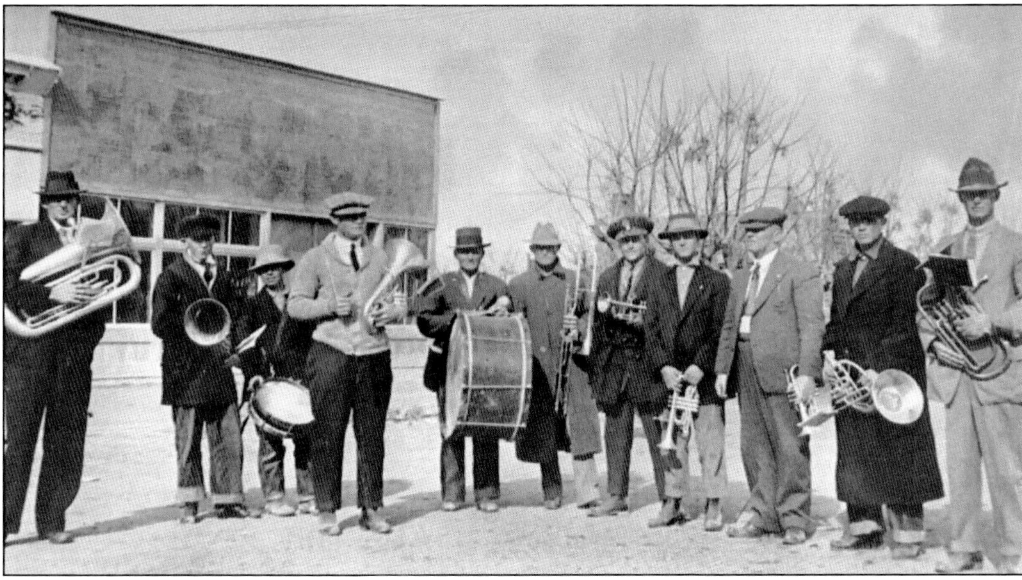

Citizen bands were in great demand. The Pima Band, together in 1913 and 1914, included, from left to right, Alford Rhone, Paul Merrill, Mack ?, Reece Green, Willie Ferret on bass drum, Sam Lines on trombone, an unidentified trumpeter in the captain's hat, Lawrence Holladay, Fred Webb, Clarence Davis, and an unidentified horn player.

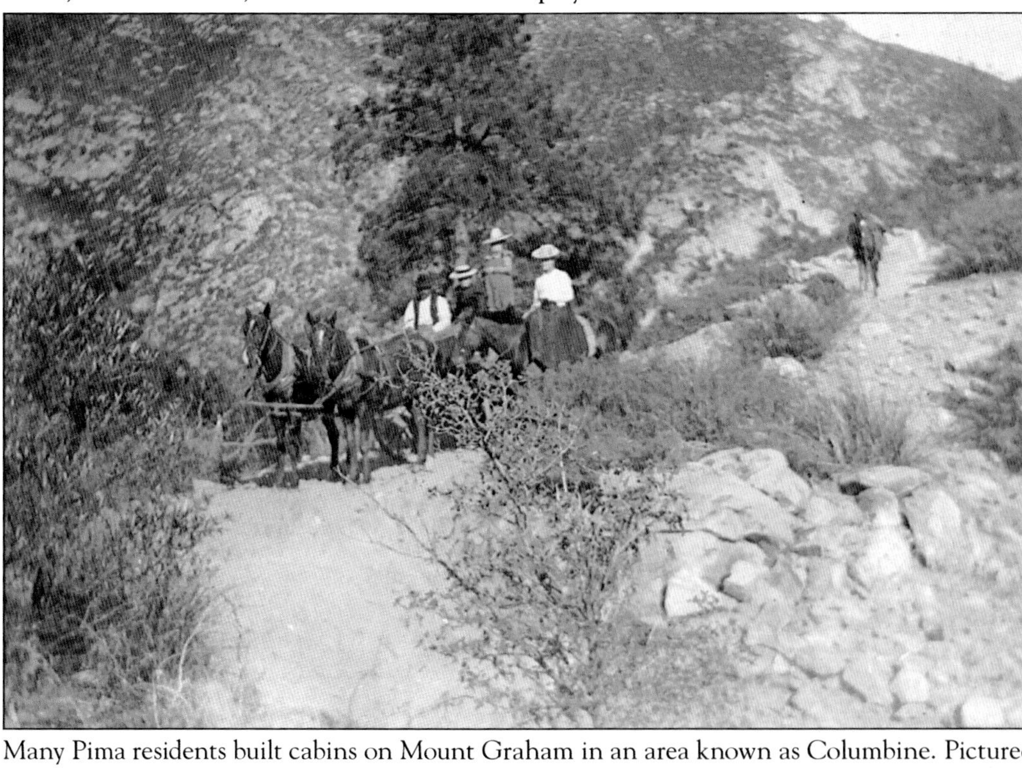

Many Pima residents built cabins on Mount Graham in an area known as Columbine. Pictured here are teachers returning from a retreat of the Graham County Teachers' Institute at Columbine in 1900. Pictured from left to right are Joseph G. Allred, Eliza Allred, Maggie Allred, and Sarah Allred. Notice the packhorse, dutifully following behind.

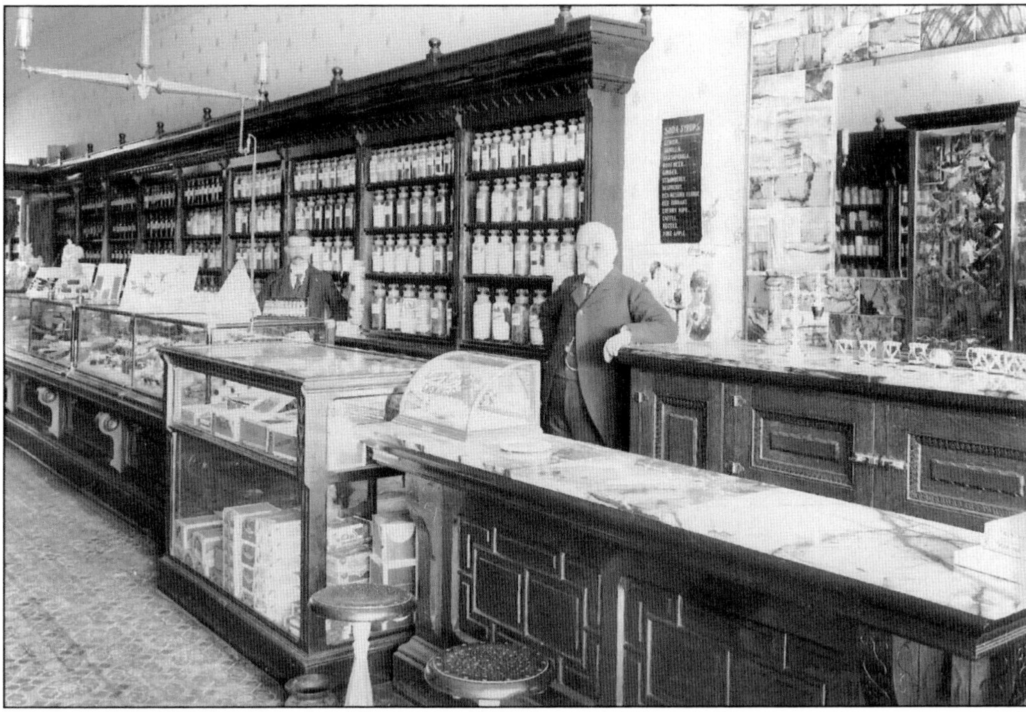

One of the most important enterprises in town was the local drugstore, where stools and marble counters welcomed customers. The counter in front of proprietor L. E. Wightman (right) contains cigars, and the flip-top display provides chewing gum.

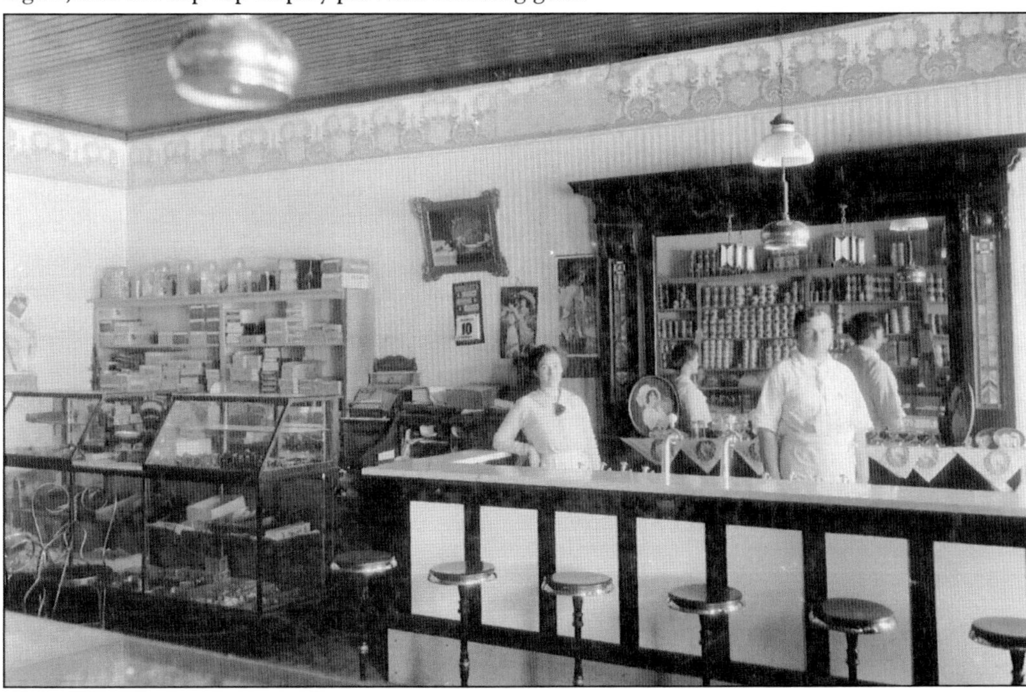

Another of Pima's popular gatherings was Cole's Store and Fountain, pictured in 1910. The shop sold candy by the ounce and a wide variety of canned goods.

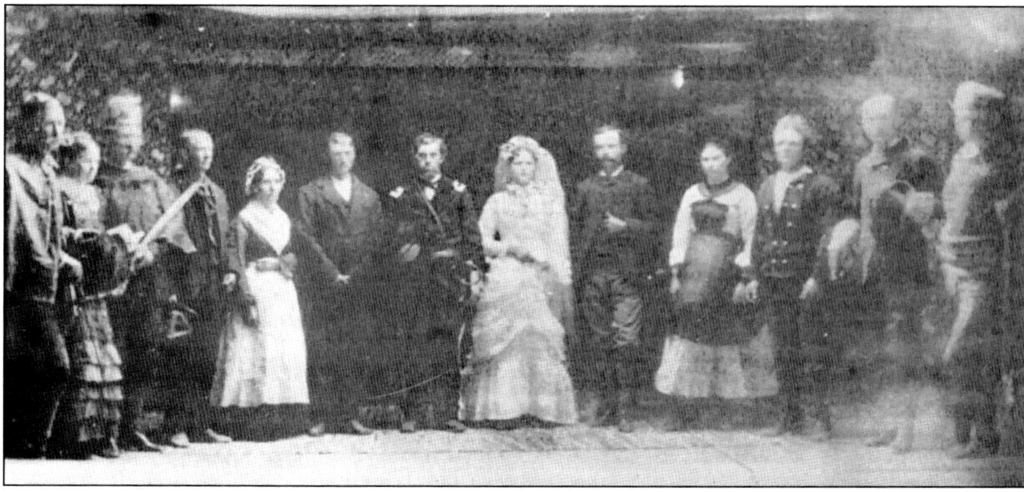

Dramatic performances were very popular around 1900. Shown here is a dress rehearsal of the Pima Dramatic Company Players, photographed in Cluff Hall in 1895. Pictured from left to right are Dave Norton, Ellen Norton, W. W. Crockett, Thomas Norton, Louise Johnson, Peter Norton, William Ransom, Zobedia Ferrin, J. M. Moody, Janetta Ferrin, George Bailey, Joseph East, and Thomas East.

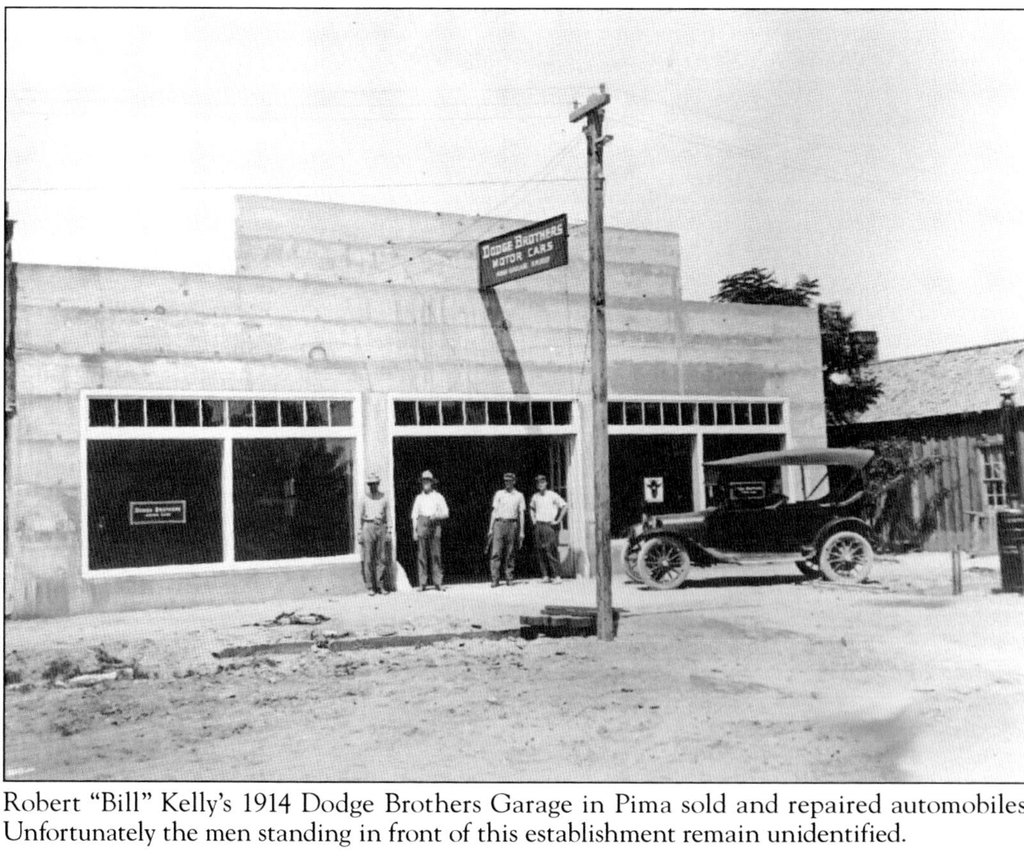

Robert "Bill" Kelly's 1914 Dodge Brothers Garage in Pima sold and repaired automobiles. Unfortunately the men standing in front of this establishment remain unidentified.

Nine

Thatcher

Education, Enterprise, and Entertainment

For most of its existence, Thatcher has been primarily influenced by the evolution of today's Eastern Arizona College. From its beginning as a branch of the Brigham Young Academy, it evolved as the St. Joseph Stake Academy, the Latter Day Saints Academy, Gila Academy, Gila Normal College, Gila Junior College, Gila College, Eastern Arizona Junior College, and Eastern Arizona College. As the college grew, so did the community that surrounded it.

The first impetus to community growth was housing for the students that came from nearby communities, farms, and ranches. At first, students lived with friends and relatives in the community or rented rooms from local residents. Local accommodations like the Brinkerhoff Hotel offered some housing at modest rates, but the need for dorms was recognized. After the completion of the first expansion in 1908, students began to arrive from all over Arizona Territory.

Thatcher was the seat of the St. Joseph Stake, a huge religious territory of the Church of Jesus Christ of Latter Day Saints. Christopher Layton had been sent from Utah to serve as its president. Several commercial enterprises were sparked by the stake president when he developed interests in stores, flour mills, farming, and transportation.

Unlike other communities of similar size, Thatcher never established a recognized main street or downtown. While its businesses faced Highway 70, Thatcher failed to develop a compact town center, instead relying on the services in Safford, only five miles to the east. The community therefore built around the college.

Following World War I, the demand for field workers and goat herders increased the number of Mexican residents and encouraged the development of a separate community north of Thatcher. Because of the white alkaline powder that covered the surface of the land there, the Mexicans called it Salitre ("salt flat"). Anglo residents of Thatcher referred to it as "Mexican Town," and people who traveled through Thatcher never knew of its existence. Salitre is no longer a separate entity, as the community is comfortably integrated today.

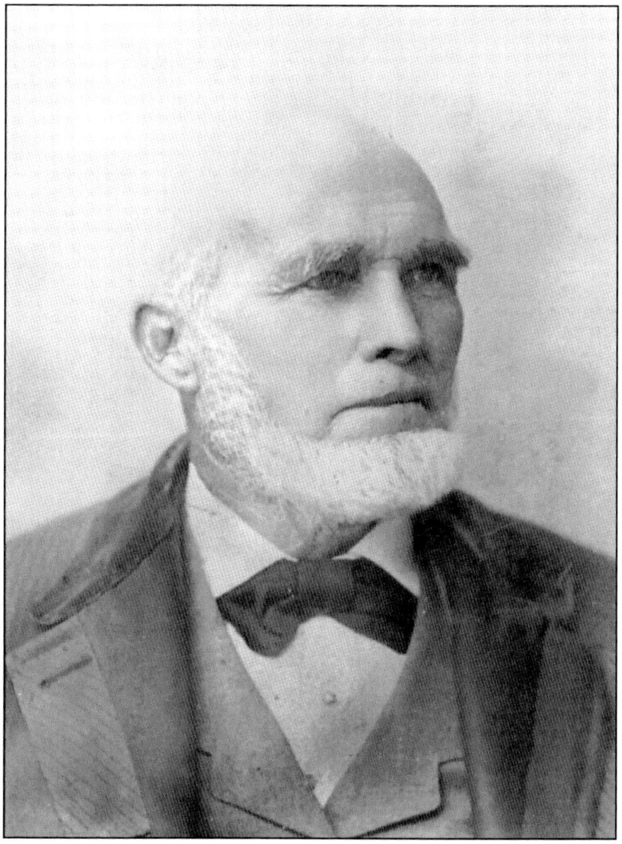

The founder of Thatcher, Christopher Layton, was sent to the Gila Valley in 1883 with the authority to organize the wards within the St. Joseph Stake. By 1885, there were 247 families in the St. Joseph Stake: 538 people in Pima, 293 in St. David, 185 in Central, 178 in Layton, 142 in Curtis, 73 in Graham, and 65 in Thatcher. Christopher Layton was serving as president of the St. Joseph Stake when he laid out plans for the town of Thatcher.

Christopher Layton's home in Thatcher stood on land that is now part of Eastern Arizona College. Layton became involved in farming, flour milling, and other businesses in Safford and Thatcher. The still-active Layton family organization recently erected a plaque and bust of their ancestor near the Thatcher Town Hall.

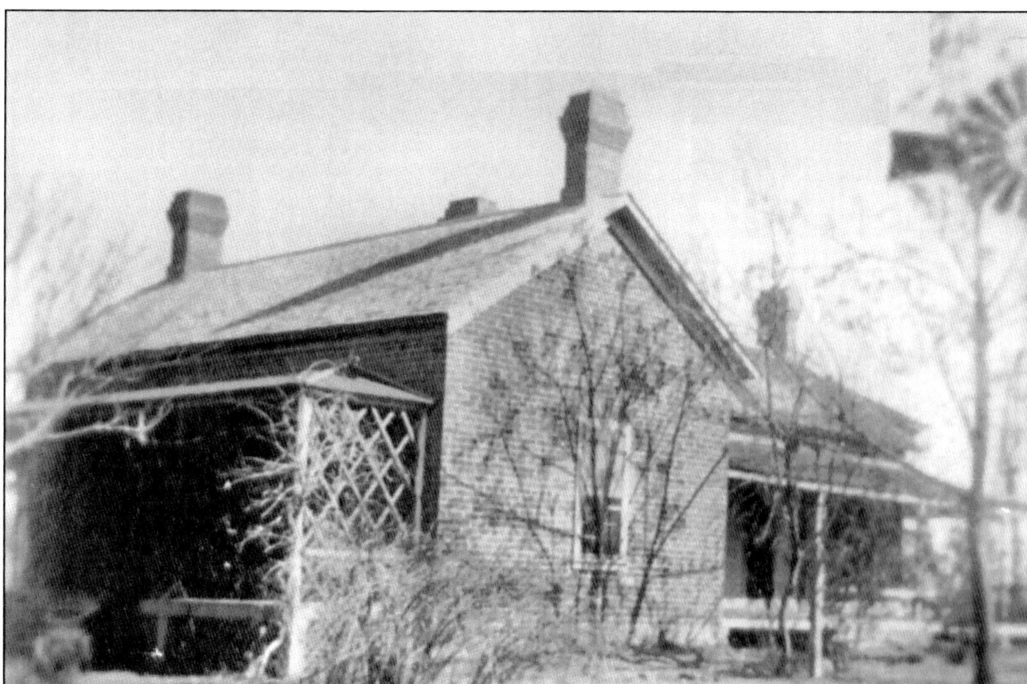

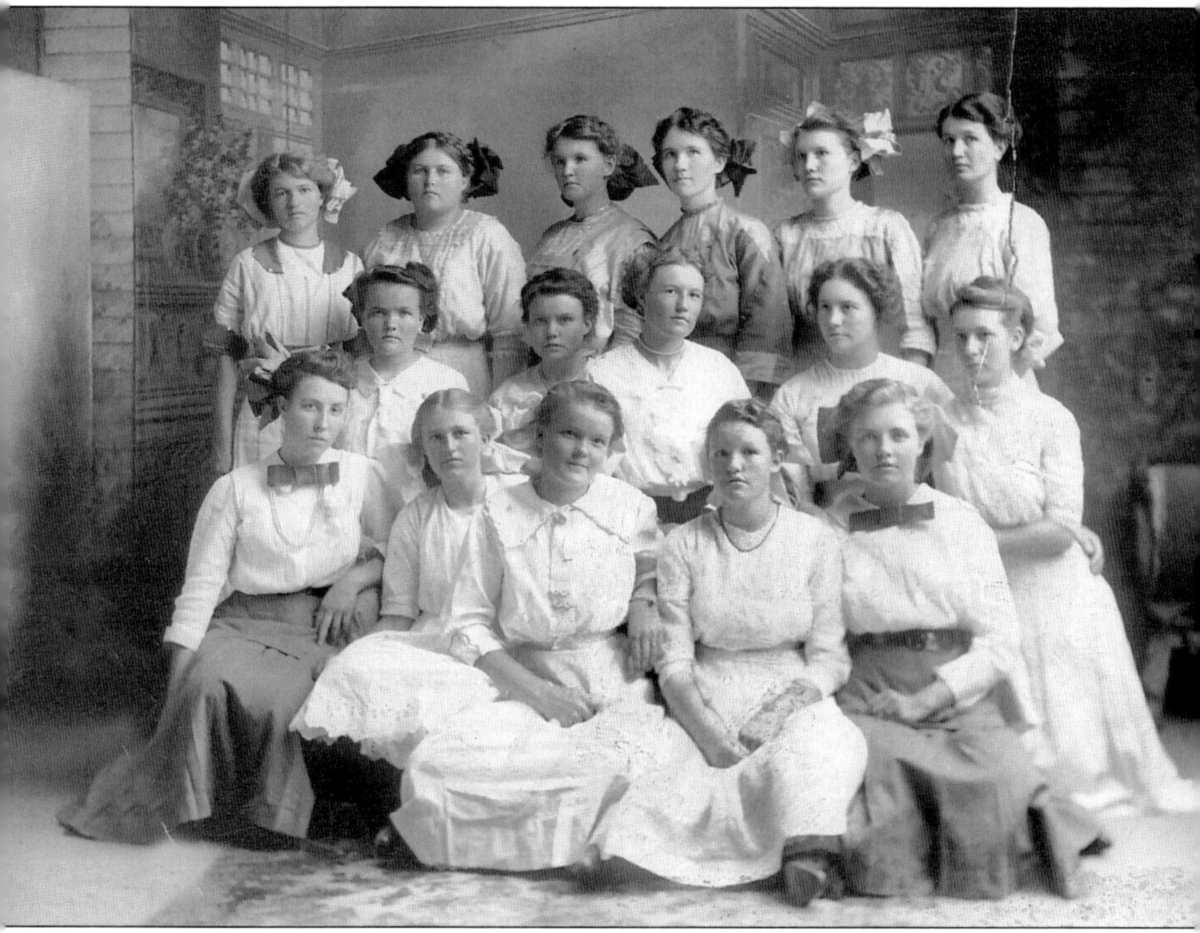

Pictured here are Christopher Layton's daughters and granddaughters. Layton built a store, initially named C. Layton and Co. and later called the People's Store. He also established a blacksmith shop, a creamery and ice plant, and, in conjunction with his son-in-law Joseph Allred, a grain mill.

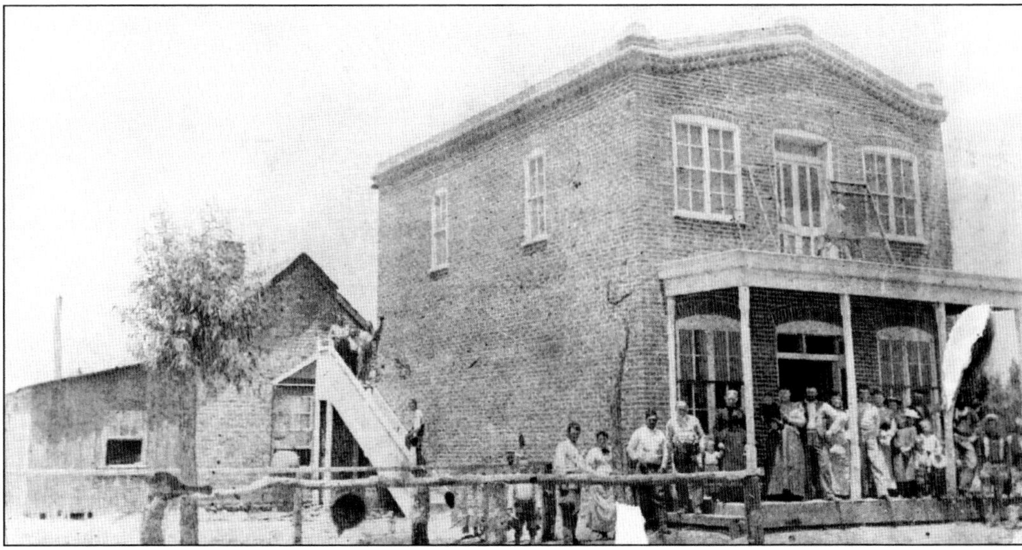

Stevens Mercantile, opened in Thatcher at the start of the 20th century, served as a popular gathering place for residents of the town. The stairs to the left provided a means for the family living on the second story to enter and exit without going through the store.

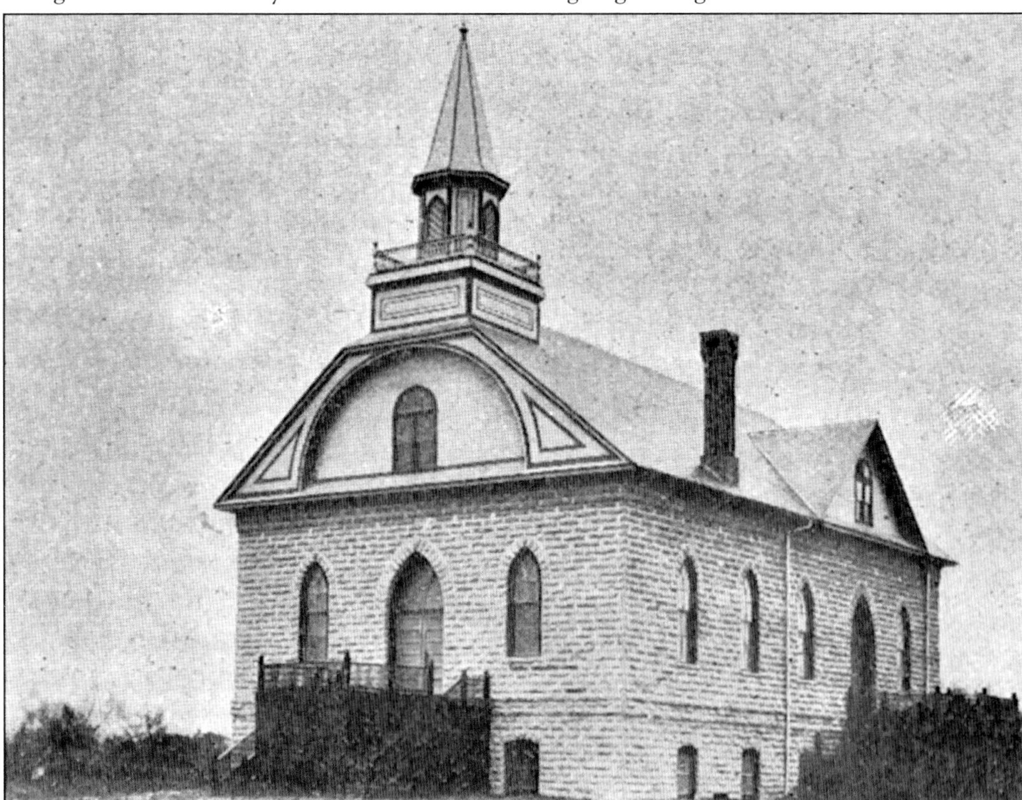

The LDS St. Joseph Stake built this grand edifice, where church services were held for half a century. The Thatcher Ward met in this building. As the population of Thatcher grew, new wards were added and assigned ordinal numbers rather than names.

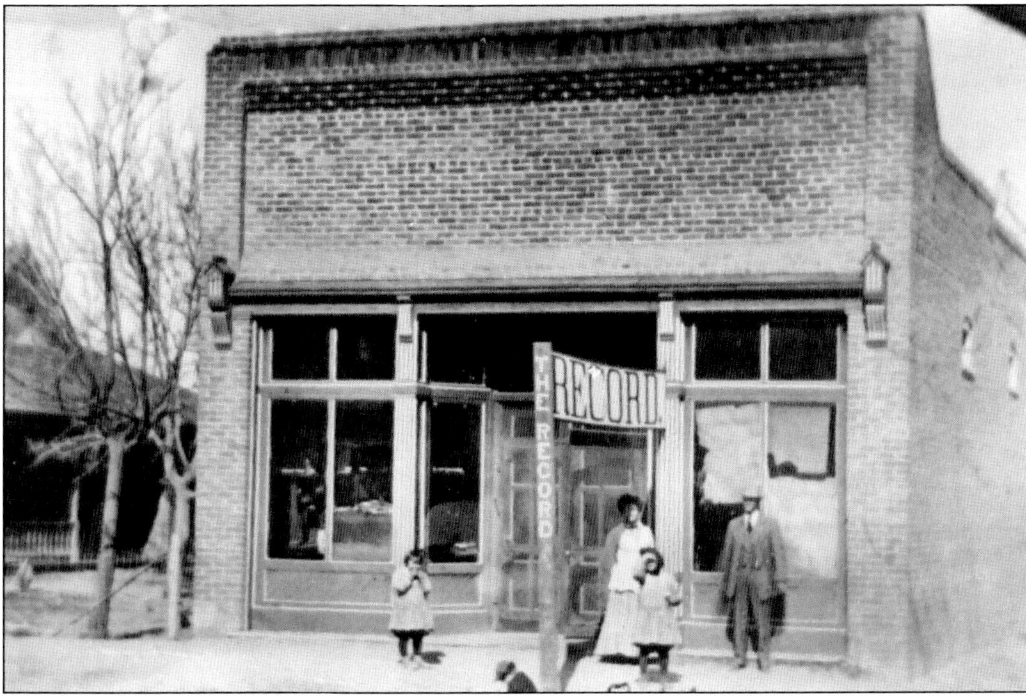

The Woods building in Thatcher housed the first local newspaper, the *Record*.

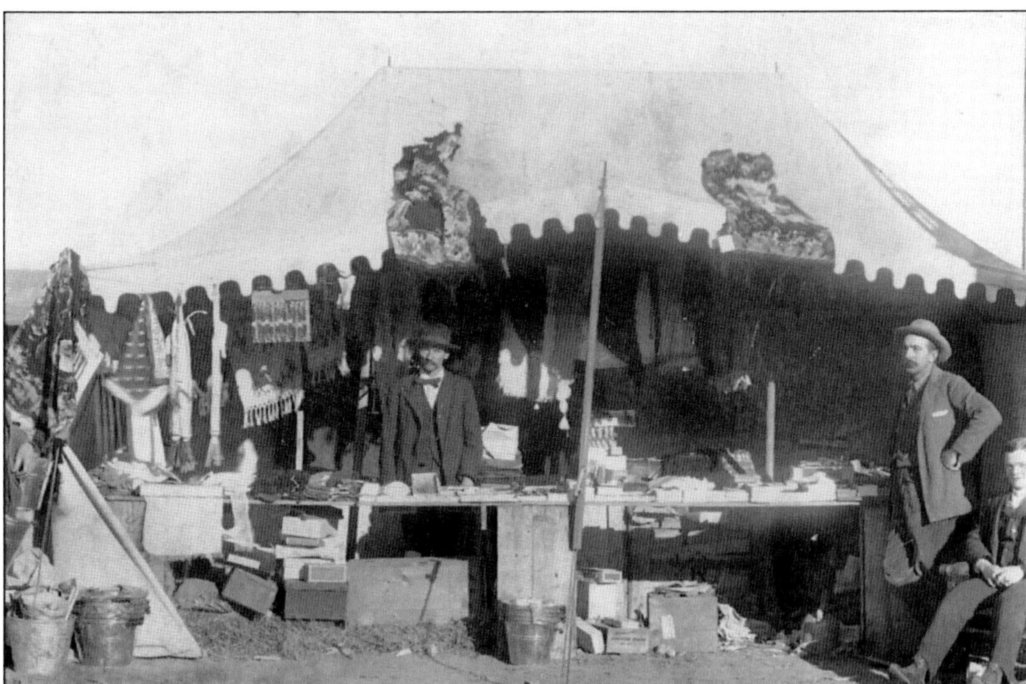

Drummers' (itinerant salesmen) tents, often placed in conspicuous places to attract attention, were a necessary part of life before mail-order catalogs became popular. Both retail merchants and individual customers were welcome. Drummers also frequented local hotels and restaurants.

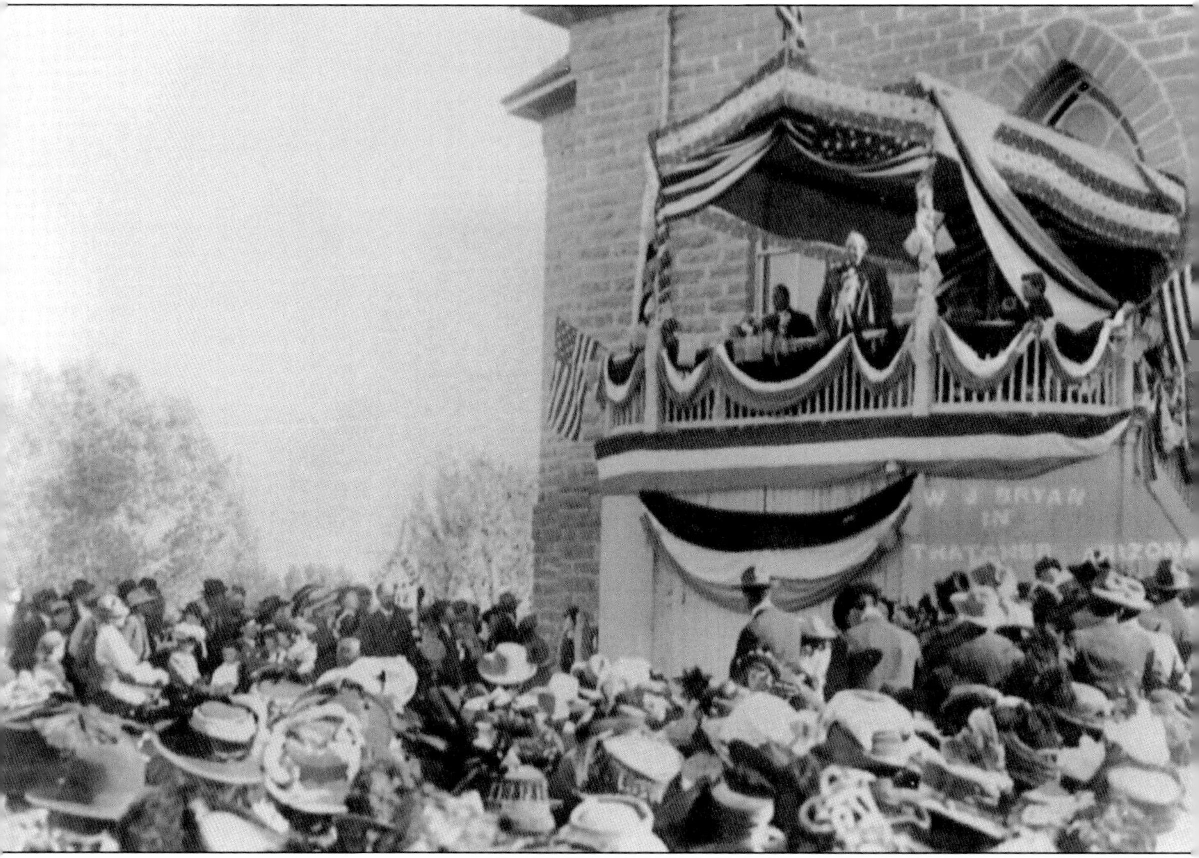

During the 1900 presidential campaign, William Jennings Bryan visited Thatcher to ask for residents' votes. As a strong anti-imperialist, he was running on the Democratic ticket. Traditional Mormons were attracted to the Democratic Party, as it was a conservative organization at that time.

Karl Maeser served as the principal of the St. Joseph Academy in 1898. As a well-respected educator, he oversaw the expansion of the academy and its move from Central to Thatcher.

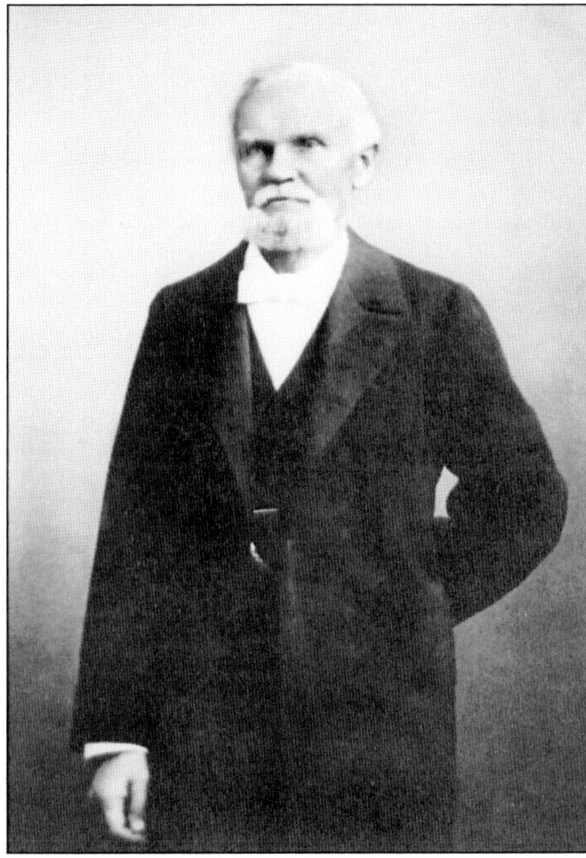

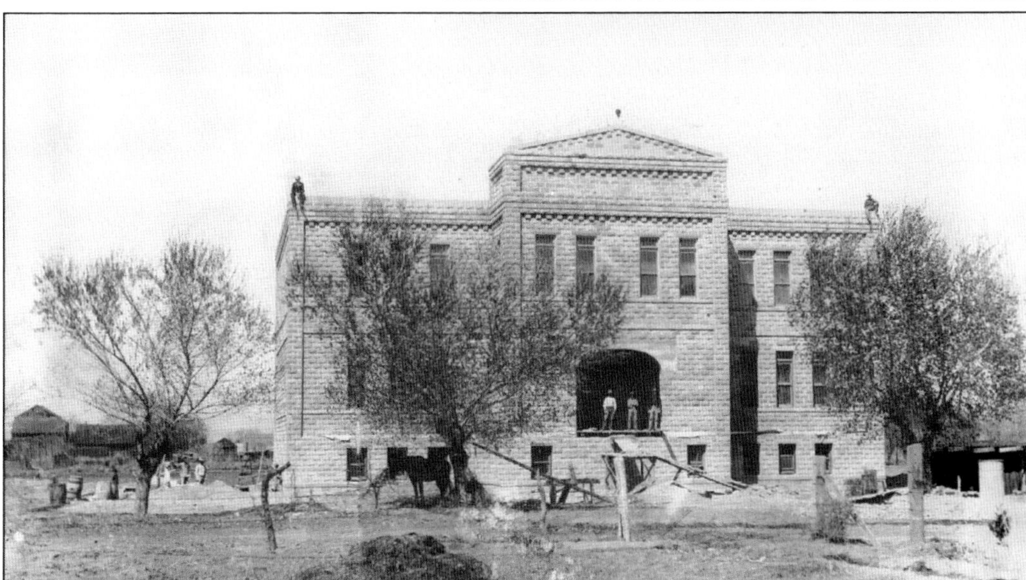

Expansion of the LDS Academy required a new building for the administration, faculty offices, and classrooms. Seen here in 1907, the facility opened in 1908. Called Old Main, the stately brick building was the center of the college for years.

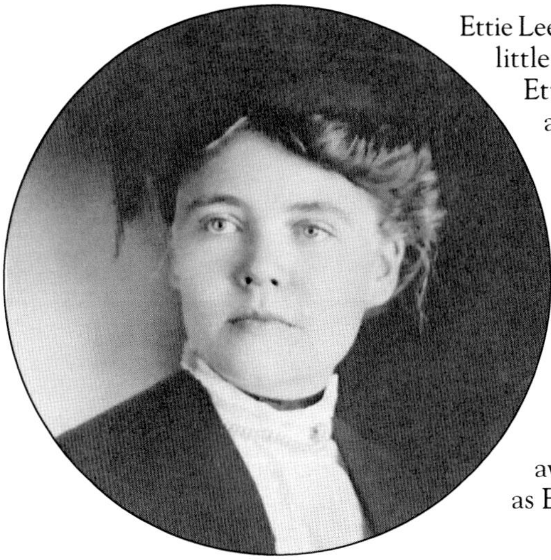

Ettie Lee's 1903 LDS Academy graduation photograph does little to foretell her distinguished future. The story of Ettie Lee reads like a true American success story: a high school teacher with a dream to start homes for troubled young men becomes a success. In 1917, after receiving her master's degree, Ettie began teaching English in the Los Angeles high school system. In 1927, she started buying and selling Los Angeles real estate using techniques learned from a library book. Her vision was to have home parents—a married couple with experience working with children—live with the young men on a ranch and teach them how to become productive citizens. Ettie Lee passed away on April 25, 1974, but her dream continues as Ettie Lee Homes.

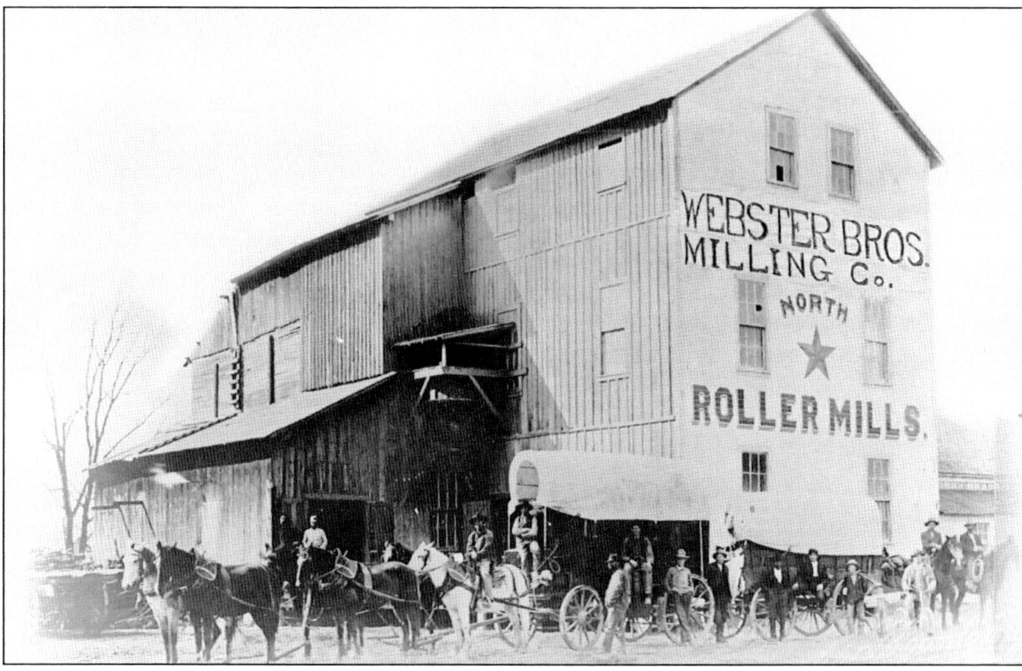

Arriving back in the Gila Valley aboard the Gila Valley Globe & Northern Railway after failed surgery to repair a deformed hip, Zola Webster was greeted by smoke rising from the direction of her father's flour mill (pictured here) in Thatcher. Zola's father was badly burned in the fire, and she undertook his immediate nursing. Doc Platt, Thatcher's only physician, recognized Zola's nursing skills and started teaching her all the tricks of the trade. While her father was recovering, a neighbor, Ted Ferguson was thrown from a calf and broke his arm. Doc Platt called for Zola to assist him. Even though she resisted, she learned—and learned well. For the rest of her life, Zola was recognized as a nurse and healer, even though she never sought formal training in medicine. Zola married Marc Claridge and became the county's first female mohair broker. She later organized the Graham County Republican Party and served as chairwoman. In 1952, she attended the National Republican Convention in Chicago, and in 1964 she was a member of the electoral college.

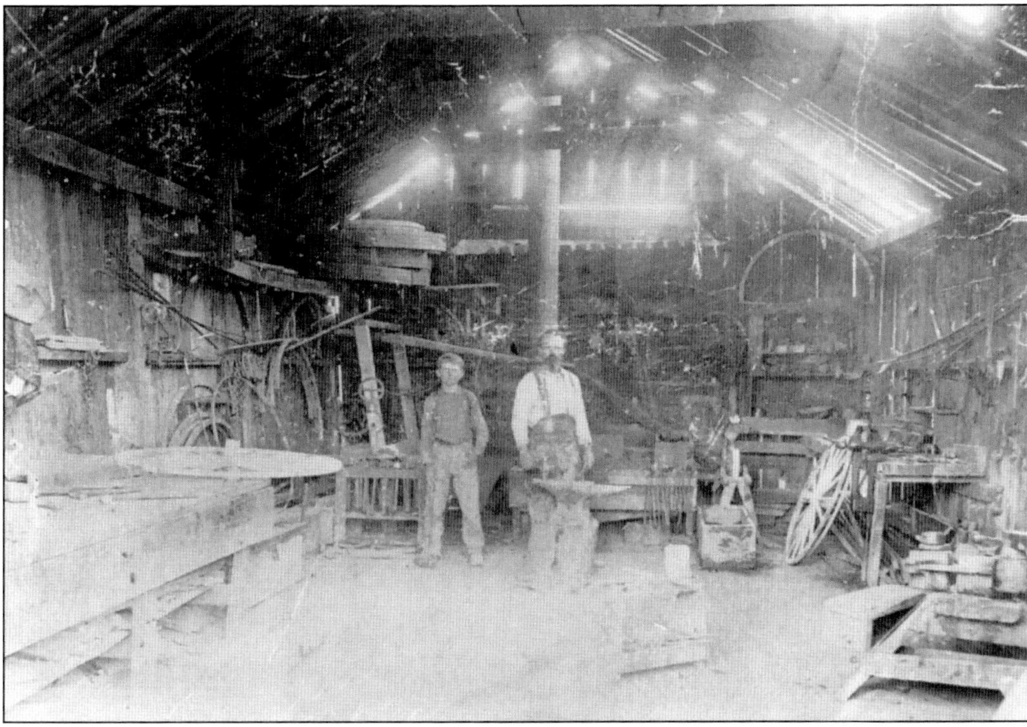

For decades, the blacksmith shop was a business that seldom closed. Here John Young plies his trade for the citizens of Thatcher at the beginning of the 20th century. The skills of a good blacksmith survived well into the 1900s. Horses and buggies coexisted with automobiles for decades, and early cars were hand built, often requiring a good blacksmith to keep them running.

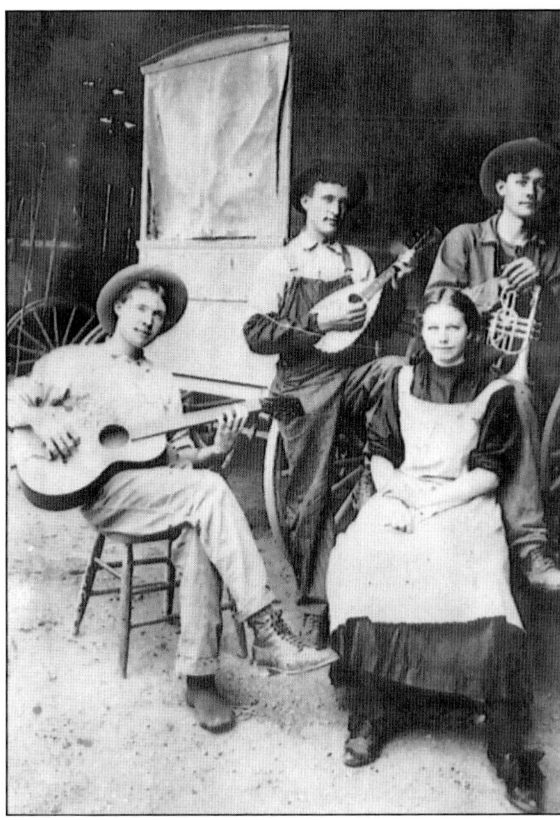

The George Ballard Band entertained audiences across the valley in 1925. Like modern youth, the members were relegated to the garage to practice.

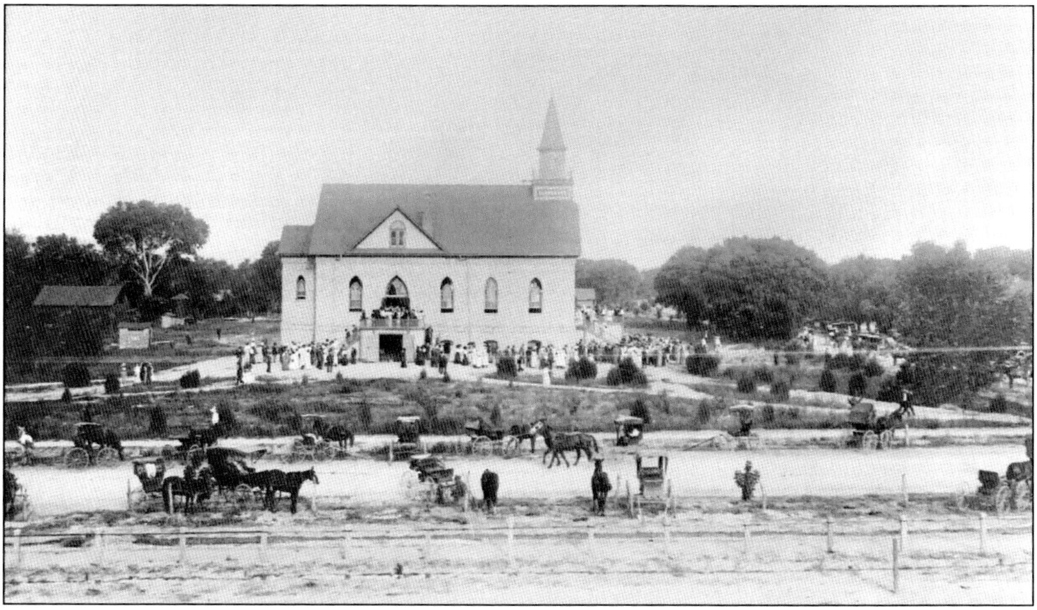

On Sunday mornings in Thatcher, residents turned their attention to the LDS Stake Center on the hill. With a large basement, this church saw countless weddings, funerals, and social gatherings.

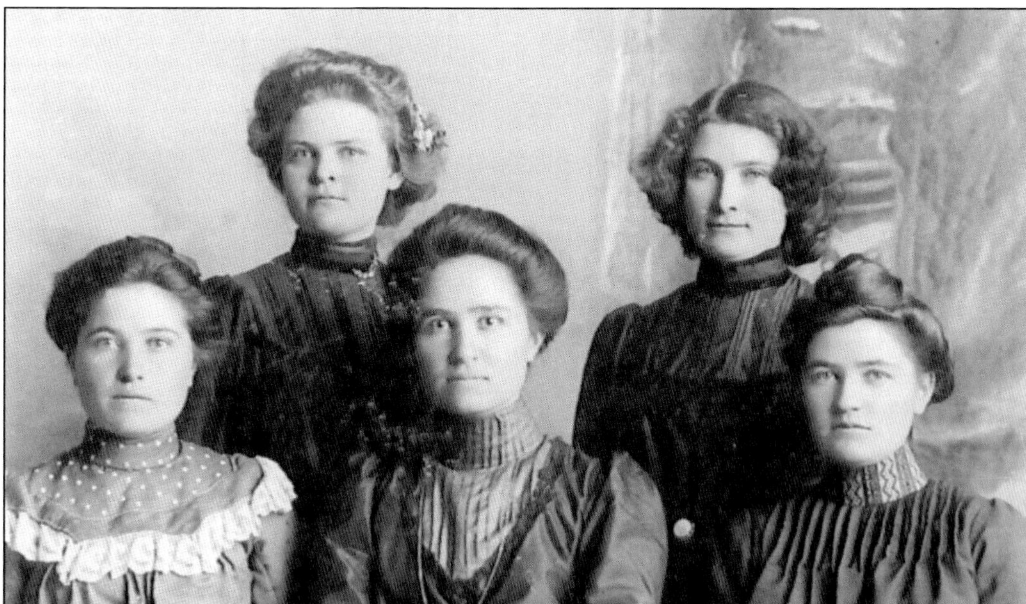

In 1903, this group of young women graduated from the LDS Academy. Shown from left to right are (first row) Della, Julia, Ina Curtis; (second row) Julia and Ethel Felshaw.

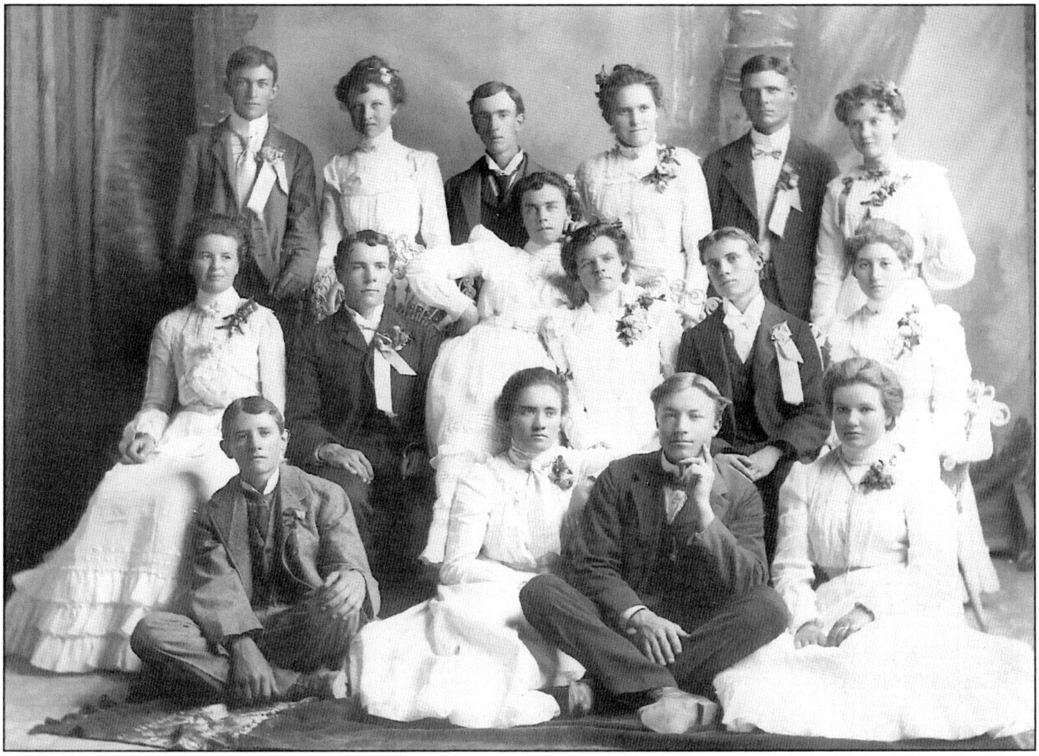

The entire LDS Academy graduating class of 1903 consisted of these 16 unidentified young men and women.

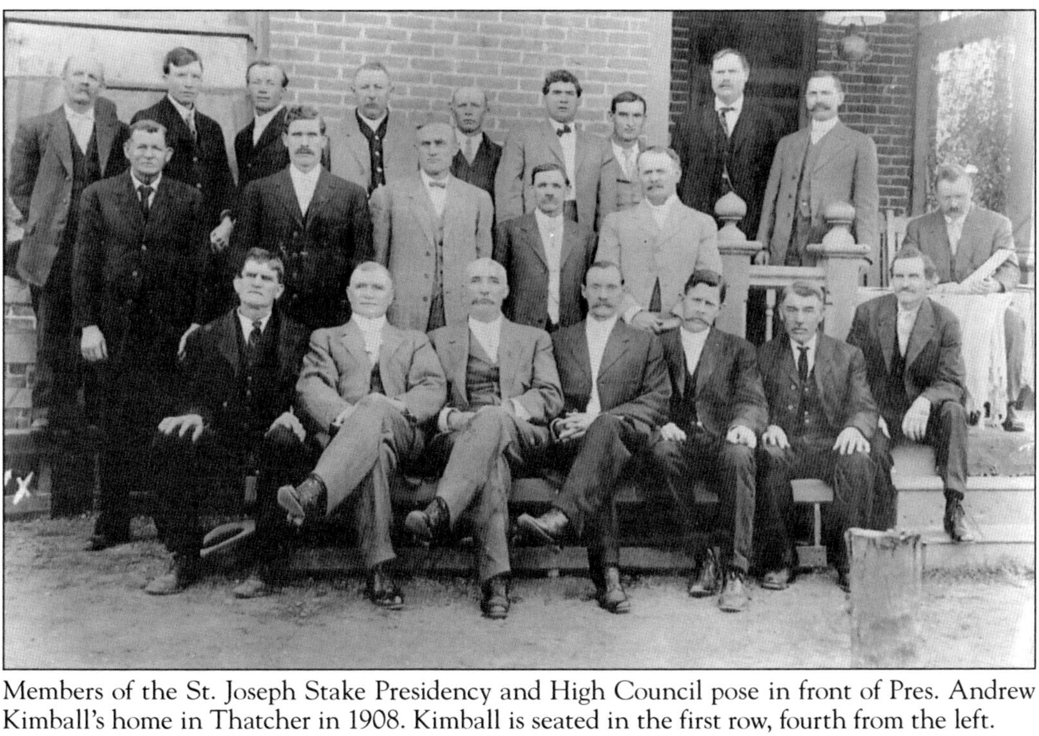

Members of the St. Joseph Stake Presidency and High Council pose in front of Pres. Andrew Kimball's home in Thatcher in 1908. Kimball is seated in the first row, fourth from the left.

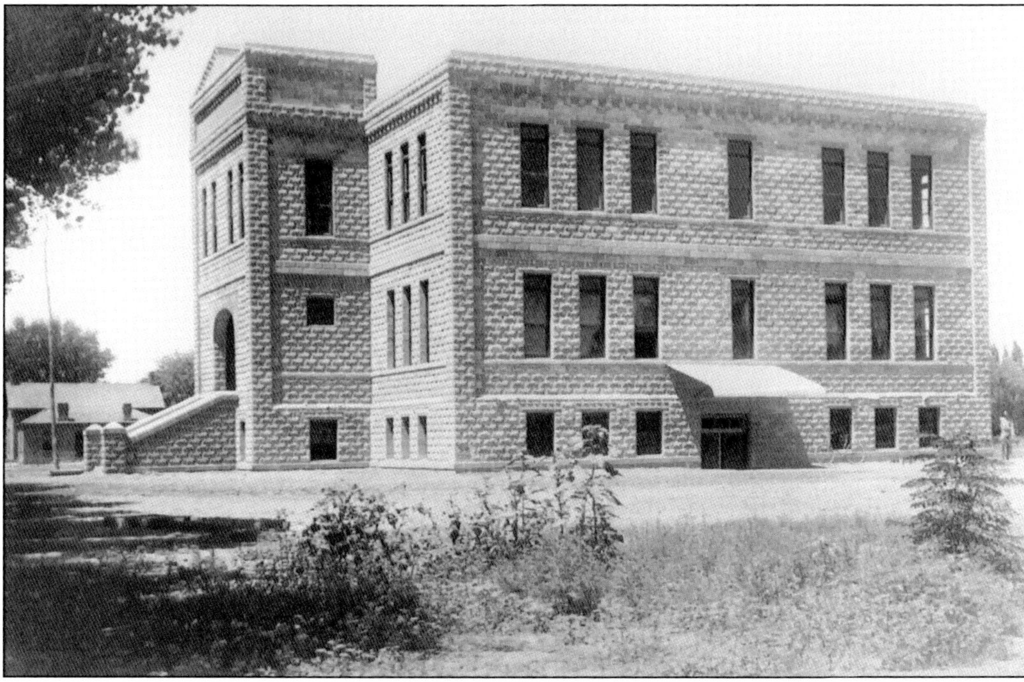

In 1908, the new LDS Academy building Old Main was inaugurated.

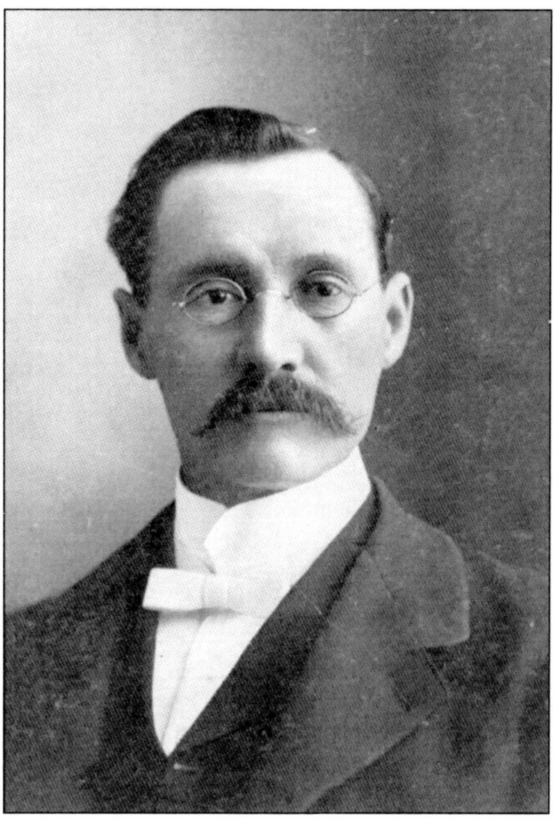

Andrew Kimball, the son of LDS patriarch Heber C. Kimball, was the successor to Pres. Christopher Layton as president of the St. Joseph Stake. Kimball was an engineer who assisted in the construction of the Morenci South Railroad. As a Thatcher businessman, he served on the boards of three canal companies and was a partner and secretary of a farm implement and general merchandise business. In November 1900, Kimball was elected to the Arizona Territorial Legislature, where he earned distinction as an expert on irrigation and water rights. Because of his acumen and personal interests, the Gila Valley grew in state-wide importance and economic significance.

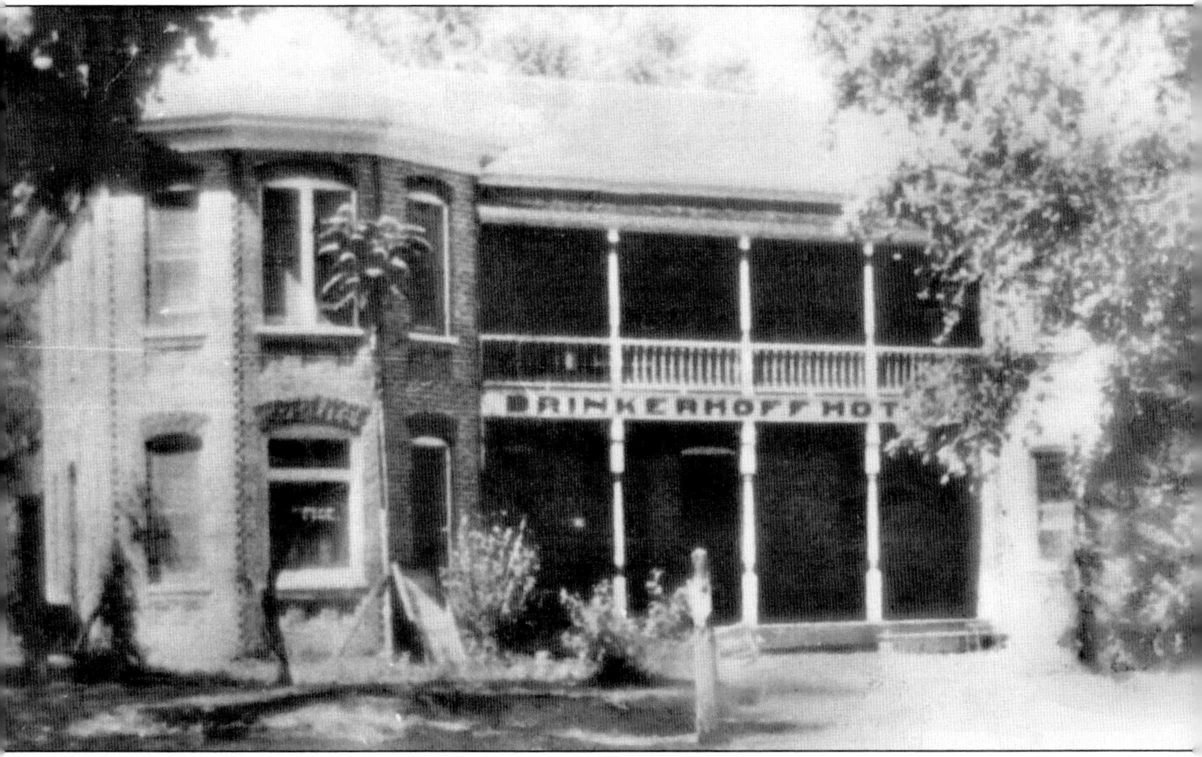

The Brinkerhoff Hotel, situated north of the college campus, was a popular place for students to reside while school was in session. Some students were willing to sleep on the porch, just to get a place to stay. The hotel became locally famous because of a box of human bones kept in the basement. Isaac C. Haight fled Utah following his participation in the Mountain Meadow Massacre. After being recognized in Mexico, he fled to Thatcher, where he died alone on September 8, 1886. His burial in the old Thatcher Cemetery was short lived. Haight's bones were dug up, and plans were made to return them to family in Utah. None of the relatives claimed them, however, so his remains were stored until Spencer Brinkerhoff paid to have them reburied in the new Thatcher Cemetery.

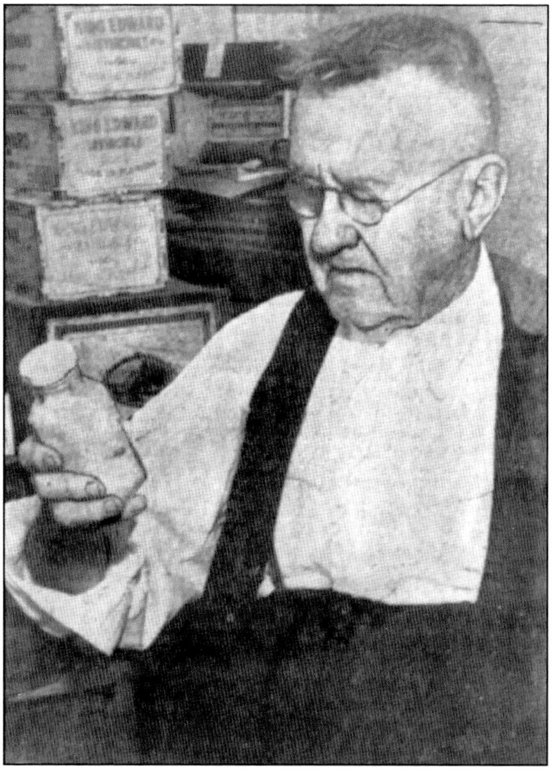

Wise Dr. William E. Platt, a local physician and druggist, was often called upon for medical advice. He often testified and served as the county's medical examiner.

Dr. Platt's drugstore was all business—no soda fountain, just medicines, health supplies, household trinkets, and shaving supplies, all dispensed with sage and kindly advice. Of course, the kiddies had to be satisfied, so he carried dolls and candies.

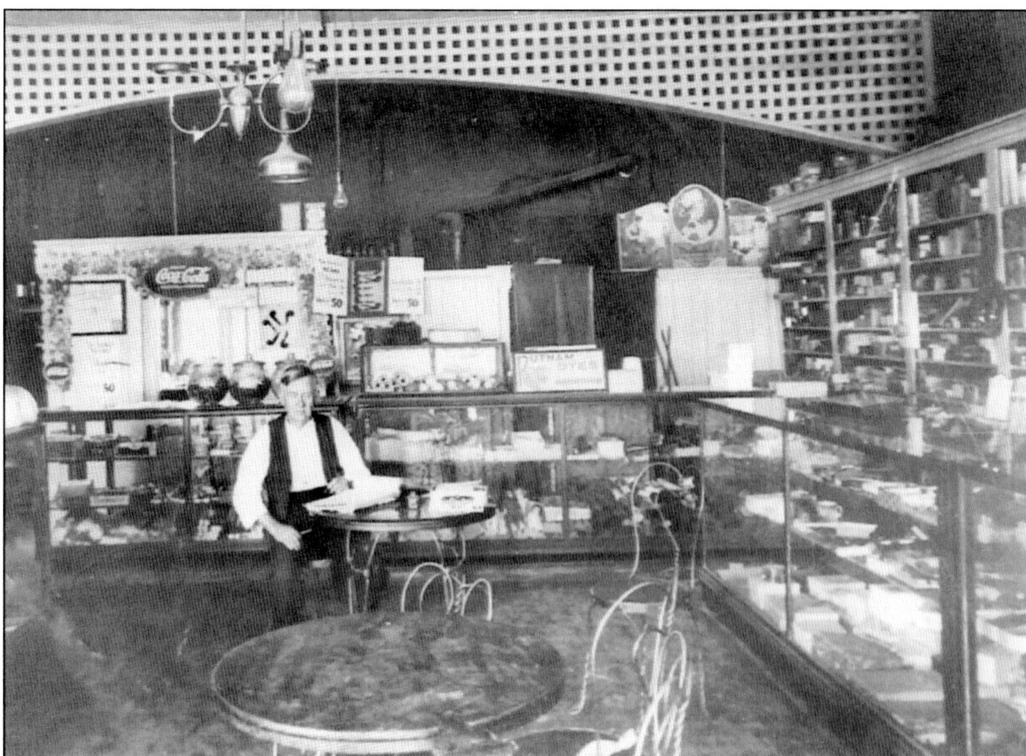

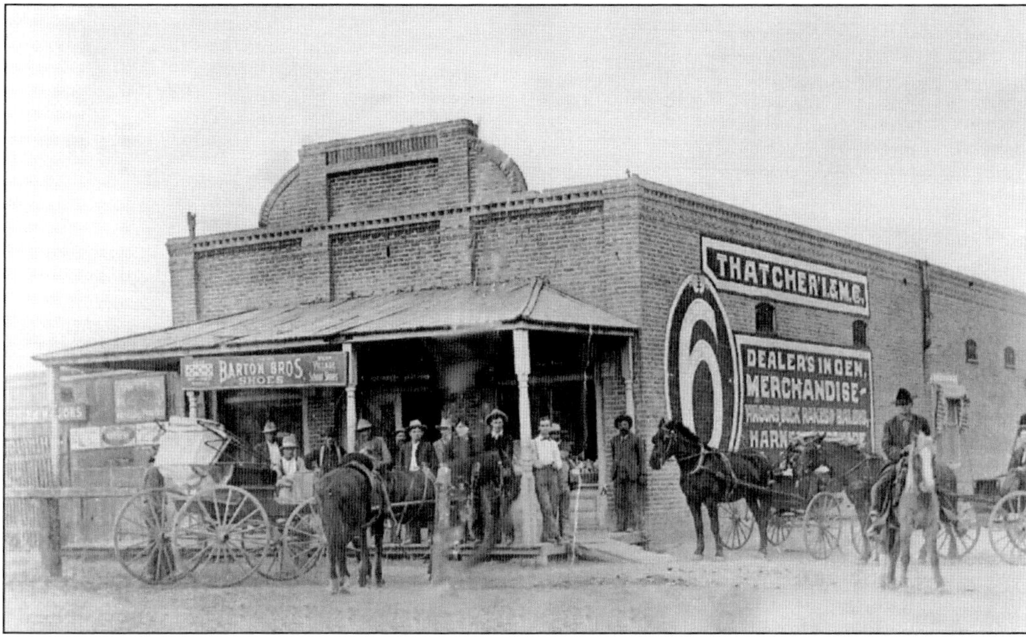

The most famous business in Thatcher was the Big 6 store. Six Thatcher residents—W. W. Pace, John Hoopes, I. E. D. Zundell, Andrew Kimball, Ed Phillips, and Frank Tyler—combined their assets to open this implement and mercantile company in 1901.

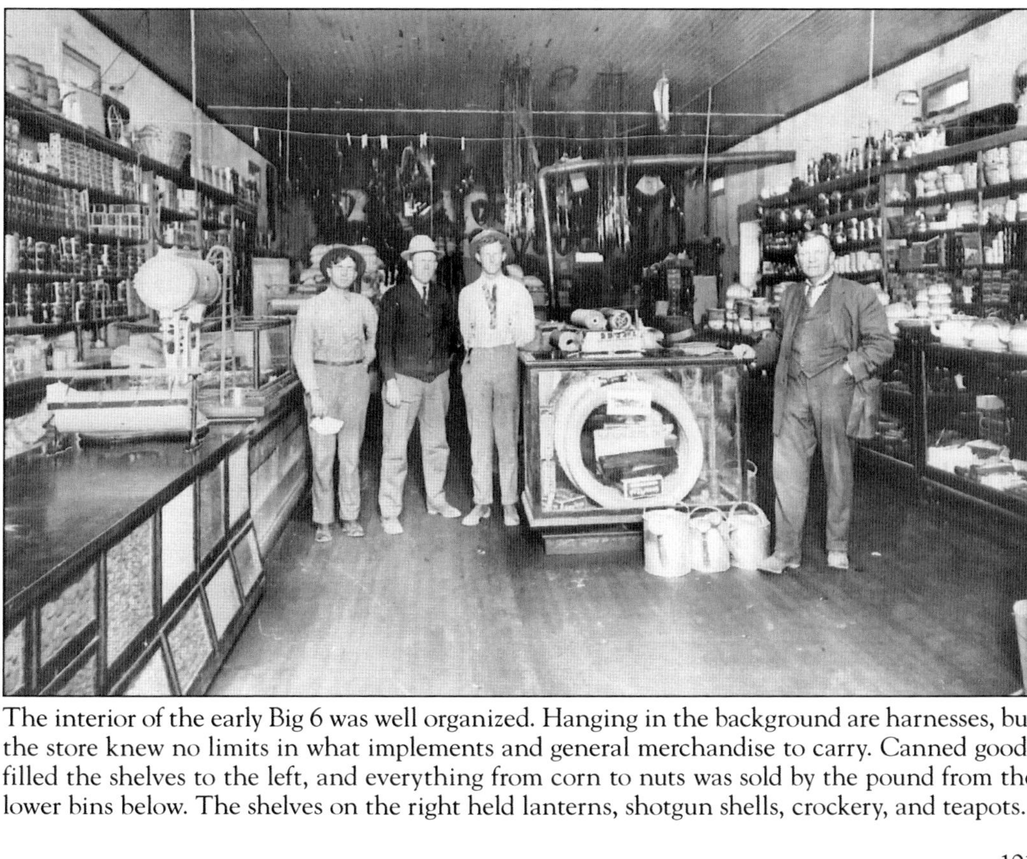

The interior of the early Big 6 was well organized. Hanging in the background are harnesses, but the store knew no limits in what implements and general merchandise to carry. Canned goods filled the shelves to the left, and everything from corn to nuts was sold by the pound from the lower bins below. The shelves on the right held lanterns, shotgun shells, crockery, and teapots.

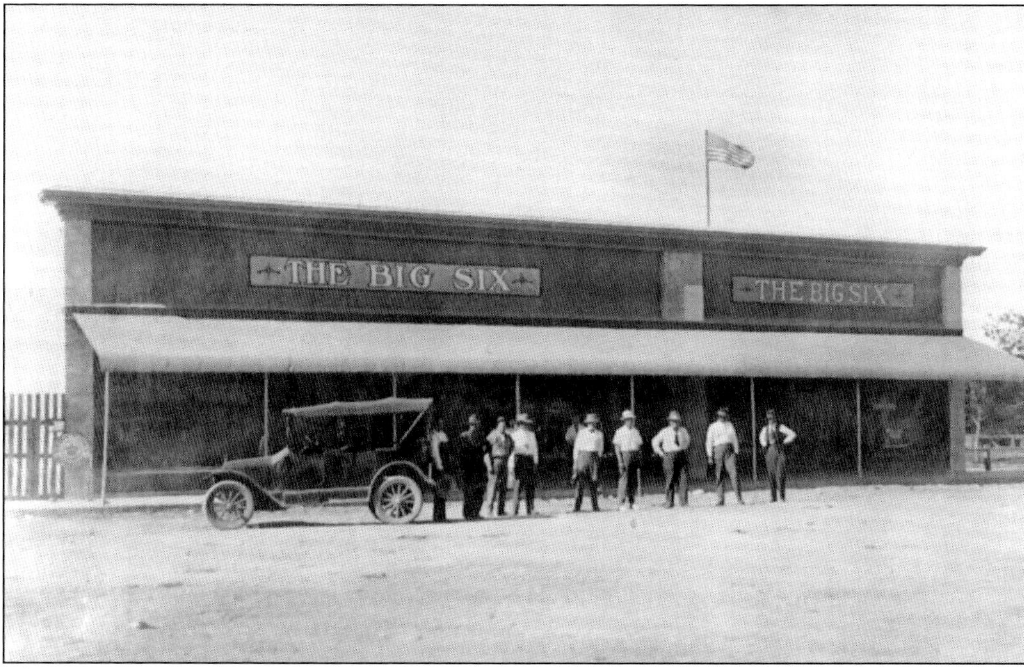

The Big 6's original partners pose in white shirts at the expansion of the building in 1920. By the time this photograph was taken, the store was under the sole ownership and management of W. W. Pace.

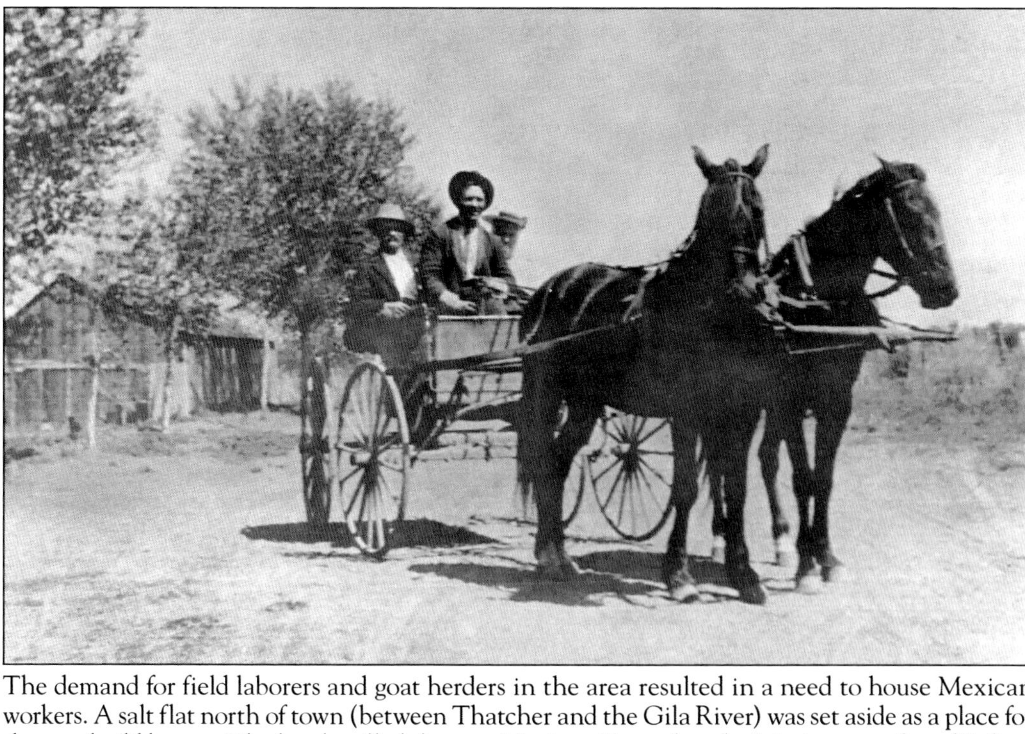

The demand for field laborers and goat herders in the area resulted in a need to house Mexican workers. A salt flat north of town (between Thatcher and the Gila River) was set aside as a place for them to build homes. The locals called the area Mexican Town, but the Mexicans preferred Salitre ("salt flats"). Here a local farmer picks up some laborers on what would become Porter Lane.

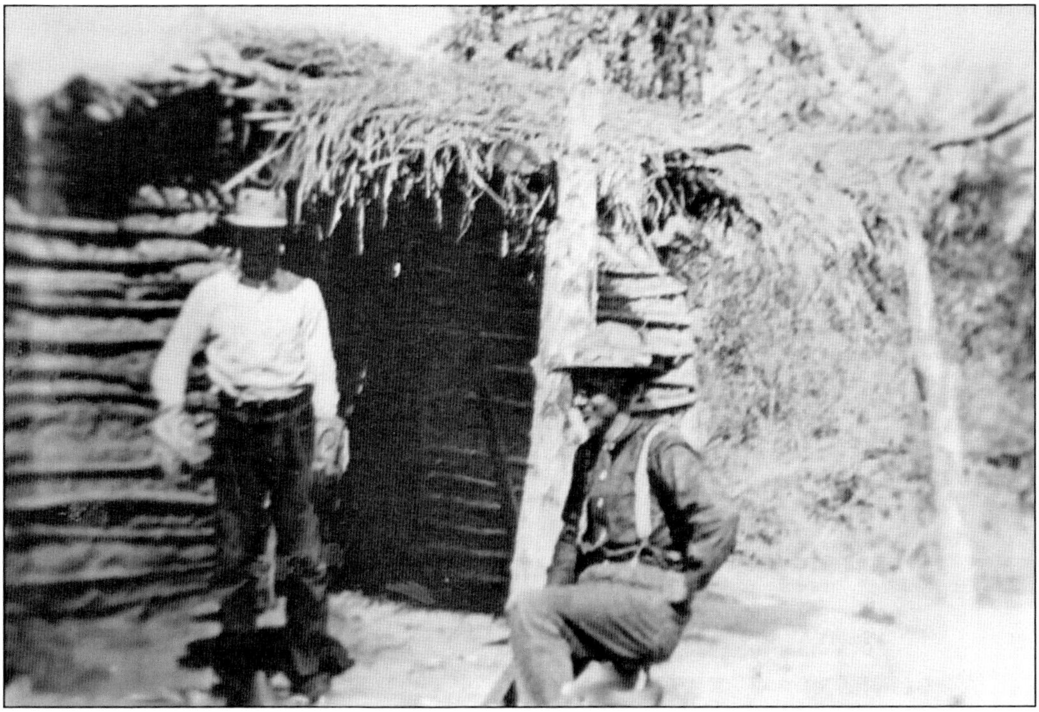

This rare view depicts one of the shanties in Salitre. It is impossible to tell what J. Myron Allred (seated) is doing here or what the unidentified gentleman in the doorway is holding in his hands.

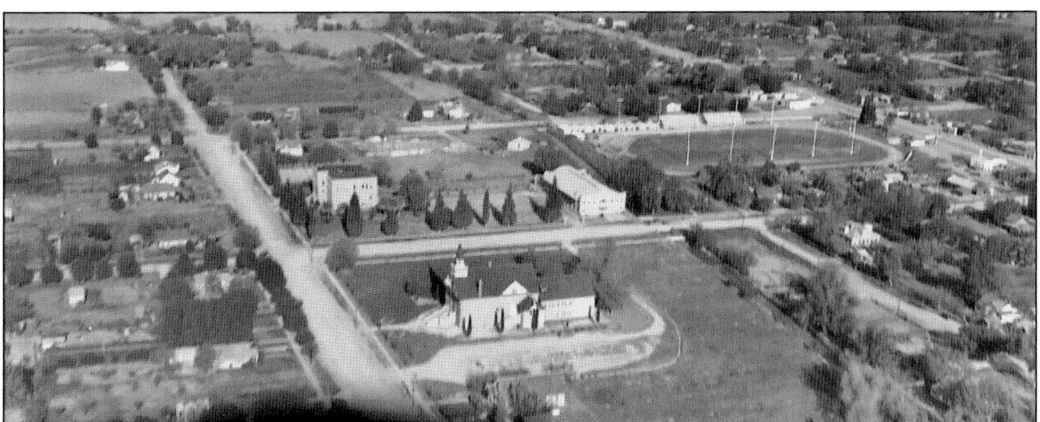

This 1942 aerial photograph of the heart of Thatcher shows the LDS Stake Center and the college, known at the time as Gila Junior College. These days, Eastern Arizona College covers much of the area pictured here.

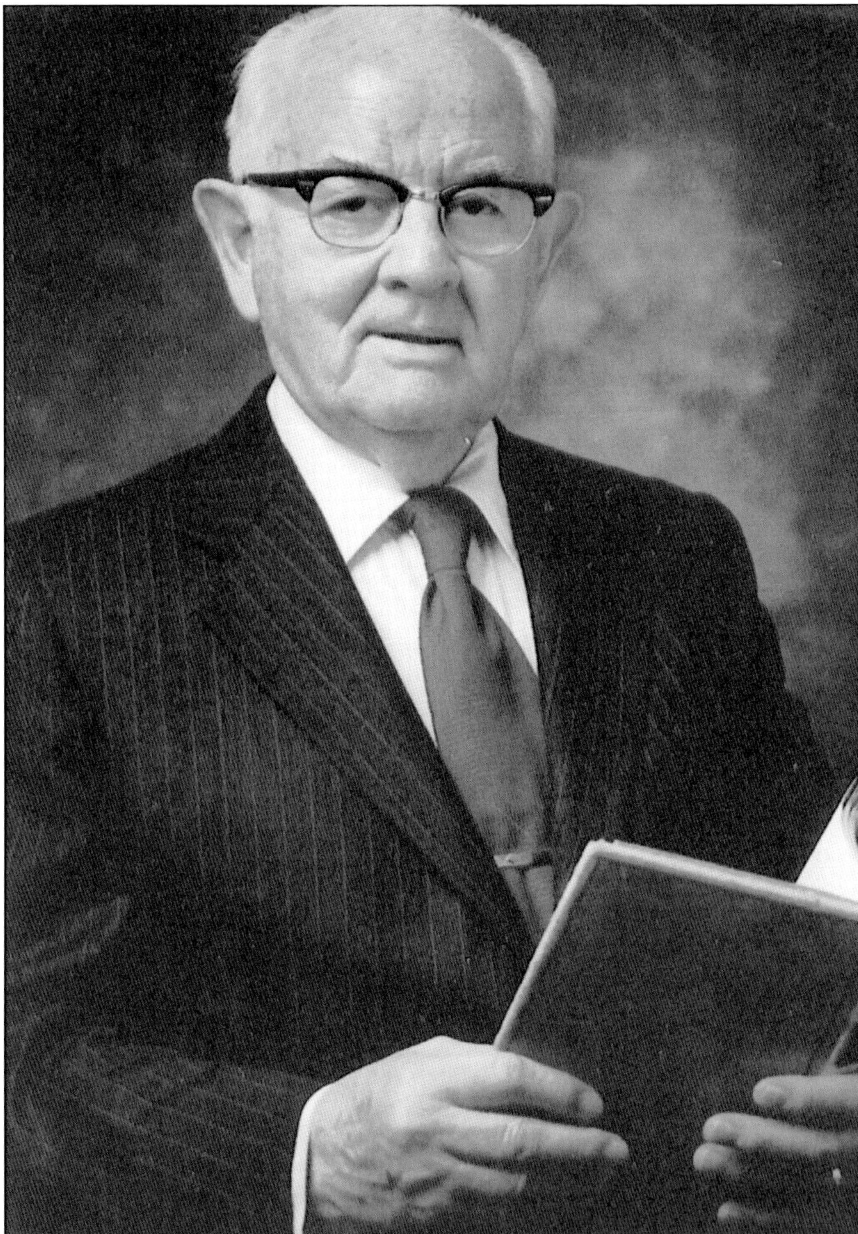

In 1973, Thatcher resident Spencer W. Kimball was ordained president of the Church of Jesus Christ of Latter Day Saints. Born on March 28, 1895, in Salt Lake City, Kimball grew up in Thatcher. After completing missionary service, he married Camilla Eyring of Pima and settled in Safford, where he raised a family and ran an insurance business. Years of church and community leadership preceded his calling as an apostle in 1943. Overcoming severe health problems, he became LDS president on December 30, 1973, at the age of 78. Kimball led the church during a period of vitality and growth. His administration produced significant advances in doctrinal understanding, member unity, and gospel expansion worldwide. In the 12 years of his presidency, the number of operating temples doubled and the number of missionaries increased by 50 percent. He died in Salt Lake City on November 5, 1985.

Ten

Safford
Commerce, Government, and Competition

The unique Safford development had a traditional main street that eventually abutted the picturesque Graham County Courthouse. The community believes the road became the inspiration for Disneyland's Main Street following Walt Disney's visit to the valley in the 1940s.

The founding of Safford has been credited to four members of the California Volunteers of Civil War fame: Daniel Hughes, John C. Glasby, Hiram Kennedy, and Joshua Bailey. Their efforts to control the flooding waters of the Gila River at Gila Bend failed, costing them all they had invested in a dam and canal head. Consequently they brought their energy and plans far upstream to the heart of Graham County. There the Gila ran slow and broad and a diversion dam and canal head could be designed to irrigate a broad expanse of flatland.

In 1875, frontiersmen Amos Perigo and H. J. Davis arrived in the valley and helped Josh Bailey create a town. Bailey named the new town after territorial governor A. P. K. Safford and built a store and bar, becoming the community's first postmaster. Unlike the LDS communities to the west, Safford attracted a diverse population of residents and developed a reputation of lawlessness.

Land speculator William H. Kirkland invested in construction and designed the new town. By 1881, the community of Safford was thriving. On March 10th of that year, Graham County was created out of Pima County, with Safford designated as its county seat. That designation lasted but two years. I. E. Solomon's ambitious plans for his own community—and the continuing practice of judges and lawyers to travel from Tucson to Solomonville to provide law and order to the valley—resulted in the change to Solomonville. County business was conducted in Solomonville until 1915, a few years after statehood.

Several changes caused Safford to add new businesses and increase in population: the building of the Gila Valley Globe & Northern Railway through Safford, and the construction of a new county courthouse at the west end of Main Street.

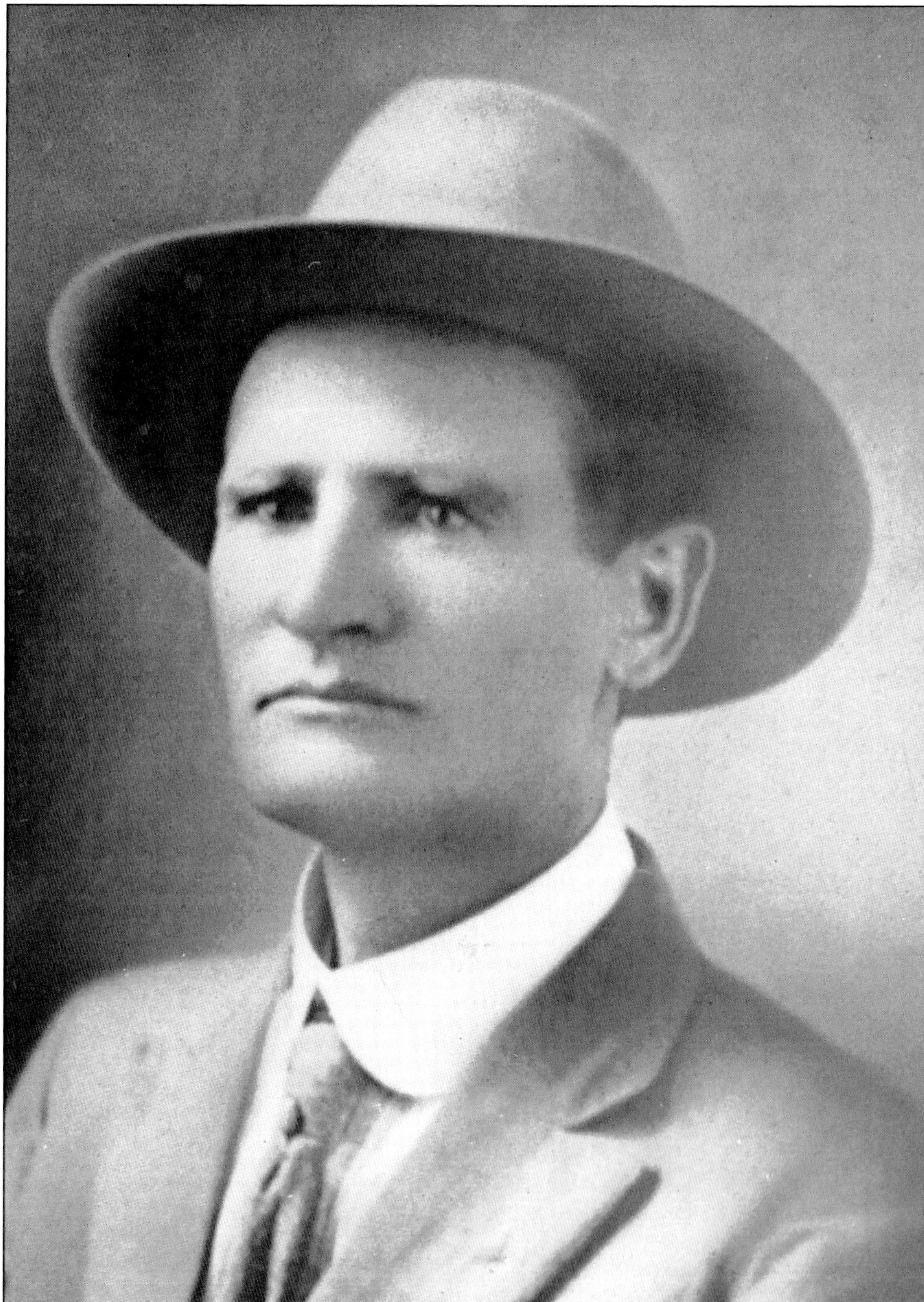

Sheriff Frank McBride is remembered here because he best represents the conflicted history of Safford. A dedicated Mormon serving in a diverse community, McBride was elected to office in 1916 and began serving in January 1917. A little over a year later, on February 10, 1918, McBride, deputy Martin Kempton, and deputy Kane Wootan were killed in a shoot-out at the Power cabin. Only Deputy U.S. Marshal Robert Frank Haynes lived to tell the tale.

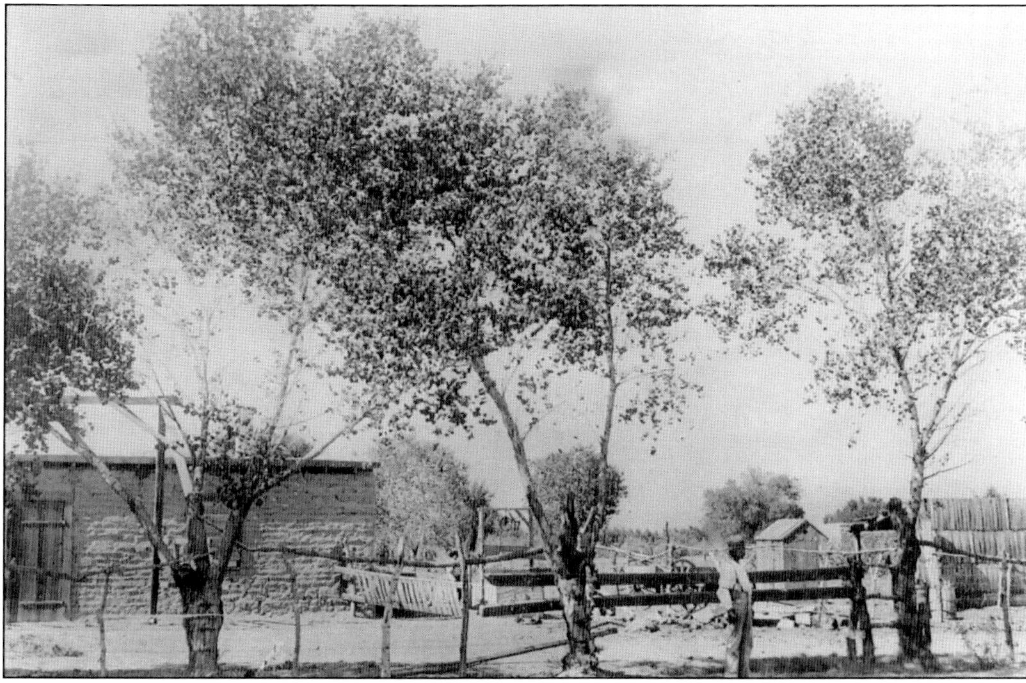

Safford was a small community of family farms. Josh Bailey was the first to build a store in the community, but moved his business to Solomonville because that town was growing much faster than Safford in the 1870s and 1880s.

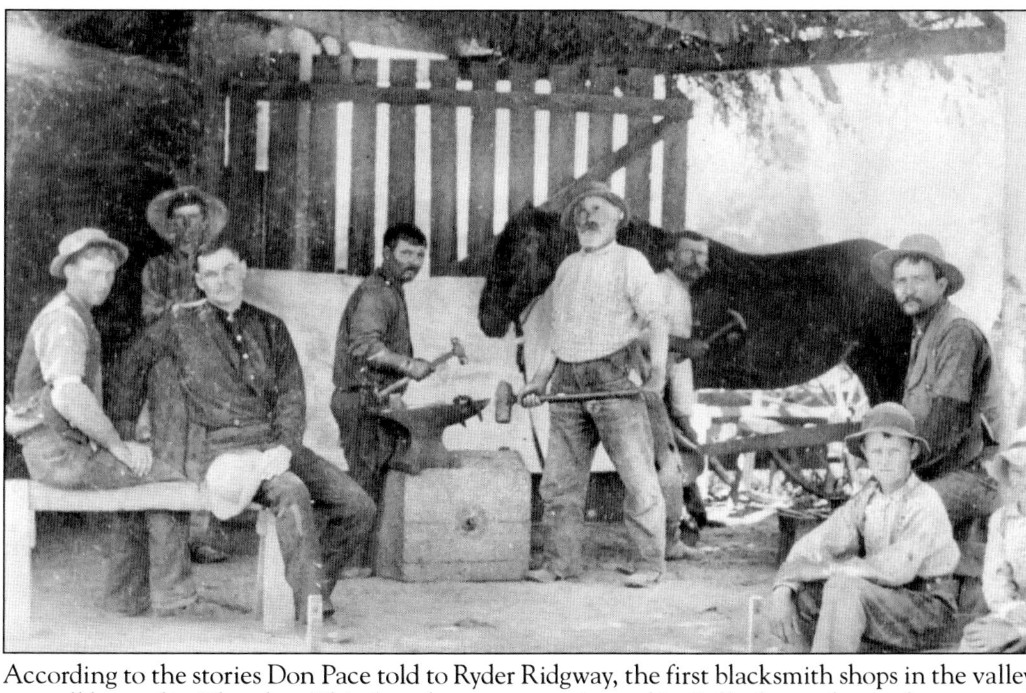

According to the stories Don Pace told to Ryder Ridgway, the first blacksmith shops in the valley were all located in Thatcher. This shop, however, was situated in Safford near the southeast corner of today's Eighth Avenue and Second Street. It was operated by brothers John and Jim Young at the start of the 20th century.

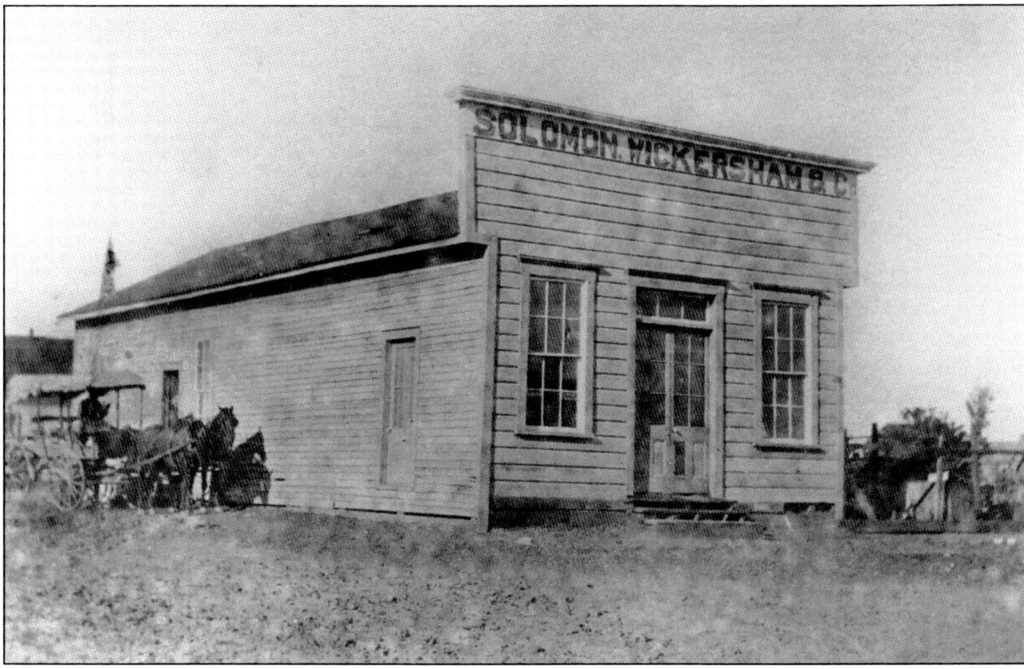

I. E. Solomon and D. W. Wickersham of Safford partnered in the Solomon-Wickersham Company, a wholesale food business. Originally established in Bowie in 1895, it grew in size and importance, moving to Safford in 1901.

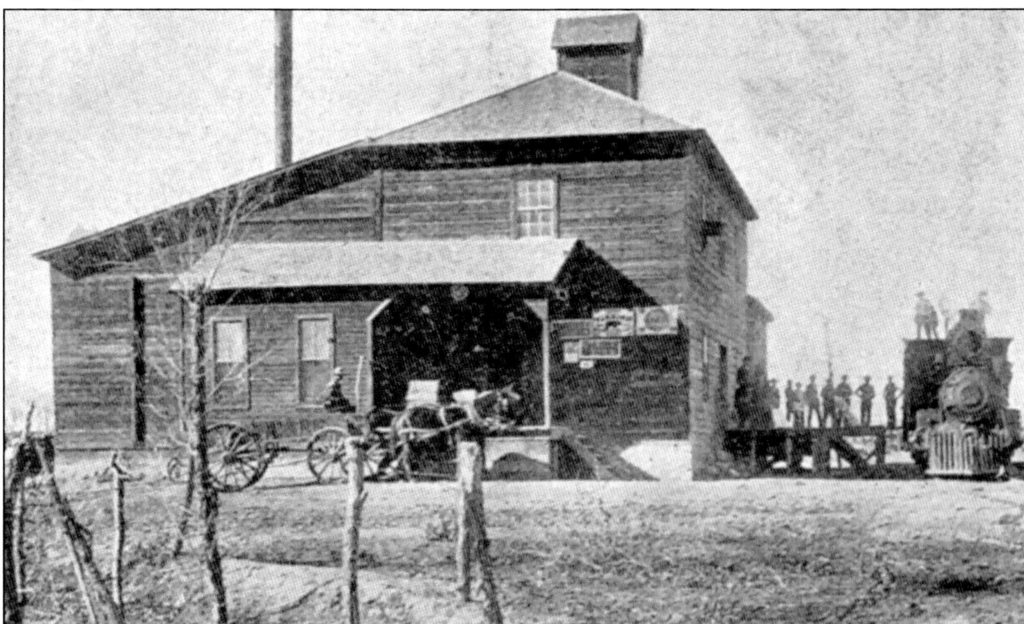

The Solomon-Wickersham Wholesale Company prospered as the railroad grew. A side track was used to unload merchandise directly from the train into the warehouse. The Gila Valley Globe & Northern Railway reached the Safford area in 1895. This engine, the first to operate on the line, was one of the two that met at Promontory Summit in Utah when the Union Pacific and Central Pacific Railroads were completed on May 10, 1869.

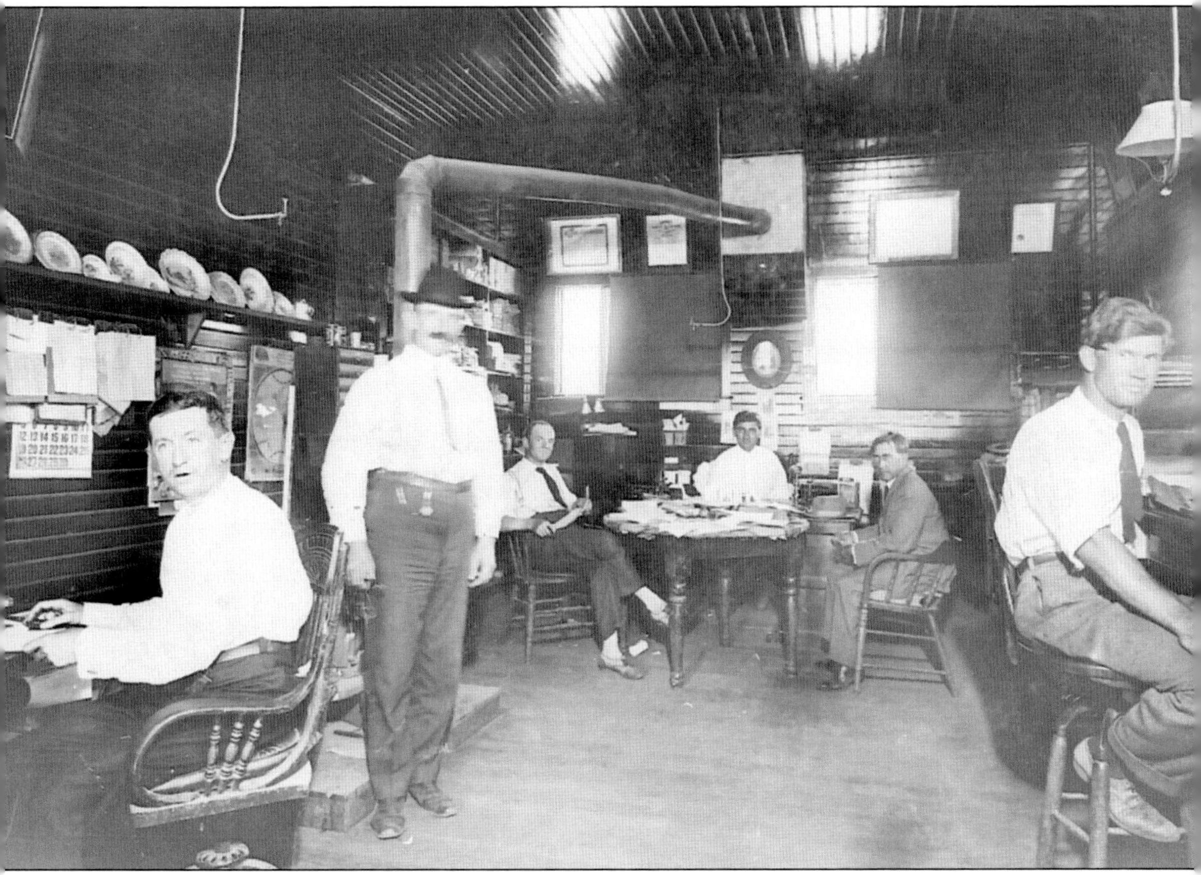

Office space within the Solomon-Wickersham Wholesale Company was crowded but comfortable. This photograph demonstrates the labor-intensive business of recording, pricing, and tracking the new merchandise that entered the valley.

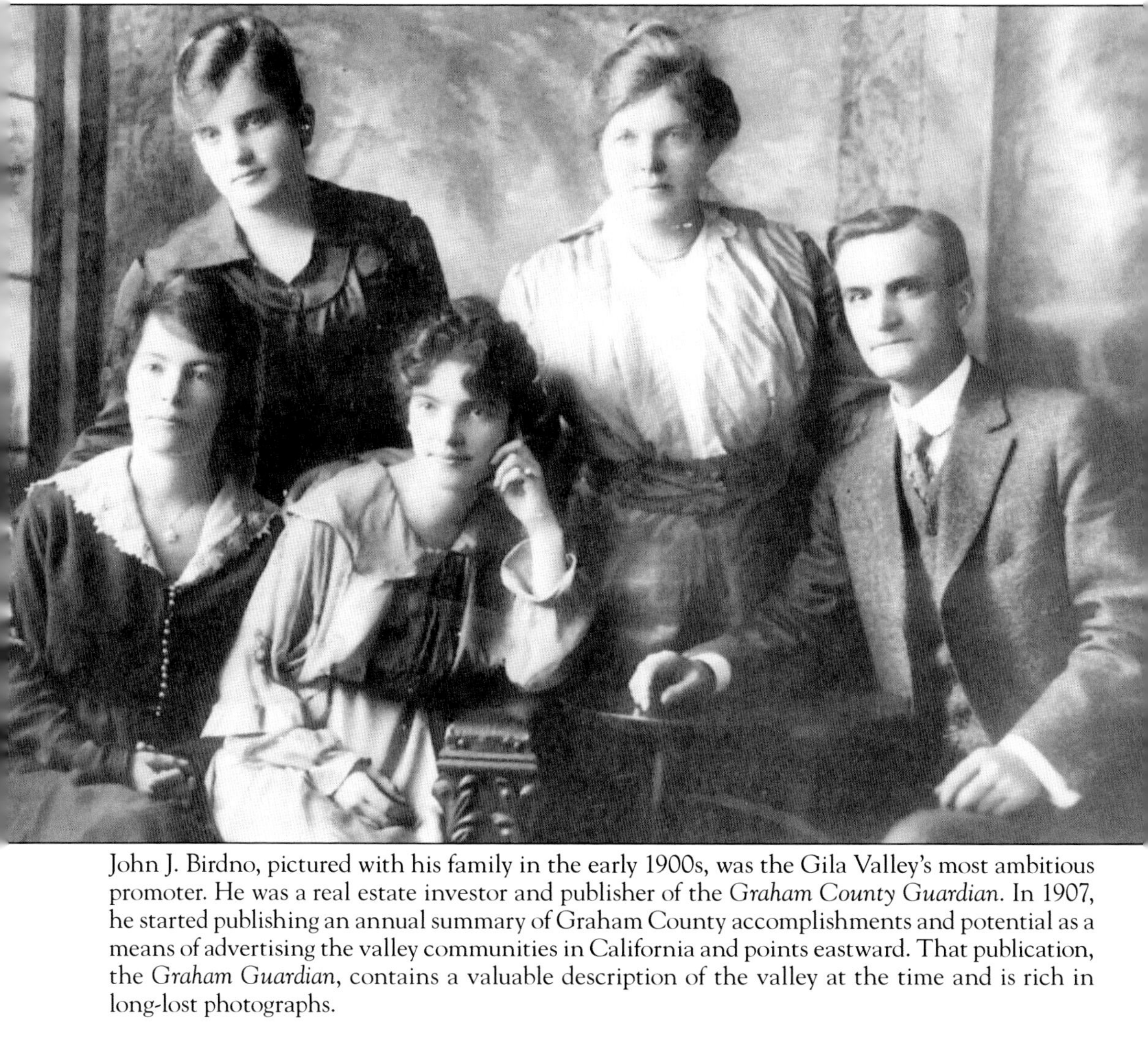

John J. Birdno, pictured with his family in the early 1900s, was the Gila Valley's most ambitious promoter. He was a real estate investor and publisher of the *Graham County Guardian*. In 1907, he started publishing an annual summary of Graham County accomplishments and potential as a means of advertising the valley communities in California and points eastward. That publication, the *Graham Guardian*, contains a valuable description of the valley at the time and is rich in long-lost photographs.

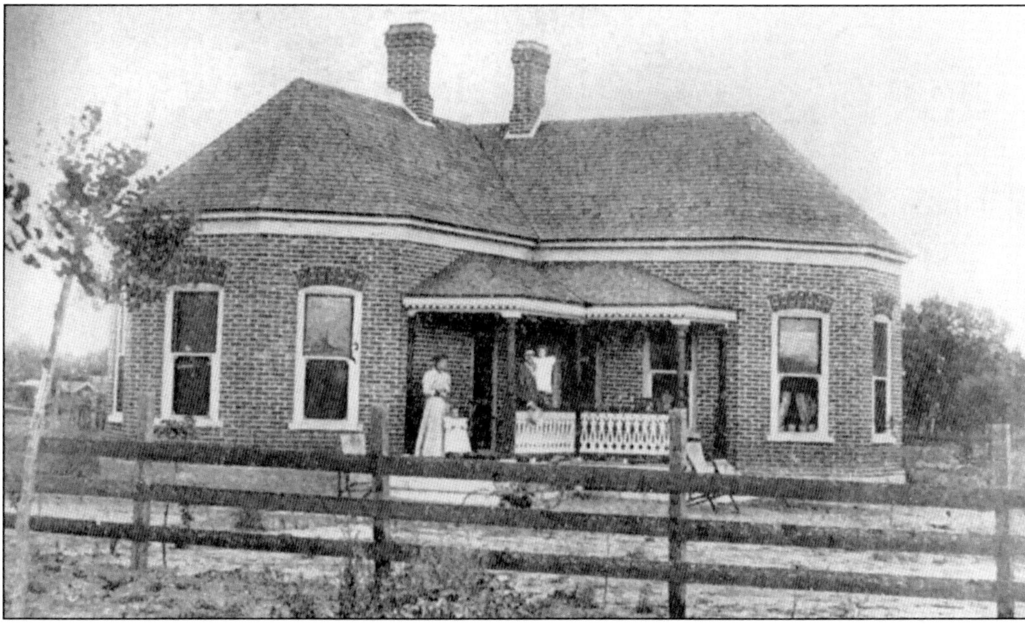

Just before John Birdno built this home in Safford, he was actively promoting the Spenazuma mining fraud. Unbeknownst to Birdno, superintendent Thomas McEniry was feeding him false information. In his ambitious design to promote all business operations in Graham County, Birdno continued to endorse the operation, even after George Smalley had exposed it as a fraud in the *Arizona Republican*.

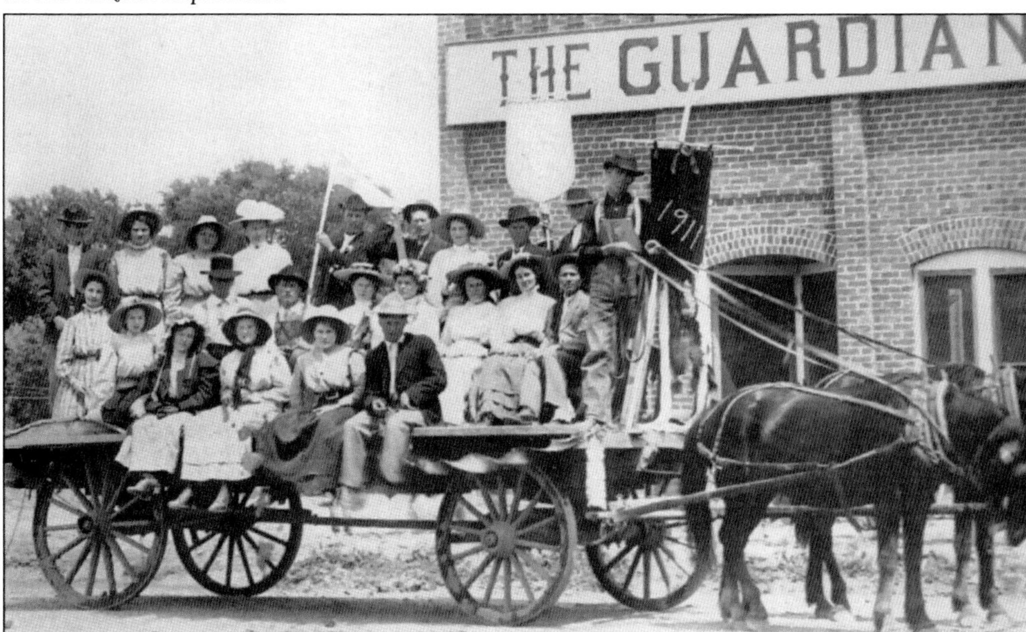

A 1911 parade passes in front of the *Guardian* office on Main Street. At that time, the *Guardian* often ran editorials and letters to the editor complaining about the dust from the dirt streets interfering with civilized commerce. The only cure was to sprinkle the streets with water. Concrete streets were in great demand, but the cost was prohibitive.

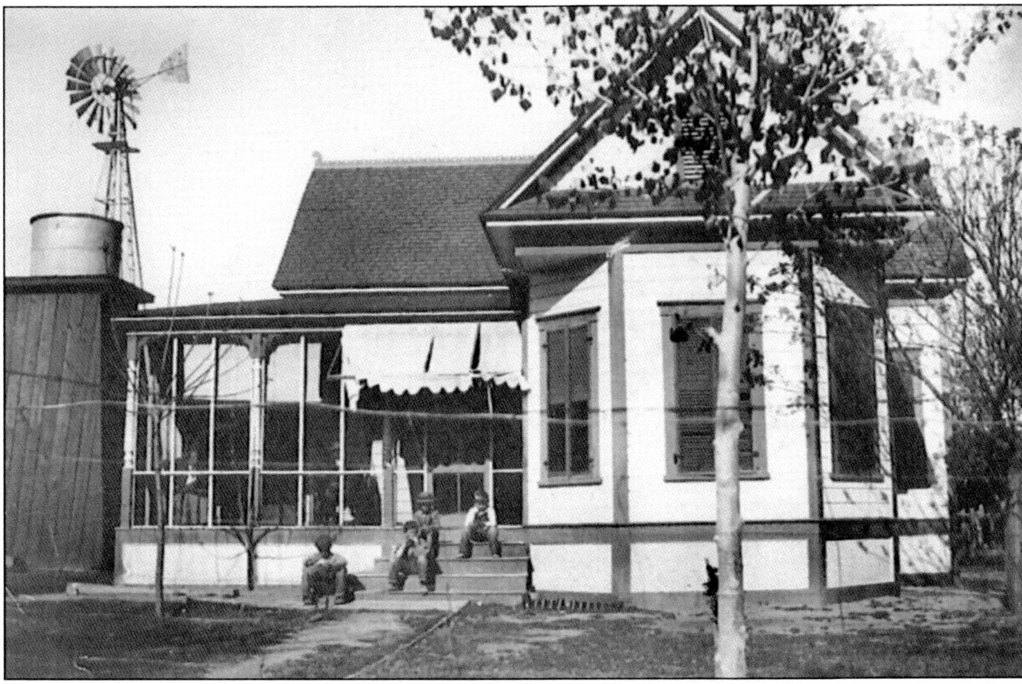

This early-20th-century Safford home proudly displays two highly prized possessions: a windmill and an elevated water tank. This house was undoubtedly furnished with running water in the kitchen. It may have had enough indoor plumbing to support a bathroom, but most homes of the era had an outhouse standing about 100 feet or so from the back door.

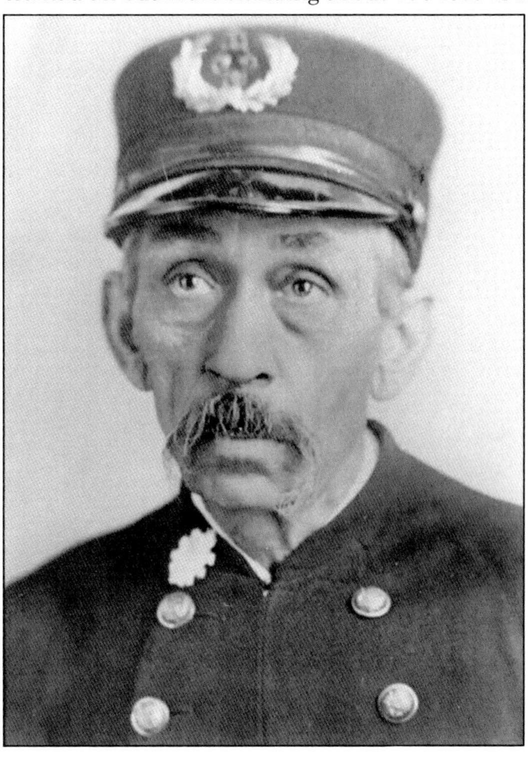

Possessing a Keystone Cops demeanor, fire chief Charles Kruger was a serious professional who protected Safford residents from the ever-present threat of fire. In 1900, the year this photograph was taken, Safford was literally a tinder box. Because of wood-framed homes heated by Franklin stoves and populated with wood-burning kitchen ovens, fires were frequent and required a quick response by hardy volunteers.

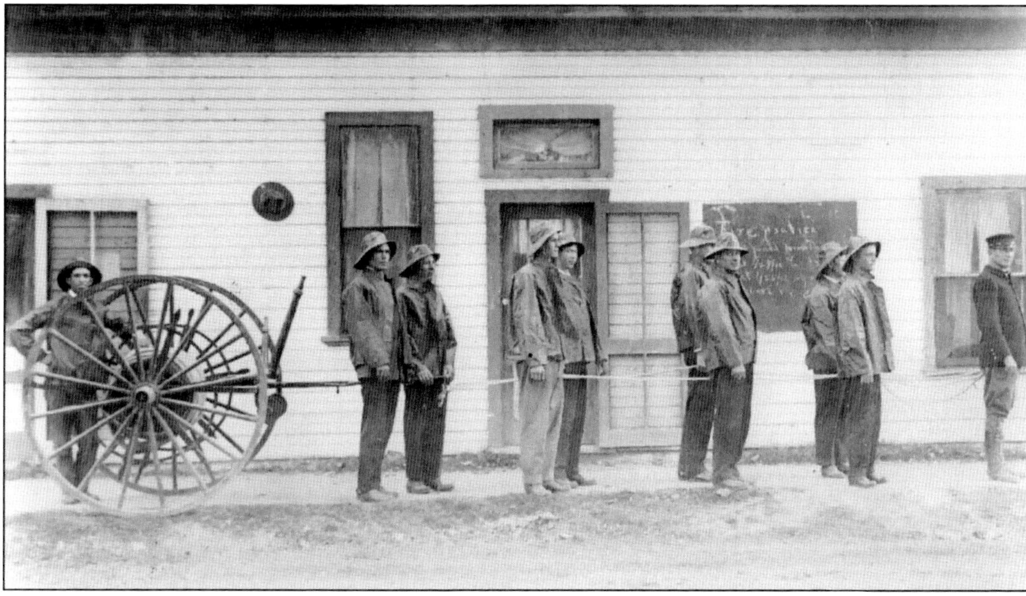

In 1911, the Safford Fire Department was manned by volunteers who were hitched horse-like to a hose reel. The use of this apparatus indicates that pumps requiring horsepower would arrive separately.

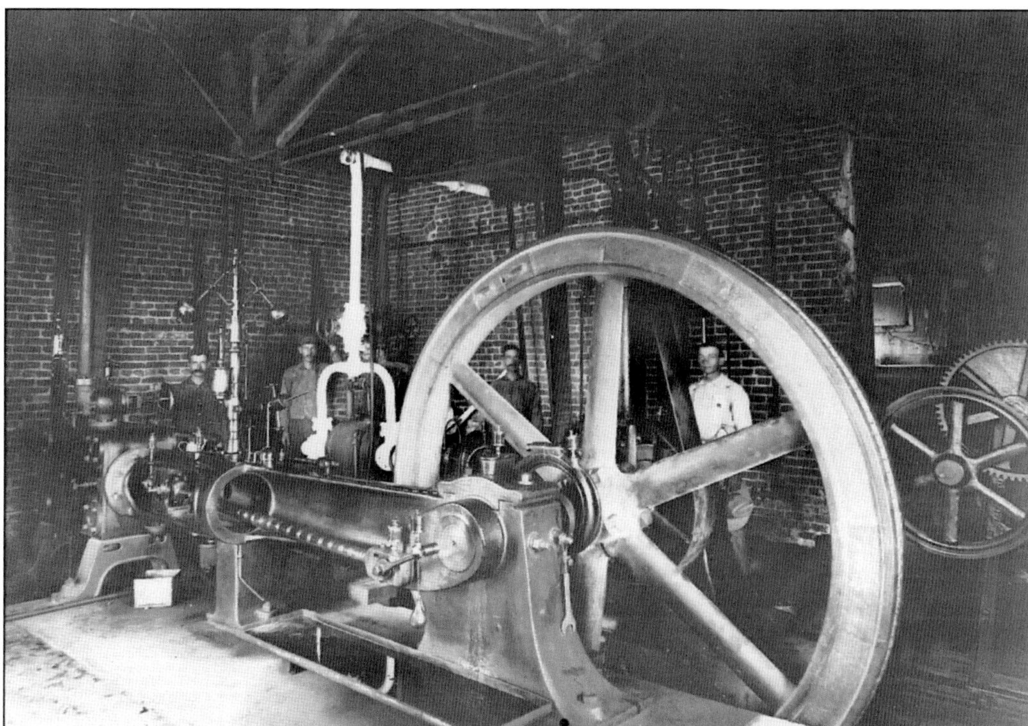

The interior of the Safford ice plant was a dangerous place to work. Long before Occupational Safety and Health Administration (OSHA)–issued safety precautions, plant workers were exposed to open gears, huge flywheels, and flying grease and oil.

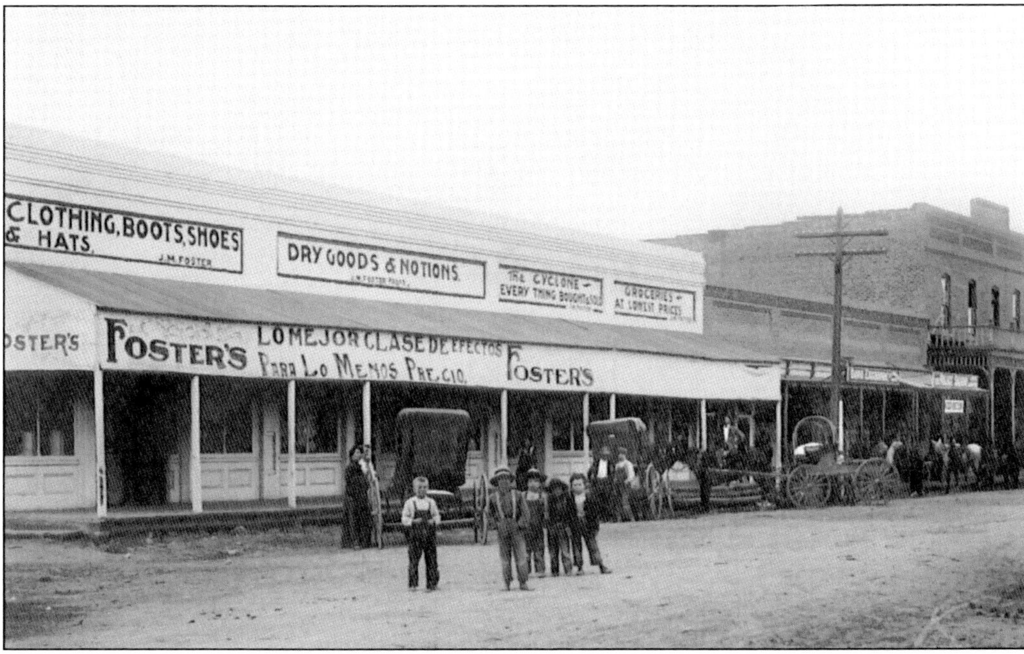

These unidentified youngsters were anxious to get their photograph taken in 1907. Main Street was a dry, dusty affair at the time, but the businesses were varied and profitable. The sign on Foster's Dry Goods and Notions, in both Spanish and English, indicates the importance of Spanish-speaking clientele.

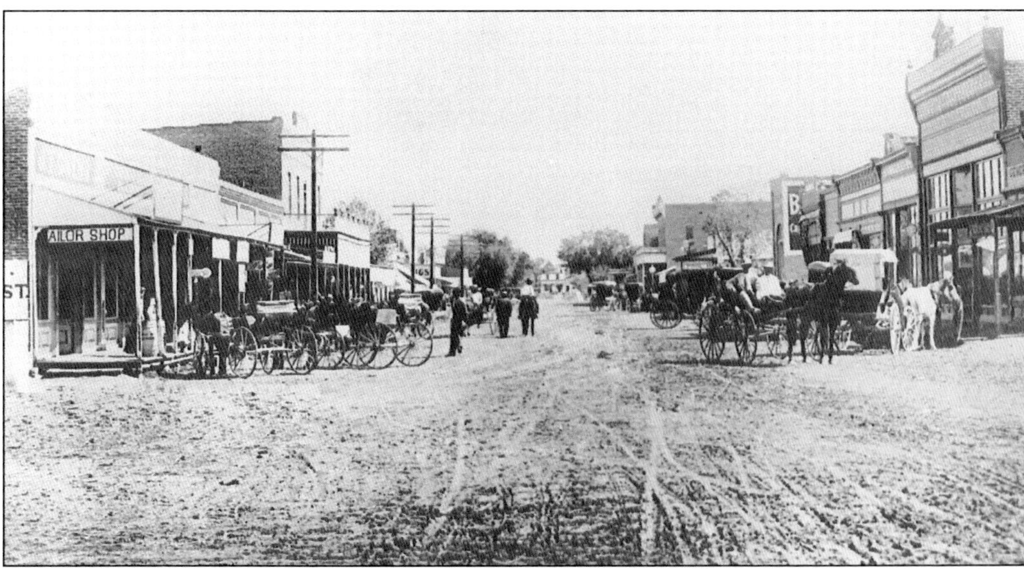

Main Street is pictured prior to the construction of the Graham County Courthouse. This 1912 scene demonstrates both the popularity of downtown business and the potential for mud and dust at various times of the year.

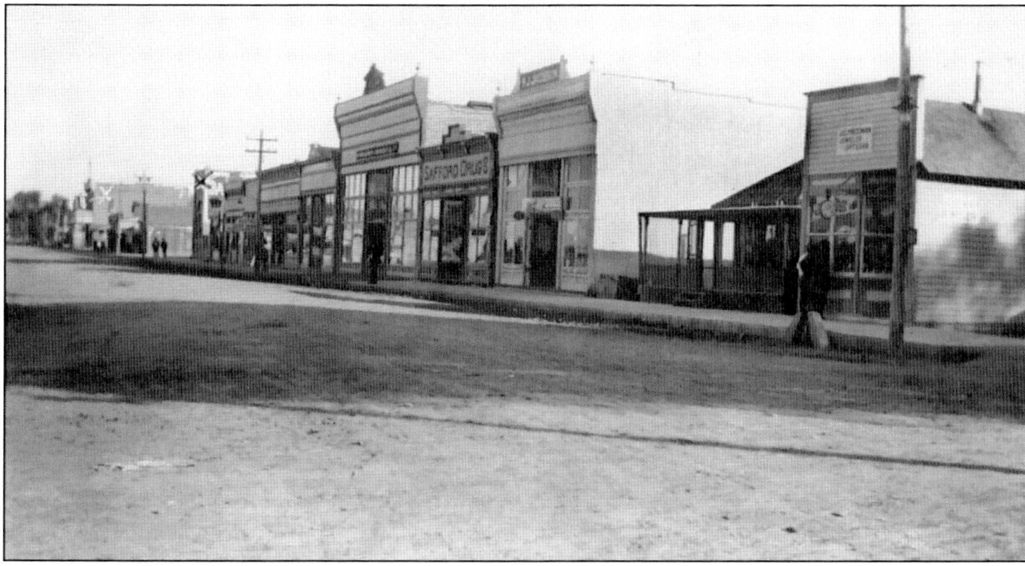

By 1914, when this photograph was taken, the wooden sidewalks had been replaced by concrete. Main Street was still unpaved, but the businesses were expanding in number. An X marks the location of the Bank of Safford.

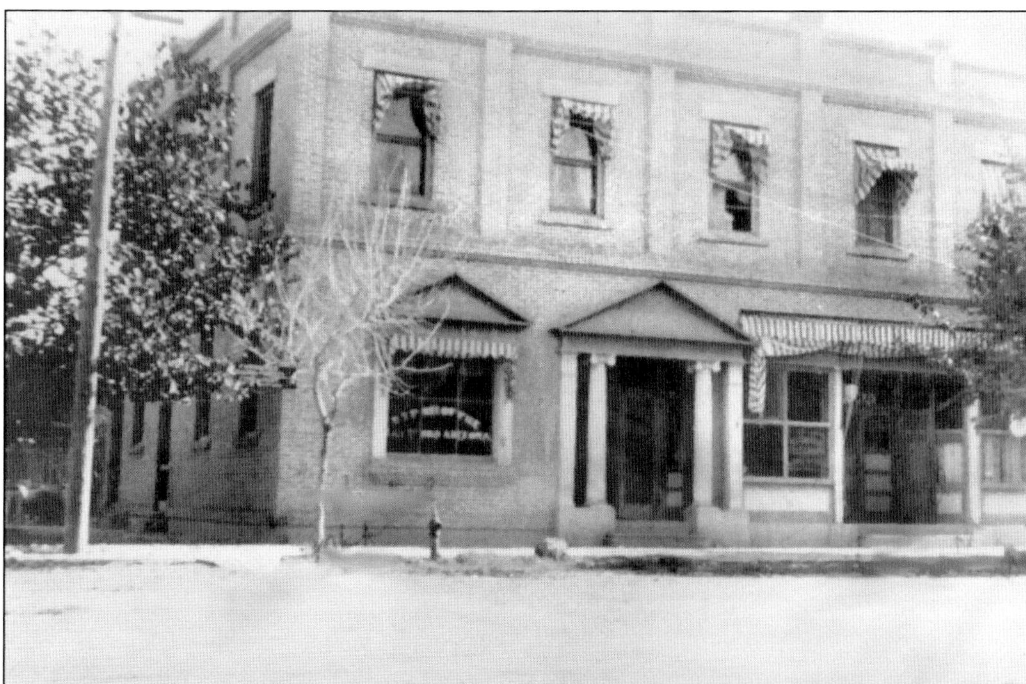

In 1907, the U.S. Post Office and telegraph offices stood side by side on Main Street. The fire hydrant in front of the post office is indicative of the capability of the water supply in Safford at the time.

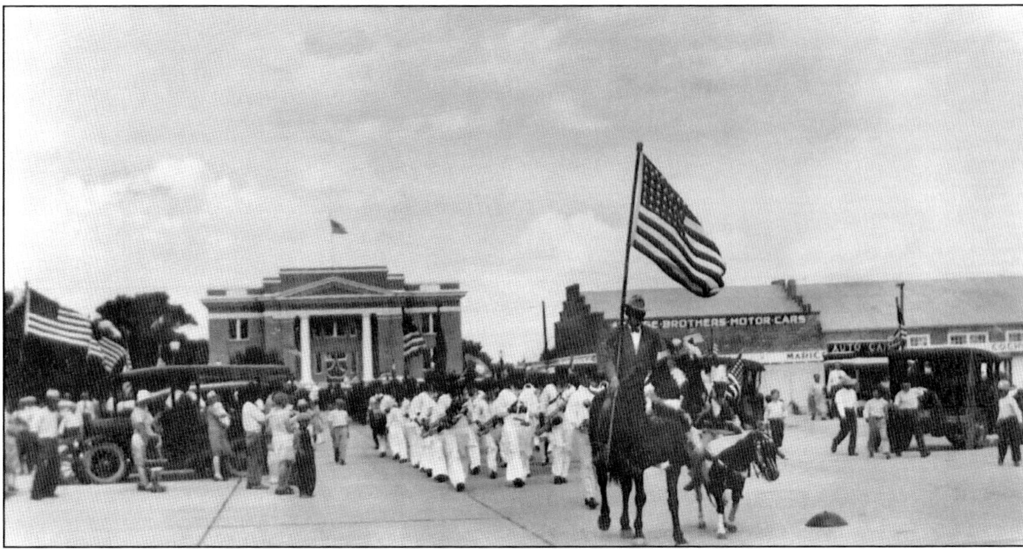

The front of a Fourth of July parade proudly marches on the newly laid concrete of Main Street. This view, taken in the 1920s, shows the marchers traveling from west to east.

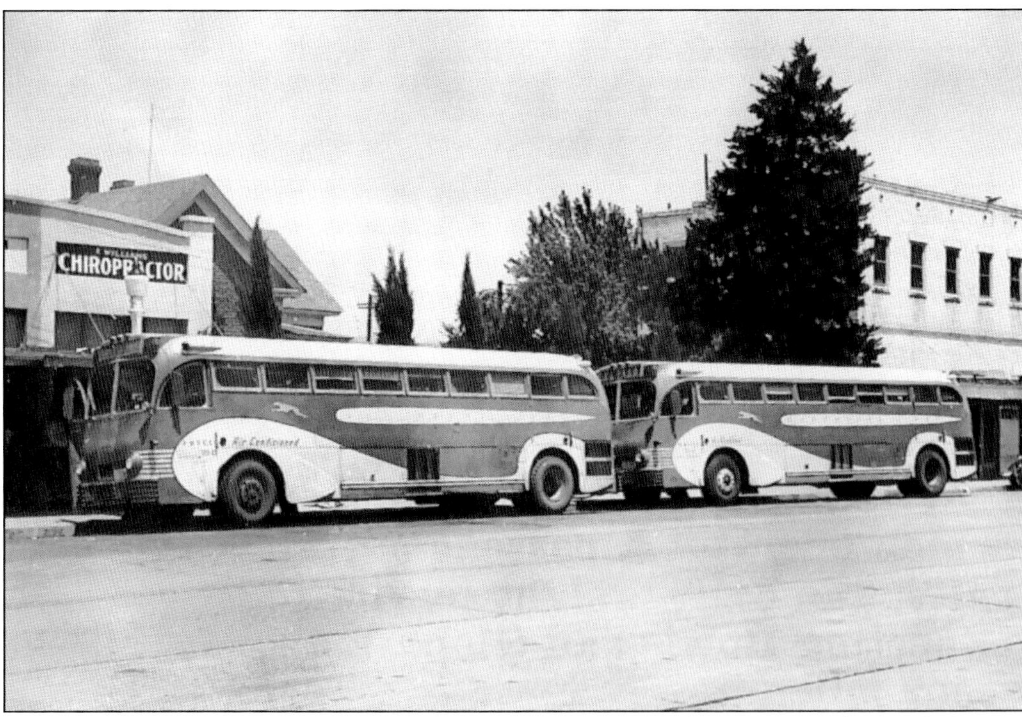

Train service out of Safford was comfortable and inexpensive; however, it only traveled in one direction. To fill the void and offer more choices, Greyhound bus service became popular during the World War II era. At that time, the bus depot was located on Main Street and had an extensive lunch counter that serviced travelers and locals alike.

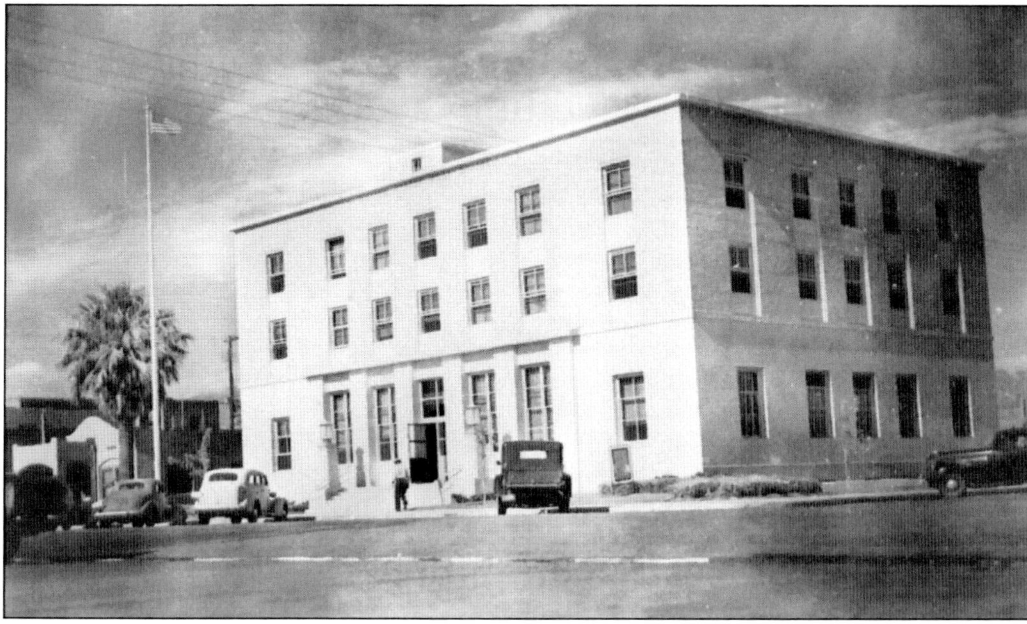

By the 1930s, a three-story post office had replaced the old. This imposing structure was the only building in town that had an elevator. It still serves as Safford's post office. Few buildings in town can boast of an elevator—even today.

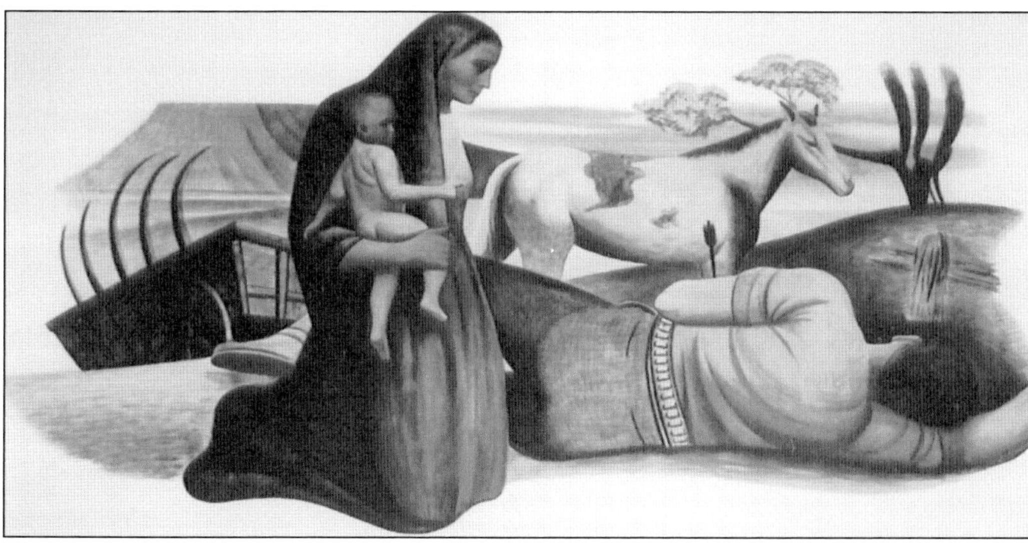

The post office lobby features six murals by artist Seymour Fogel. In 1939, a federal project was initiated to commission artists to paint murals and oversized paintings for post offices across the country. The new Safford Post Office was selected to receive this honor. Fogel had created his designs before leaving Washington, D.C., and his idealized representations of Apaches were soundly rejected by a local population who had been raised on stories of Apache bloodshed their entire lives. The bereaved woman kneeling by her slain husband was a compromise for the artist. The scene had started out as a sleeping pioneer with smoke signals rising from the background mesa.

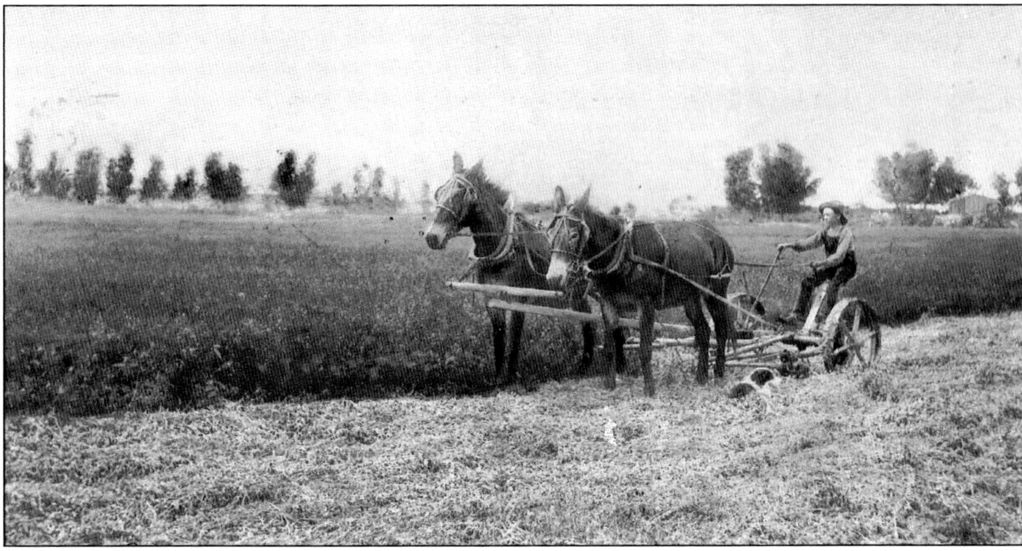

Dr. Edward Brenner owned this farm in 1912. The young boy cutting alfalfa is probably the Brenner's second-eldest boy, Bruce. The farm, which later became Jenning's Orchard, was located in the Artesia district, southeast of Safford.

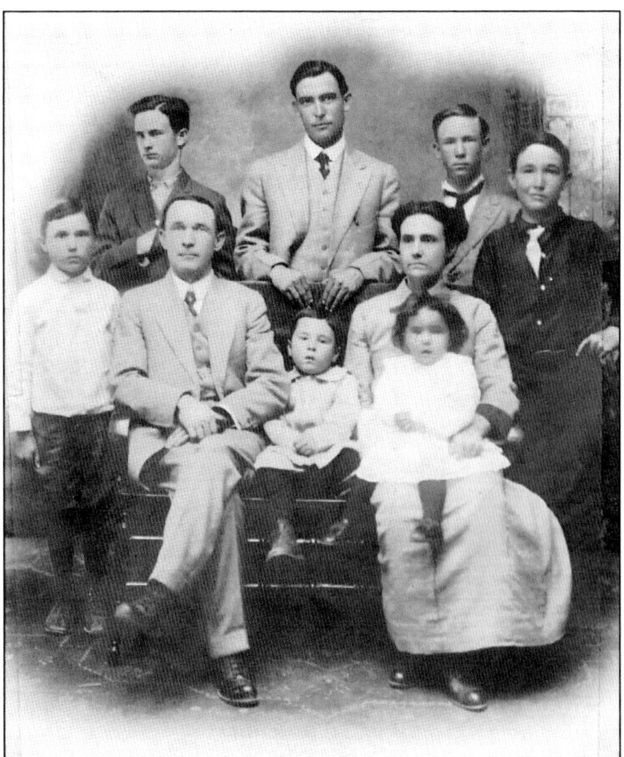

Dr. Edward Brenner was a popular medical doctor and farmer. He is shown here with his family in 1914. Pictured from left to right are (first row) Morris (died soon after this photograph was taken), Dr. Brenner, Wayne Earl (Bud) [killed in 1942 while serving in the U.S. Navy], Maude Barnette Brenner (holding Daisy Cochise, age 2); (second row) Bruce Artem, Fred, Edley (whose twin Eric had just died), Laurence (lost his right arm at age 13).

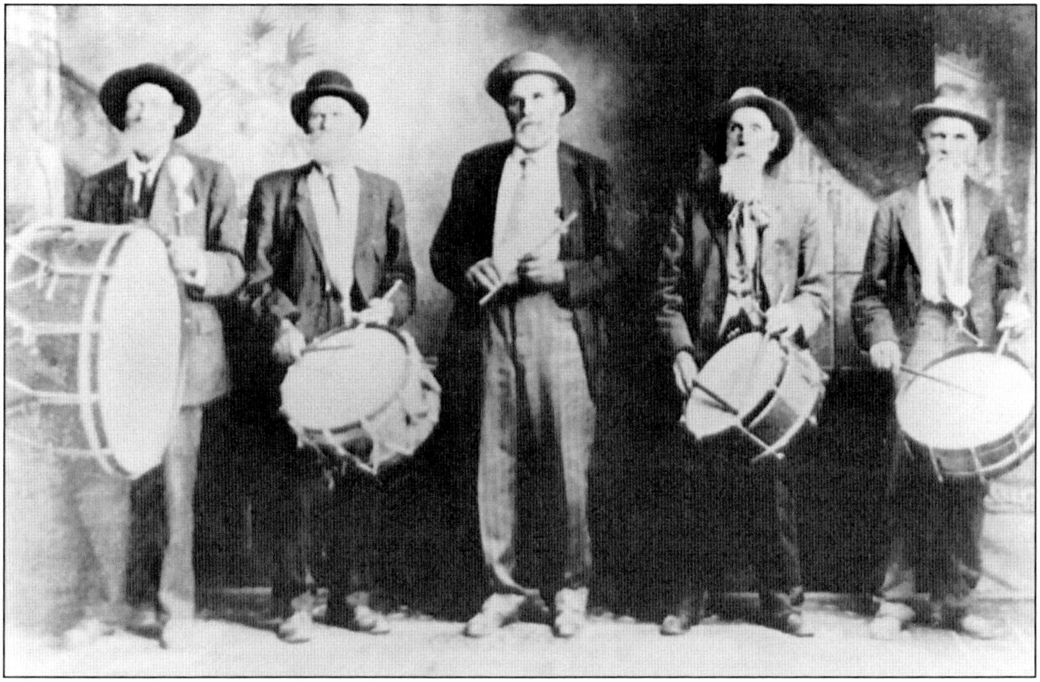

Like Thatcher and Pima, Safford had a volunteer band. Here the old-timers' fife and drum troop displays its form in 1912. This troop supported the efforts of the official Safford City Band. From left to right are Alonzo Packer, James R. Freestone, Peter J. Jacobson, William Ballard, and Thomas Nelson.

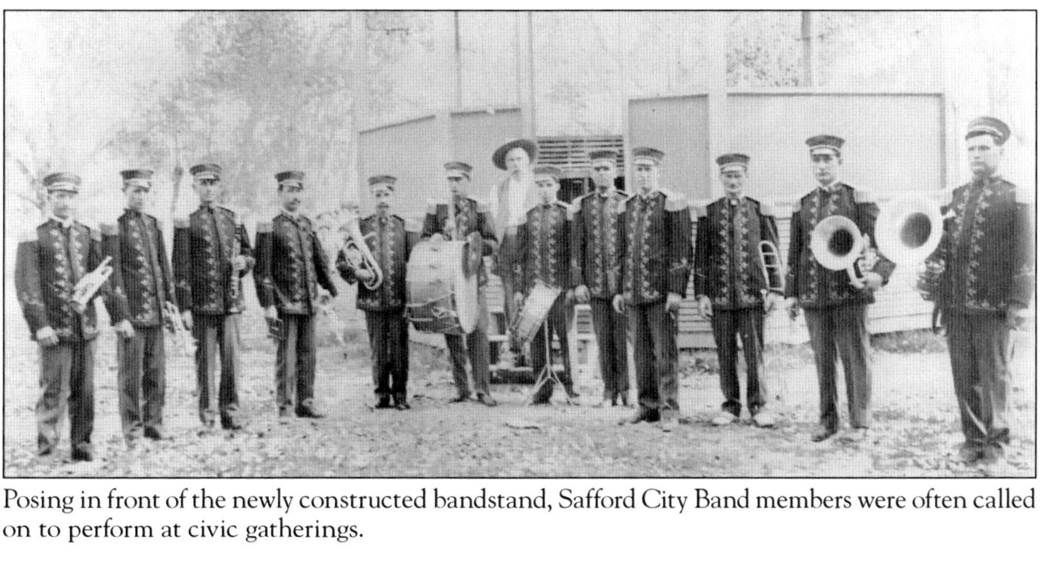

Posing in front of the newly constructed bandstand, Safford City Band members were often called on to perform at civic gatherings.

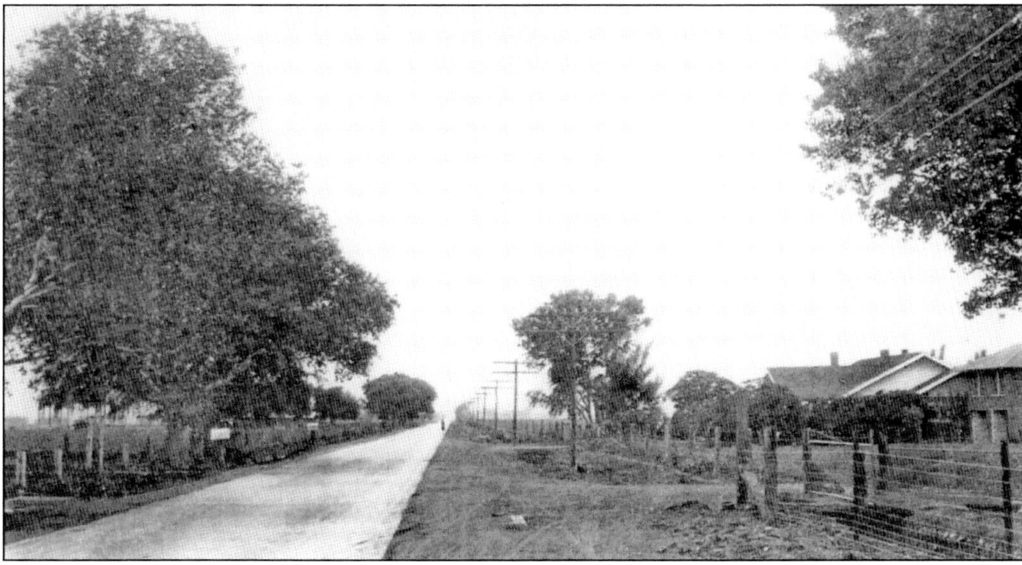

In the mid-1920s, the county took a major step to improve the most traveled route from Pima to Solomonville. This concrete road was built roughly parallel to the railroad track, making a much shorter drive out of what had been an all-day trip for buggies and automobiles. This view looks west toward Safford from a place west of Solomonville. The white house on the right belonged to Ed and Lillian Claridge.

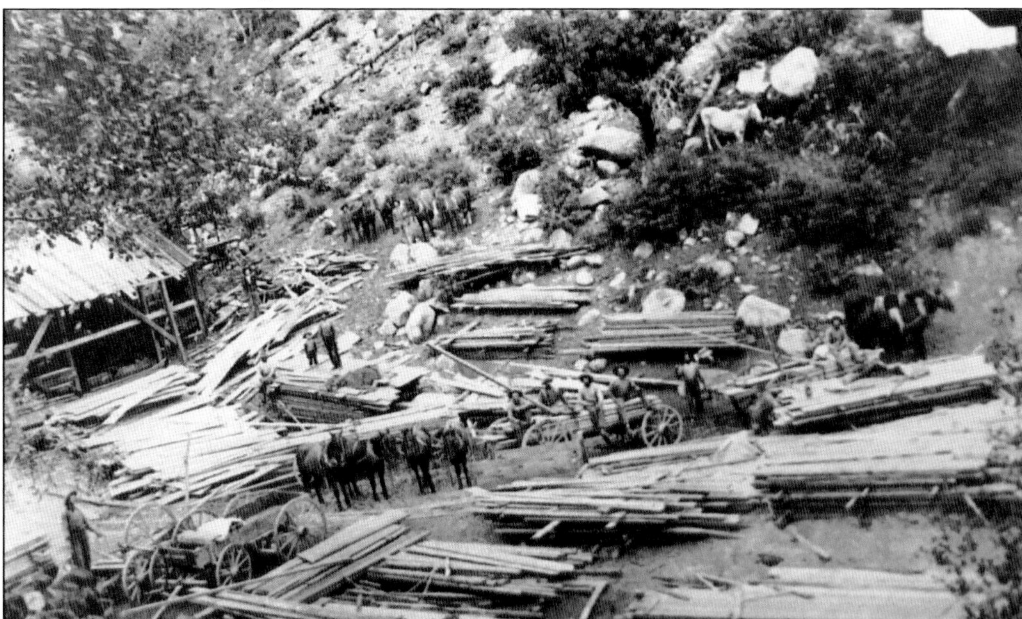

Pima residents did more than any other community in the valley to build and operate sawmills on Mount Graham. Pictured here is the Hunt Lumber Company mill in 1914. Rough-cut lumber was sent to finishing mills in Pima and other communities via a cable tram. Because the original mills had access to virgin forests of tall, straight timber, planks of long lengths and widths were processed. Those planks were in great demand in the mines in Globe and Clifton and provided good profits for the mills.

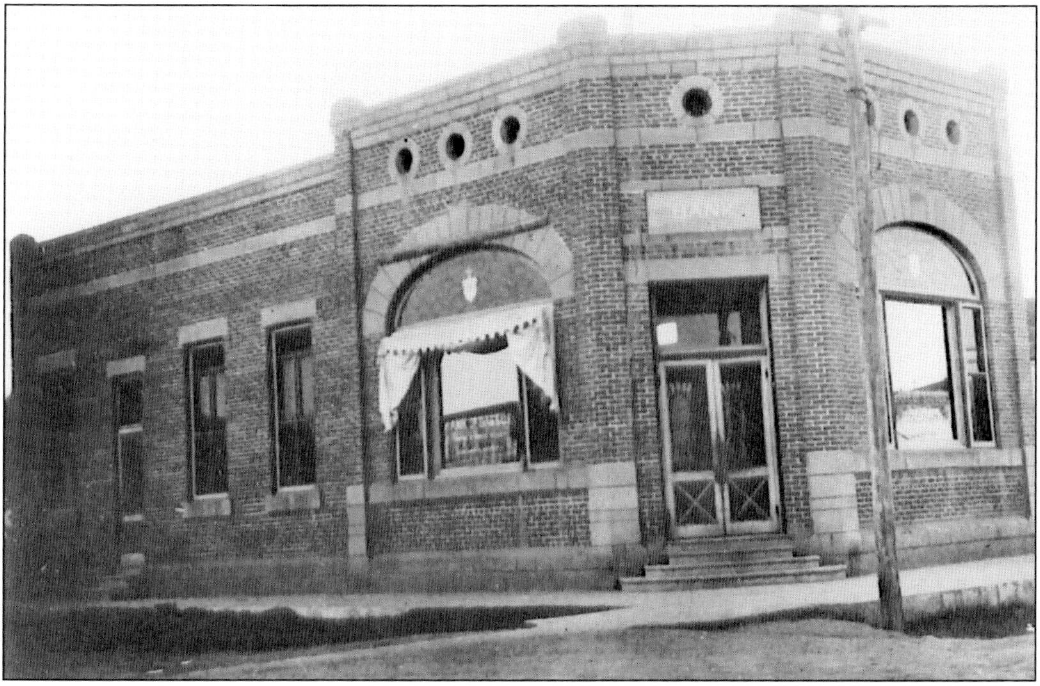

The Bank of Safford is shown in 1914, nine years after the brick building was constructed. Created by new arrival W. F. Holt and two prominent ranchers—J. N. Porter of Geronimo and J. C. Pursley, a founder of the Chiricahua Cattle Company—it was a successful enterprise from the beginning.

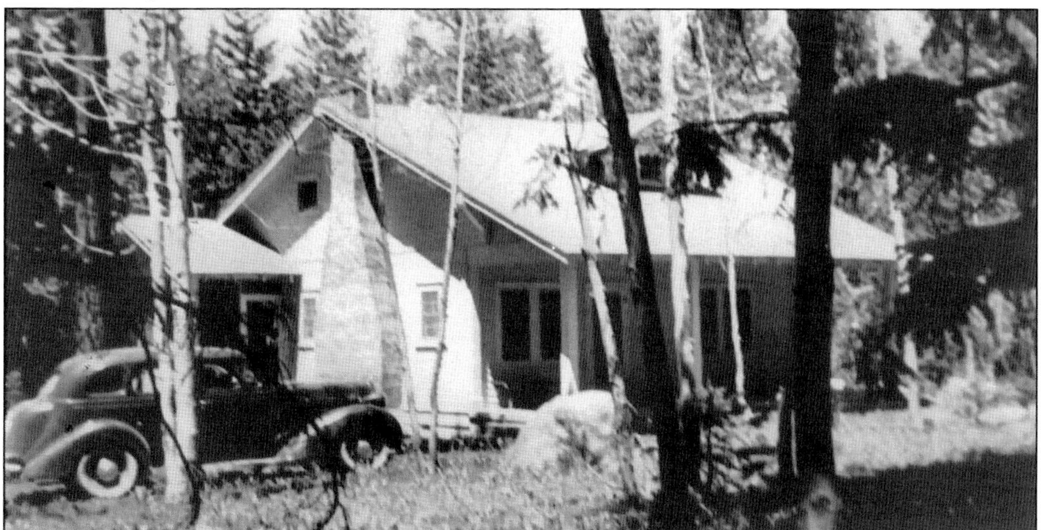

Escape from the unforgiving heat of summers to Mount Graham has become a tradition for many valley residents. This picture shows an important factor in the construction and maintenance of family cabins at several locations on the mountain, including Turkey Flats and Columbine. Pictured here is the Ranger Station in 1934. The creation of the National Park Service allowed for year-round protection of private property on the mountain, but it also limited the number of building sites available for expansion.

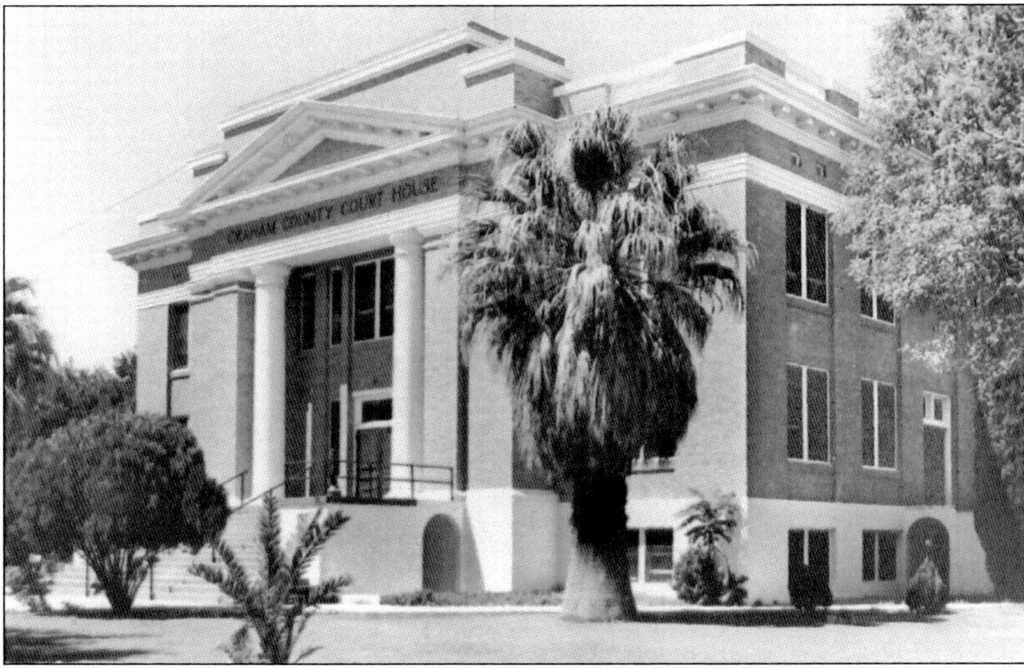

The anchor and pride of Safford has long been its stately courthouse. Standing at the west end of Main Street, the classically designed structure was built in 1916, only one year after the county seat was returned to Safford. An election on June 28, 1915, had decided the location of the county seat. It was a close call, with Safford receiving 1,286 votes and Pima receiving 982 votes.

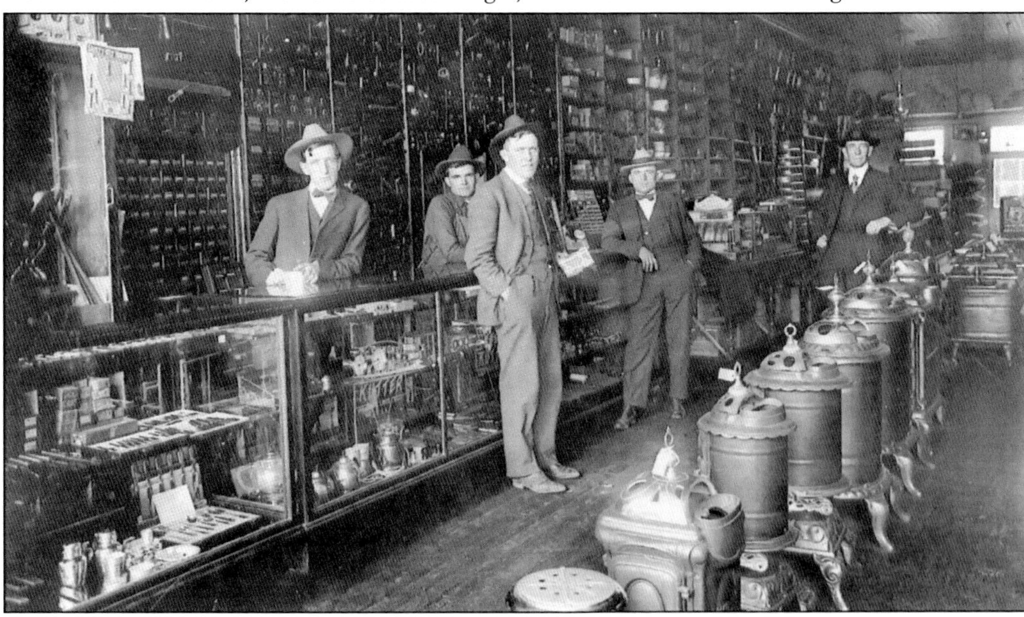

Pace Hardware, situated on Main Street in Safford, was well stocked in 1916. Here wholesale representatives Charles F. Davis of the Zork Hardware Company (fourth from the left) and Cliff Parson of the Hibbard, Spencer, and Bartlett Company in Chicago (far right) have come to confer with store owner Willard Pace (center). The two clerks are Thomas H. Haralson (left) and Charles Kirtland (second from the left).

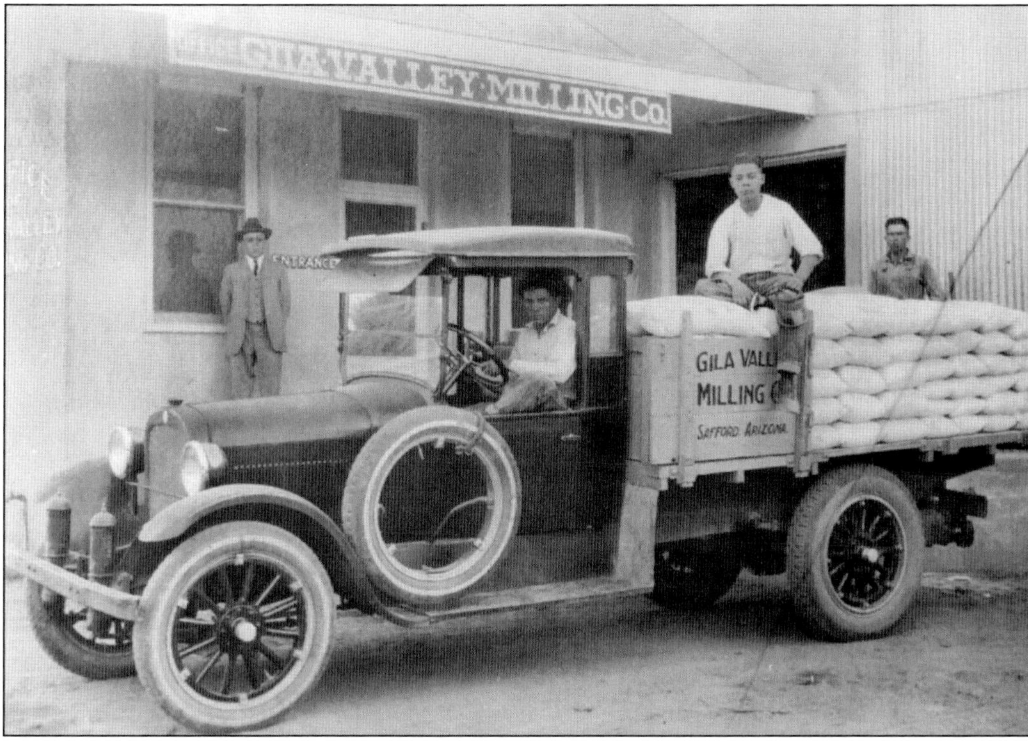

During the 1930s, the Gila Valley Milling Company not only supplied flour to local stores and markets but successfully exported to Globe, Silver City, Lordsburg, and Tucson.

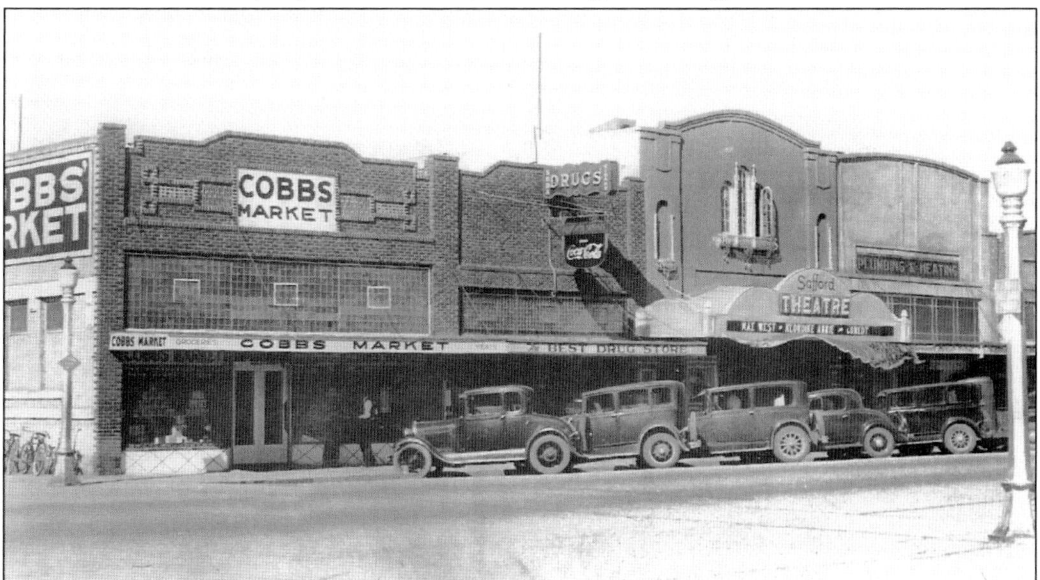

The Cobb's Market building, next to the Safford Theater in the 1930s, began as the Gila Valley Bank in 1909. The bank, started by I. E. Solomon, moved to Safford from Solomonville in that year and later crossed the street to become the Valley National Bank. One of the most popular businesses to occupy that same lot was the Misak Variety Store. Every kid in the valley could—and did—spend hours in there, begging Mom and Dad for this and that.

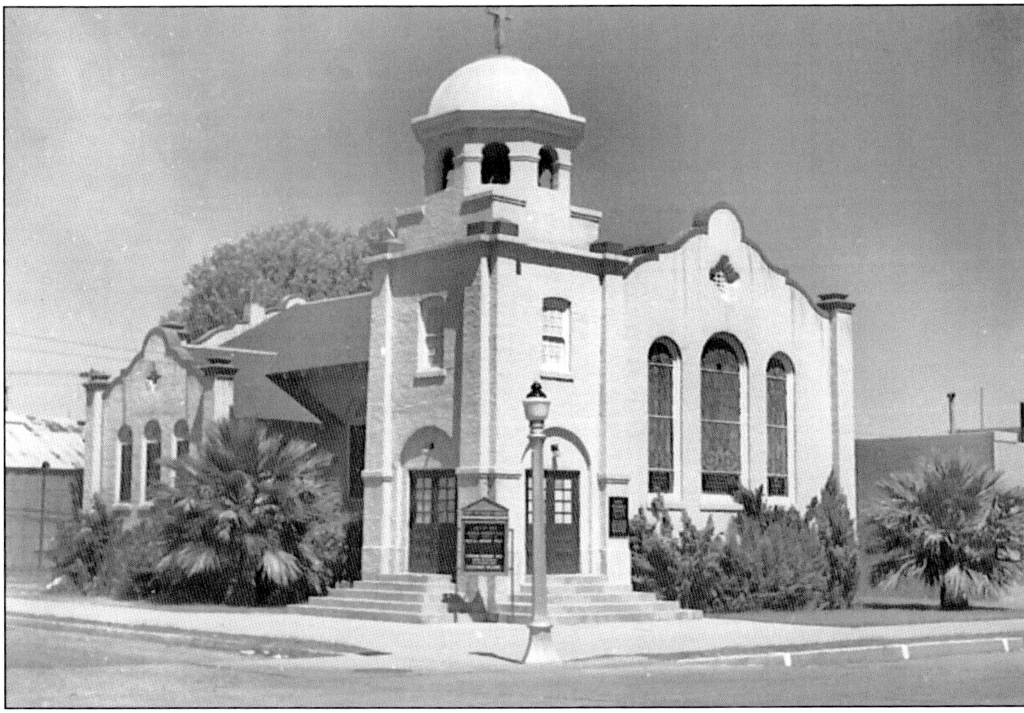

In 1940, two Methodist churches were located in the Gila Valley. This stately edifice graced a corner near the downtown area. The other church stood in Fort Thomas, where it served ranchers and farmers who had arrived from Texas and points eastward.

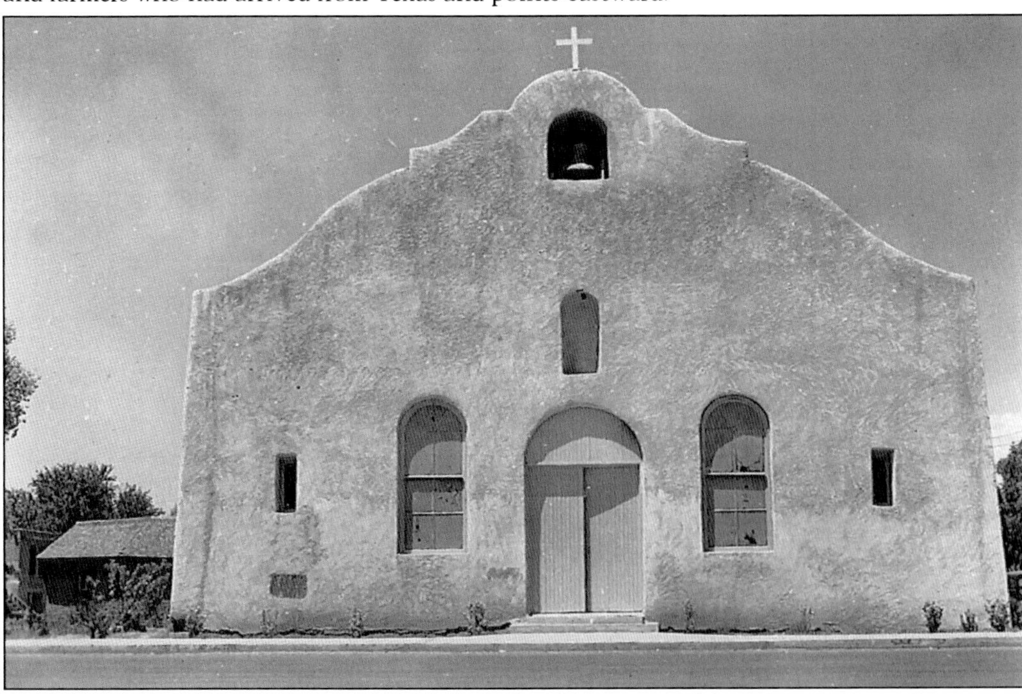

The first Catholic church in the valley was built in Solomonville in 1884. It burned down and was rebuilt in 1911. The church pictured here was built in 1924.

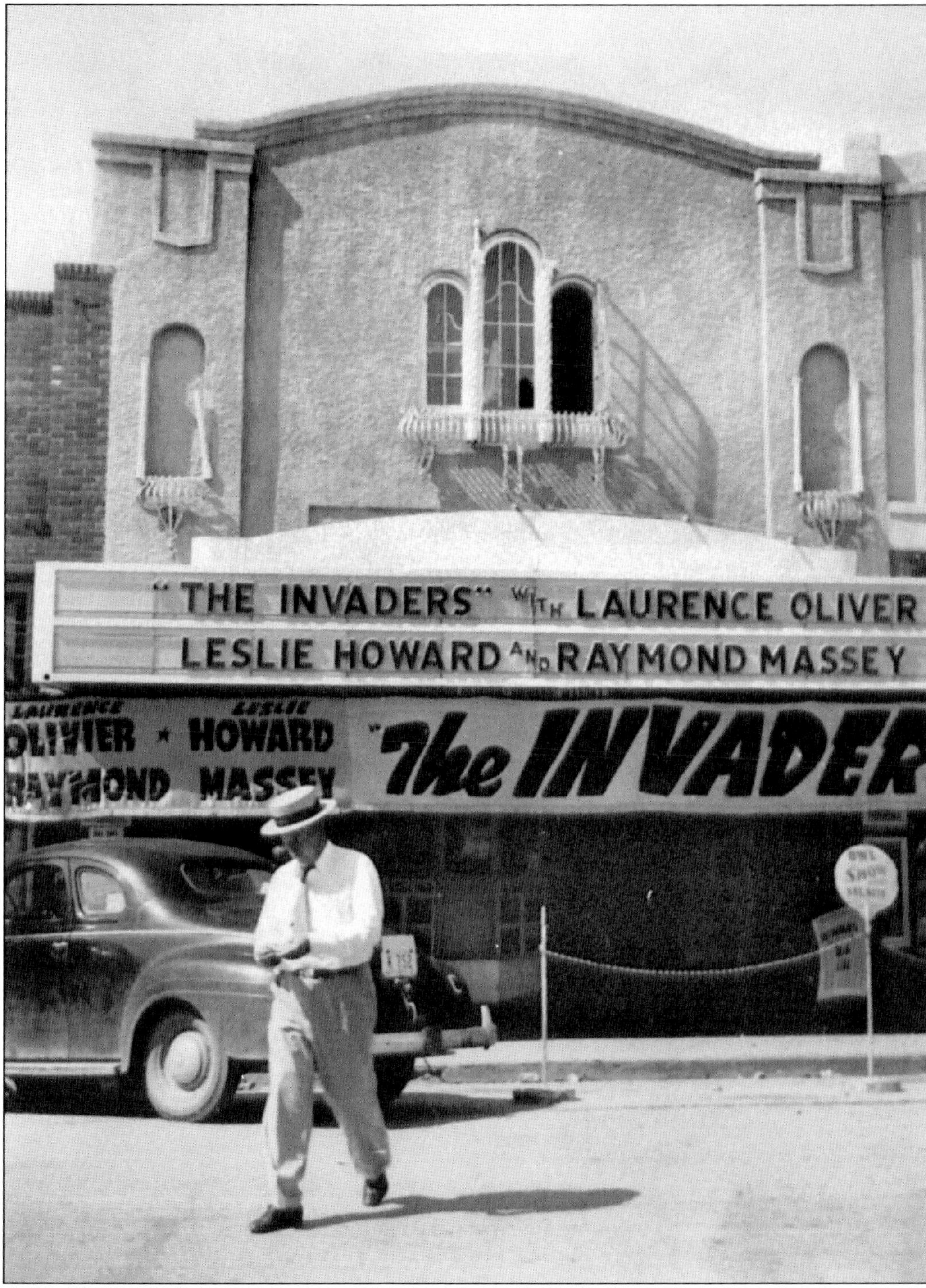

Louie Long's Safford Movie Theater is pictured in 1942. *The Invaders* was released on April 15, 1942. It was not a science fiction movie, but rather a violent World War II propaganda film made in Great Britain. The movie attracted big crowds. Louie Long, a great promoter, worked hard to get every penny he could out of potential audiences.

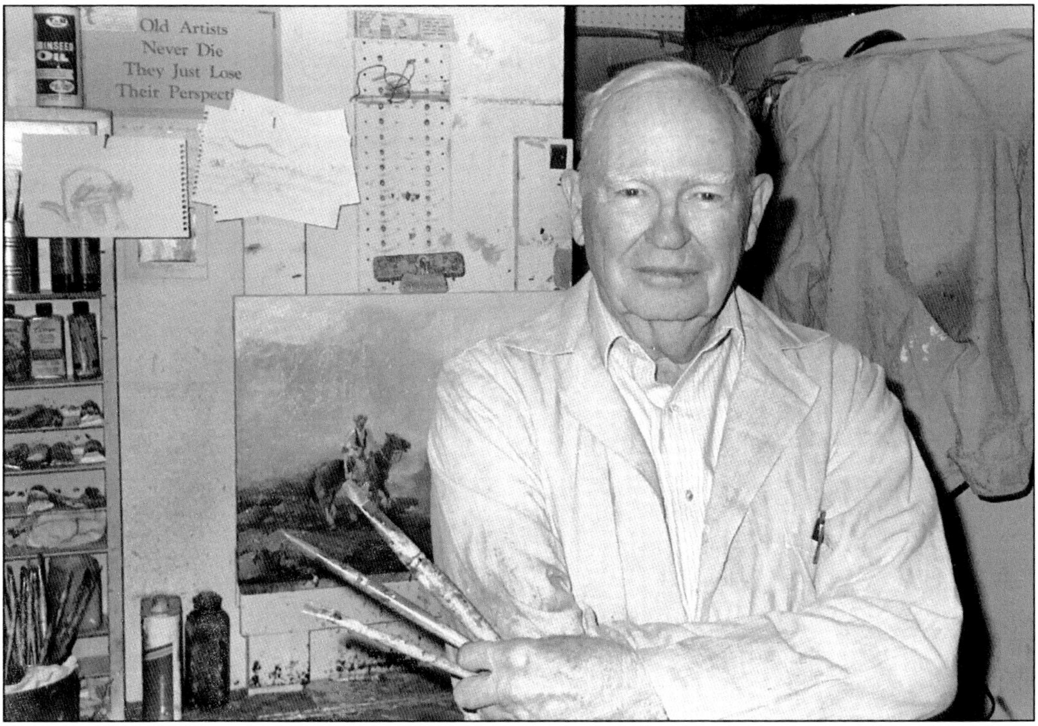

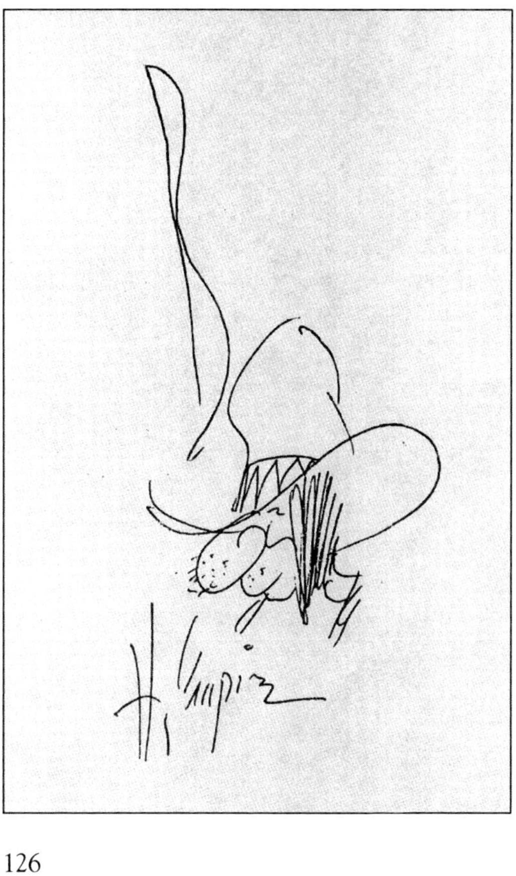

Hal Empie started his career as a druggist in Solomonville and plied that trade in Safford and Duncan while simultaneously perfecting his skills as an artist and teacher. His Duncan drugstore included an art studio in the back, and students came from all over the country to study with this prolific artist. Empie retired to a studio in Tubac, where he sold his art and never tired of sharing stories of his younger years in the Gila Valley.

The Graham County Historical Society and Museum is the proud owner of several Hal Empie works. All of his pieces are properly copyrighted and require permission for reproduction. Hal once wrote a letter to Maude Porter, an early president of the historical society, with this characteristic signature. The society highly prizes this possession.

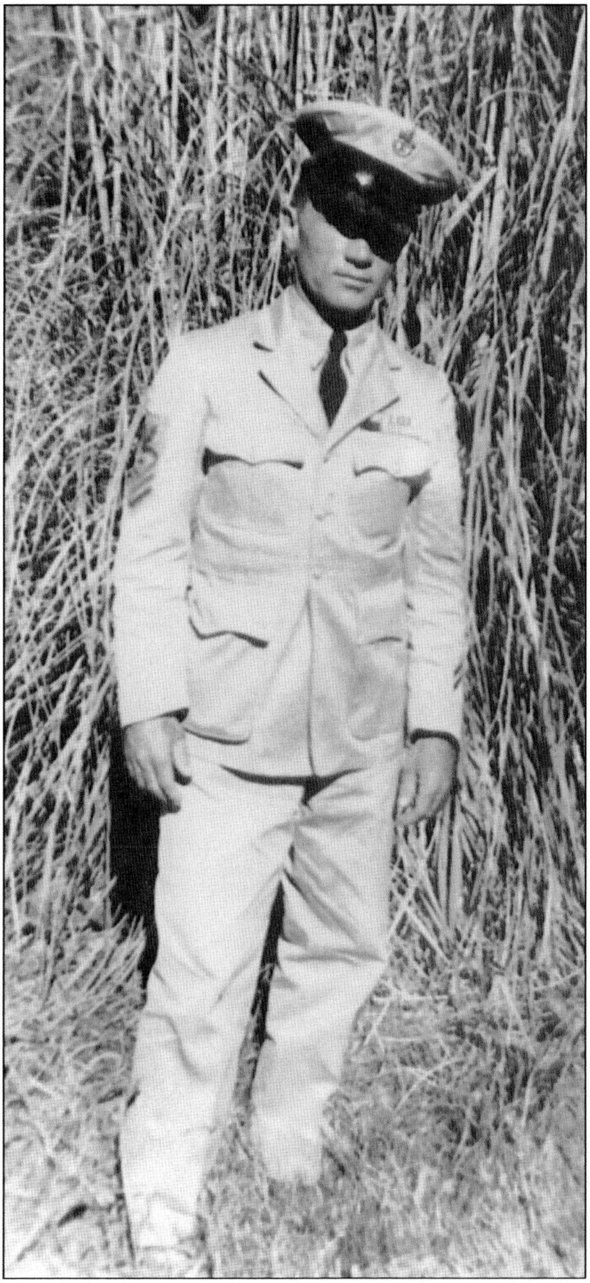

Erwin Eugene Curtis, the son of Eugene and Pearl Woods Curtis, was born in Thatcher on March 27, 1911. Joining the U.S. Navy in 1931, he earned the rank of chief turret captain and served on several warships, including the USS *Indianapolis.* After delivering the world's first atomic bomb to the island of Tinian in the South Pacific, the USS *Indianapolis* was struck by a torpedo from a Japanese submarine on July 30, 1945. Of the 1,197 sailors and marines on board, approximately 900 were able to get to lifeboats or don life jackets. Help arrived after three days and three nights. Only 317 men survived the dehydration and frequent shark attacks. The details of Erwin Eugene Curtis's death remain a mystery, but we honor him and his fellow servicemen for their ultimate sacrifice.